SOUTHWESTERN COLLEGE LIBRARY/LRC

3 3200 00155 3236

P9-DTN-272

THE

INTIMATE

HOUR

Books by Susan Baur

The Dinosaur Man:
Tales of Madness and Enchantment
from the Back Ward

Confiding: A Psychologist and Her Patients
Search for Stories to Live By

Hypochondria: Woeful Imaginings

The Intimate Hour:
Love and Sex in Psychotherapy

2-13-97

THE
INTIMATE
HOUR

Love and Sex in

Psychotherapy

SUSAN BAUR

RC
480.8
B384
1997

SOUTHWESTERN
COLLEGE
Library
CHULA VISTA
CALIFORNIA

HOUGHTON MIFFLIN COMPANY

Boston   New York   1997

Copyright © 1997 by The Mot Company
All rights reserved

For information about permission to reproduce selections from this book,
write to Permissions, Houghton Mifflin Company, 215 Park Avenue South,
New York, New York 10003.

For information about this and other Houghton Mifflin trade and reference
books and multimedia products, visit The Bookstore at Houghton Mifflin
on the World Wide Web at http://www.hmco.com/trade/.

Library of Congress Cataloging-in-Publication Data
Baur, Susan.
The intimate hour : love and sex in psychotherapy / Susan Baur.
p.   cm.
Includes bibliographical references and index.
ISBN 0-395-82284-X
1. Psychotherapists — Sexual behavior.
2. Psychotherapy patients — Sexual behavior.   I. Title.
RC480.8.B384   1997
616.89'14 — dc20   96-31380
CIP

Printed in the United States of America

QUM   10 9 8 7 6 5 4 3 2 1

For

Ethel Naugle,

Richard Blake,

Warren Freeman,

Mary-Pat MacKenzie,

and Keith Morehouse

Contents

THE

INTIMATE

HOUR

Introduction

> I have again and again been faced with the mystery of
> love, and have never been able to explain what it is. . . .
> Here is the greatest and smallest, the remotest and
> nearest, the highest and lowest, and we cannot discuss
> one side of it without also discussing the other.
>
> — *Carl Jung*

How do two people sit across from each other in therapy, becoming closer and more intimate by the hour, without sometimes giving in to the full and natural expression of love? What happens when they do?

When, as a psychologist, I first began imagining how I could rescue a charming and literally motherless young woman, when I spun fantasies about a handsome man or thought of trekking cross-country with a schizophrenic who believed she owned everything that began with the letter *B*, including me — when, in short, I first found myself becoming surprisingly fond of certain patients, I tried to find a book that would describe in detail what Jung calls the opposite sides of love. Parental concern, friendship, attraction, love — where did all this "heart-revealing intimacy" fit into the work I had chosen? It was easy to find books describing the place of warmth and empathy in psychotherapy, easy to find articles warning against overinvolvement — even easy to find material on hating a client — but I could not locate any firsthand accounts of love. Where were the clinicians who would come right out and say, "I am in love with my patient" or "I want to take this child home with me," and who would then go on to think the situation through out loud and tell me what took place? Nor could I discover what intense affection in therapy felt like to a client. I found stories of sexual exploitation, but they had nothing to do with love — on the part of neither therapist nor client. No one, it seemed, was comfortable addressing questions that I considered fundamental to psychotherapy.

Initially, I attributed this lack to the recent and dramatic wave of lawsuits and legislation that have brought to public awareness the nearly unanimous belief that sex and sexual harassment have no place in therapy. New codes of ethics state that any behavior that is sexually exploitive — whether physical or verbal, and whether undertaken with a patient, former patient, or immediate relative of a patient — will be punished. Being relatively new, the ethical guidelines are being interpreted in a great variety of ways. Some complaints are taken extremely seriously. In 1994, a woman won $7.1 million in a sexual abuse suit against a psychiatrist who fostered her dependence on drugs and sexually abused her. Some are brushed off. The charges against a male psychologist who, fully clothed, climbed onto a hospital bed to comfort a client awaiting surgery and against a female psychologist who wore short skirts were dismissed. The majority of complaints lie somewhere between these two extremes and are settled inconsistently and unhappily. Most are so complex and rest on so little evidence beyond what is said in private therapy sessions that typically, after years of legal fighting, both accuser and accused feel battered and resentful. "You're all bastards," said a woman who received $287,000 for damages allegedly done by a promiscuous psychiatrist. "Some day I'll have enough money to have you all castrated." "Why are these women so vengeful and horrid?" asked a renowned analyst. "It's turned into a witch-hunt." "Hug a client, hire a lawyer," said a psychologist who trains doctors to practice defensively.

In spite of bad feelings on both sides, the attempt to clean up therapy goes forward. Licenses to practice are revoked, clinicians sued, groups started for the abused, and, in a growing number of states, legislation passed making sex with a client a criminal offense. Given all this activity, it is no wonder, I told myself, that clinicians are reluctant to discuss feelings of attraction. They are afraid that any admission will be interpreted as unethical or as a prelude to punishable behavior.

"Both students and experienced therapists are so anxious now," said a woman who lectures on sexual attraction, "that they either pretend erotic feelings don't exist or believe them to represent a therapeutic error."

Yet in spite of denial, silence, regulations, and some spectacular lawsuits to support these regulations, surely the problem of therapists and clients becoming too fond of each other still exists. After all, as millions have noticed, love does not wait for an invitation before barging in. And as surveys investigating the incidence of doctor-patient liaisons have also noted, it happens at some point in the careers of *at least* 3 to 12 percent of all clinicians. There are well over a million counselors and clinicians in the United States. So where are the stories?

I went in search of what I anticipated would be a great many accounts and found two sources — an old one and a recent one. In the letters and diaries of analysts and patients who lived thirty or more years ago, I discovered dozens of anecdotes describing strange and potentially exploitive practices as well as full-blown stories of love — usually troubled love with all the tenderness and nastiness that comes with it. For example, Anton Mesmer, whose studies on "animal magnetism" led to the discovery of hypnosis, seemed to have so much power over his patients that Louis XVI ordered an investigation of the dangerous technique that "inflamed" the senses. Mesmer himself became so enthralled by one of his patients, a blind pianist, that he separated permanently from his wife. Sandor Ferenczi, who let his patients kiss him, became enamored of a married patient whom he later married. (He also fell in love with her daughter.) Frieda Fromm-Reichman (the analyst portrayed in *I Never Promised You a Rose Garden*) analyzed Erich Fromm (later the author of *The Art of Loving*) and then married him. Carl Jung credited one of his most important discoveries to "the love of S. for J.," namely the love that his young patient Sabina Spielrein lavished on him, her married doctor, for more than a decade. And Julius Spier, briefly a student of Jung's, had a remarkable affair with Etty Hillesum that in less than two years radically changed both their lives. The list of entanglements goes on and on and includes every imaginable sort of relationship. Among them, the Spielrein and Hillesum liaisons are particularly interesting, for both women kept diaries that describe in detail their violently alternating moods of hope and despair — and their eventual resolution. In other words, both shabby treatment and love are clearly described.

"I saw almost too well what I mean to him," wrote the twenty-five-year-old Spielrein after spending an afternoon discussing sex, death, history, and schizophrenia with Jung. "It gave me the greatest satisfaction. So I am not one among the many, but one who is unique, for certainly no girl can understand him as I can." Yet a month later, fearing she is nothing but a useless dreamer, Spielrein writes, "I do believe I am capable of destroying myself with cyanide."

Or, from Etty Hillesum's diary, kept during the Nazi occupation of the Netherlands, "Sometimes when he [her therapist, Spier] just strokes my face with his great, warm hand, or, with that inimitable gesture of his, runs his fingertips over my eyelashes, I begin to rebel. 'Who told you that you could do this to me, who gave you the right to touch my body?'" A year later she writes, "I once quietly bemoaned the fact that there is so little space for our physical love in your two small rooms, and no chance of going elsewhere because of all those notices and prohibitions. And now it seems a veritable paradise of promise and freedom: your little rooms, your small table lamp, my lilac soap and your gentle, caressing hands. God knows how much that means to our relationship, to all that may lie in store for us. Not that I worry unduly about the future. You can't tell how things will turn out in the long run and so I don't bother too much about it. But if things are to be harder for us I am quite ready to bear it."

When I turned to recent accounts of doctor-patient intimacy, I found a curious progression. Articles from the 1970s, when the topic first received national attention, were somewhat tentative. The idea was put forward that many kinds of intimate relationships developed between doctor and patient. Whereas all of them were understood to represent a therapeutic failure the moment the attraction was acted on, the liaisons themselves could be good or bad. Some patients got hurt, these few articles recounted, some got helped *and* hurt, and some seemed pleased. A minuscule number went on to marry the therapist. No one was sure of how widespread the practice of sleeping with patients was, why it led to such varied outcomes, or what to do about it. In these early years of concern, most therapists believed that former patients as well as patients should be off-limits, but roughly a third believed that once therapy was over, adults were free to do what they wanted. In the 1970s, it appeared that clinicians were approaching the problem, or rather the embarrassing secret, cautiously, for it had remained hidden a long time. Sound information on who was doing what to whom and with what results would be difficult to come by. It always is when the object of investigation is unethical or punishable behavior.

So I read on — on into the 1980s and '90s — and, to my astonishment, all tentativeness disappeared from the discussion in the blink of an eye. Suddenly all questions were raised and answered.

Reading articles like "Sexual Exploitation in Professional Relationships" or "The Prevention of Psychotherapist Sexual Misconduct," I learned that the politically correct view is that "a psychopathic male therapist preys on a victimized female patient." Further, any and all overt expressions of affection are motivated by the sadistic feelings of "distressed and impaired practitioners." The harm these therapists inflict is devastating because "the woman patient . . . is in a state of psychological regression [and] becomes the helpless child again." This is true 90 percent of the time, I read, and in the other ten percent, when the patient walks away from or even survives an erotic entanglement, she is in denial concerning her true helplessness. As I read article after article about women "caught in the coils of a sexually abusing therapist," I began to feel caught in the coils of arguments that had suddenly become self-righteous, political, and tautological. I didn't recognize the caricature of the abusive therapist among my colleagues or from the accounts of famous therapists whose relationships I had been studying. Nor did I recognize the caricature of the helpless, regressed female among my friends, my patients, or the patients of Jung, Ferenczi, Otto Rank, Karen Horney, or Fritz Perls. Yet it appeared that any position on the matter of doctor-patient attraction that differed from the politically correct one — even a position of inquiry — was off-limits. For example, at a seminar on sexual abuse at a big, liberal university, a female psychiatrist started to present a case that involved an apparently satisfying romantic relationship between a male patient and a female doctor. Several members of the audience were outraged. They yelled and heckled. Two women tried to bring charges of sexual harassment *against the lecturer*, arguing that she had upset them by presenting a dangerously biased illustration. "We all know," they said in effect, "that more than 90 percent of sexual encounters occur between male therapists and female patients and all of them are abusive. To discuss any other scenario is to distract our attention from the real problem." When I read about this seminar and attended similar ones myself, my hope of finding a broad sample of current doctor-patient stories in the literature — in the public forum — disappeared.

What was happening? Why had clinicians, who usually want to ask questions, stopped asking about lust and love? Were they embarrassed to acknowledge their own feelings and actions? Were they afraid of being politically incorrect? Or were they too naive to know there was a problem? After all, current surveys show that 98 percent of clinicians adamantly oppose sex in therapy, yet it continues to happen among far more than 2 percent of practitioners. Who, then, is saying sex in therapy is bad but slipping into an affair anyway? It became clear that I would have to turn to unpublished material to find out what today's therapists and clients are thinking when attraction enters the consulting room and joins the intimate hour.

Let me make my own position clear. I do not believe that sex can coexist with therapy. This is my personal belief, and I hold it for a mixture of reasons that I will describe in the second section of *The Intimate Hour.* I have spoken to respected doctors who say that perhaps in some tiny percentage of cases, in theory, somewhere, it might be possible, but I believe this to be a male fantasy. When desire is expressed for a patient (not just discussed, but acted on), therapy walks out the door and a different relationship walks in. But this is not the same as saying that the sexual or romantic attractions that develop between doctor and patient are always examples of a thoroughly evil man preying on a helpless woman. There is a lot more to the relationship than that. I picture a wheel, half in a cool zone, half in a warm zone, within which are arrayed various doctor-patient relationships. The cool half represents therapy as a business deal, a contract; the warm half represents it as an intimate, caring relationship. Each half of the wheel produces good treatment for different people in different settings, but each has its dangerous excesses. In my opinion, sexual exploitation occurs in the coldest region of the cool zone when a doctor with no understanding of or respect for his patient and no concern for her well-being willfully indulges his sexual appetite. On the opposite side of the wheel, where warm becomes too hot, is the lovestruck clinician who overidentifies with his client, cares too much about her, and lacks the self-control and collegial support to rein in his troubled love. Both extremes can create dreadful messes, but they are different. Naturally enough, the strengths of the patient entering therapy — whether she is overwhelmed by sadness and confusion or seeking confirmation of a brave new step in her life — make an enormous difference in how the erotic entanglement will be experienced and dealt with. As we will see, some patients are like children in need of a powerful and benign protector, whereas others enter treatment as adults seeking advice from a colleague or peer. Any failure to recognize the difference either between the "hot" and "cold" motivations of a therapist or between the strong and weak positions of a patient leads to a common but unproductive oversimplification, namely, that every doctor-patient affair is an example of incest. This is false. None is good therapy, but doctor-patient liaisons — and doctor–former patient liaisons, which are far more common — exist along a broad continuum.

Sexual attraction in therapy is common. No matter what school of thought a therapist follows or what side of the wheel he or she practices on, more than three quarters admit that they are sexually turned on by certain patients. That's a lot of therapists. Rather than telling all these clinicians to be on guard against these feelings and to stifle them as quickly as possible, which is what the politically correct attitude tends to do, I think we should pay more attention to these warning signals. The training young therapists receive, which is discussed in the chapter "Repairing the Damage," needs to be radically revised. Rather than having graduate students sit around a table giving prissy responses to silly scenarios — What would you say if your patient asked, "Are you attracted to me?" — we need open discussions of actual cases, which is how all the other aspects of psychotherapy are taught. The supervisors who guide therapists need to be able to discuss their own, real experiences of powerful sexual attraction. If they cannot tell all, then the therapists coming to them will not trust them with their embarrassing secret feelings while there is still time to avoid an affair.

Sexual attraction is an occupational hazard for therapists — a legitimate, serious problem — and, as we often tell our patients, it is not wise to solve serious problems quickly. It is often more instructive to stand under a problem and experience the uncomfortable ambiguity it brings to us. What does a problem like attraction want from us? For example, the dilemma "I am powerfully drawn to a patient. What should I do?" may want us to notice something specific about our life or more general about the practice of psychotherapy. The problem says, "Watch it. Something is out of balance here and needs to be put back together in a new way." It gives this warning to an individual, and it gives it to a group and a society as well. If the problem is either denied ("I didn't feel a thing") or solved without thinking ("Drawn to a patient? *Wrong!*"), the warning goes unheeded. We don't learn what changes need to be made and, untaught, we remain children or fundamentalists, acknowledging only black and white in a world of a thousand grays. If instead the problem is entertained — literally invited in, fed, questioned, and cared for — it will eventually tell all. It may tell a therapist a personal story about loneliness or a dissolving marriage, or it may tell an angry story about feeling exploited by a managed care company and wanting to pass on the exploitation. It may tell a universal story about how difficult it is for people who are different from each other to come together with true and abiding respect, especially in a society that is so large and complex that a sense of solidarity is rare and confusion common. This is the heart of my argument. I do not advocate sex in therapy on either side of the wheel, but I do advocate questioning — everything.

So where could I go to find the ambiguities — the questions — that I suspected still exist in the minds of psychotherapists and clients, not to mention among clergy and parishioners, professors and students? To the people themselves, of course. Purposely excluding rapists and psychotics, whose behavior seems off the wheel, so to speak, I turned to men and women who are or have been involved in a doctor-patient relationship. I also decided to talk with lawyers, students, advocates, spouses — with all who are or were affected. To my delight, I rediscovered in these interviews a bubbling cauldron of questions. Here too was both the concern and respect for other opinions that have largely disappeared from the public debate. It seems that before stories of involvement settle into a mold, not only is the full mixture of emotions still present — hope, disappointment, affection, anger — but puzzlement is there too. The uncomfortable process of standing under a problem and listening goes on — privately.

"I still don't know whether I've been sexually exploited or deeply loved," began one woman eighteen months after she left a psychiatrist who wanted to have an affair.

A graduate student in psychology asked, "Why is it that the people who do the kind of work I aspire to do, and who have such strong beliefs and total devotion — why are they so often the ones brought down by sex?"

Or, from a mental health counselor in a halfway house who, when he left, had started a relationship with a resident: "I would never have believed things could get so complicated. . . . Perhaps our relationship is making it harder for her. Maybe I am thinking of myself too much."

From an entirely different perspective, a member of a board of examiners wondered why, "in most of the cases we handle, there is nothing approaching complete agreement. Someone feels wronged by us."

And a psychiatrist, a woman who fell in love with a former patient and established a relationship that evolved through a number of stages over several years, spoke of the unwanted secrecy of the relationship. "I can't be open about this relationship with colleagues because the new rules say we can't be feeling real affection for each other. The rules also say I can't be a good person. Six or seven years ago I could, but not now."

After I had read or listened to scores of accounts — old and new, public and private — it became apparent that the stories could be divided into a few broad categories. I had expected that the outcome of the relationship, whether it hurt or helped, would separate the accounts; instead, it was the kind and amount of thinking that had gone into the stories that separated them. Some accounts are thoughtful and complex. They wander through changes of heart and inconsistencies. Other stories hammer away at a single theme as if presenting a case in court, where the only objective is to annihilate the other point of view. Still other stories hold together in the sense that all the players — therapist, client, and community — speak the same language. They agree, for example, that the experience being discussed is some form of abuse or some variation on the theme of troubled or impossible love. Such an account may be angry and disputatious, but it is cohesive. On the other hand, when the speakers do not start from anything like the same basic assumptions, the story is incomprehensible. If both the board of examiners and a client call an experience abuse but a therapist genuinely believes it was love, the account will be told in two mutually exclusive languages. Because neither side is willing to translate, the result is senseless confusion and the level of frustration unpleasantly high. This kind of talking at cross purposes from entirely different sets of expectations happens in more and more areas of our lives, as our society becomes increasingly diverse and its members increasingly anxious to speak out for special rights rather than general liberties. Thus, when physical intimacy enters psychotherapy, the accounts that emerge are either complex stories or single-minded arguments, and each of them may or may not fit the accounts told by the other people involved and the public's ever-changing expectations.

The battles that commonly rage over sexual exploitation in psychotherapy and more broadly over the role that love should or should not play in good treatment are part of several larger battles — one in the field of psychotherapy, the other in society as a whole. Within the overlapping realms of psychiatry, psychology, and social work, tremendous changes are taking place. The largest is the shift from individual enterprise, an independent clinician handling his or her own cases with little comment from anyone else, to managed care, a system in which administrators control the volume and allocation of services. As health management organizations increasingly determine what problems are worth treating, who goes to the hospital, and what records must be kept, the power and responsibility of the average clinician have been reduced as never before. Paralleling changes already made in education, medical care, organized religion, and other "services" — and motivated by the same social and economic desires — psychotherapy is becoming a standardized service provided by a system rather than a private interaction between individuals. The hope is that costs can be held down while services are provided to more people. Perhaps unfortunately, the new way of doing business also weakens the doctor-patient, clergy-parishioner, and teacher-pupil relationship and changes the nature of the interaction. What were once open-ended explorations in each of these fields are now the monitored and modified "lesson plans" made jointly by insurance companies, social service agencies, and licensing boards. "The [current] standard of care itself conspires against the genuine meeting of persons," wrote one psychiatrist, adding that "professionals work very hard at living up to this impossible demand to be nonpersons."

Carrying this line of reasoning a step further, I will argue that to the extent that changes in clinical practice block genuine intimacy in psychotherapy, they push more and more clinicians into the blue zone of the business world. This has its advantages — one of them a possible reduction in lovestruck affairs — but it also has a downside, which includes the various sins of insensitivity. Although the slogan "Hug a client, hire a lawyer" may accurately describe a sad truth, so do sayings like "A pill and a pat and skip the chat." As teachers, therapists, and clergy bid a distracted farewell to intimacy, and as both the helper and the helped feel the frustration of being in a managed relationship instead of a real one, it is possible that the rate of blatant sexual exploitation could rise rather than fall. As we will see, several investigations into doctor-patient sex have found that sexual exploitation occurs when therapists become cynical and disillusioned with their profession.

A second change is occurring in psychotherapy. At the same time that treatment is being paid for and delivered in new ways that are quicker and more efficient but that also rule out long-term caring, the field is being taken over by women, who traditionally value intimacy more and give it more room in their work. In the past twenty years, therapy has changed from a man's profession to one in which women form the clear majority, and this is changing the way therapy is performed, delivered, and regulated. Counteracting the pressures of managed care, the feminization of psychotherapy tends to make treatment more honestly intimate and less sexually exploitive. It is also likely to reduce the incidence of therapist-client sex. All the surveys run to date as well as court records suggest that female clinicians are far less likely than their male colleagues to have sex with patients, and that when they do, their male clients are less likely to complain. (This is not true of their female clients.) However, roughly 85 percent of the reported complaints involve a male therapist and a female client. Thus I believe that the dominance of psychotherapy by women will reduce both sexual exploitation and lovestruck affairs, at least in the heterosexual population.

A still broader context in which to view sex in therapy is the civil rights movement in general and the women's and consumers' movements in particular. Like managed care and feminization, these changes have also shifted power away from the professional clinician and handed it over partly to the "consumer" and partly to those in the middle, specifically consumer groups such as the Alliance for the Mentally Ill, women's organizations, lawyers, members of ethics committees, and licensing boards. With all this advocacy, well-intended regulations are introduced by the dozen to protect the consumer. Each takes away another area where clinicians had previously used their own judgment. Like the economic changes, these regulations push the therapeutic relationship away from a flexible, private duet toward a business contract. The resulting retreat from the patient has already occurred in clinics and is now starting in private practice. Such abrupt changes and the accompanying loss of power make therapists nervous and irritable. Casting around for remedies, they enroll in training programs that teach them to be wary of litigation, affection, their own progress notes, overinvolvement, political indiscretion, patients who can't pay, and boundary violations. They are taught to practice defensively — to be afraid of the people they are trying to help.

"If a patient approaches you with her arms out for a hug," wrote Thomas Gutheil and Glen Gabbard in an article on the defensive practice of psychiatry, "grab her wrists and cross her arms in front of her body." Or, from a policy statement issued by an Episcopal diocese for its Sunday schools: "*No* adult should be alone with a child. . . . Doors should be left open and someone needs to 'pop in' at random intervals."

These are extremely sad statements. When the shepherd has begun to fear his flock as well as the wolves, what has happened to the helping professions? Does affection have any place in psychotherapy anymore? Or is intimacy of any kind too risky?

To weave these several themes together — to use stories of intimacy in psychotherapy to examine our changing expectations and to illustrate the risks and benefits of caring — I have divided *The Intimate Hour* into three parts. In "A History of Sexual Encounters in Psychotherapy," I explore the kinds of relationships doctors and patients, clinicians and clients, pastoral counselors and parishioners, have formed over the past hundred years. Drawing on diaries and letters as well as interviews and biographies, I let all the parties "talk." In viewing a far broader sample of relationships than is publicly available, we can compare statements such as "Professional organizations invariably will act to protect the therapist" and "*He* invariably ends the 'relationship' leaving the woman distraught" with a fuller accounting of actual lives.

In the second section, "The Current Situation," I present a kind of life cycle of both sexual exploitation and troubled love in therapy. How large a problem is doctor-patient and doctor–former patient sex, as measured by surveys? What kinds of doctors take advantage of what kinds of patients? What recourse do women have, and what laws or codes of conduct have been instituted to protect them? How can a person repair the damage done? And how can clinicians be better trained and, if necessary, rehabilitated? Is it true that for the lovestruck, love listens only to love?

The third section asks, "Why Can't We Talk About Love?" Here I try to identify the fears that arise when clinicians are asked to examine the deep emotional bond that draws and holds doctor and patient together. At least for the past two hundred years, practitioners have been alternately approaching and avoiding this topic. Mesmer discovered that the very presence of the doctor — his animal magnetism — had unsettling yet salutary effects on female patients, but it sounded too much like sexual attraction to be therapeutic. His methods were banned. A century later, Freud rediscovered much the same phenomenon, but he called the patient's amorous reaction transference love, by which he meant an attraction transferred from an earlier love to the therapist. Again, clinicians stepped away from any personal involvement in and serious investigation of the doctor-patient bond. It was as if they were saying, "If the therapeutic alliance feels in any way sexual, look the other way for an explanation." Because of this fear of violating sexual taboos, clinicians have consistently failed to see and appreciate the deep, irrational components of the doctor-patient bond.

This third section also discusses what makes for good doctor-patient relationships, or to put it another way, what constitutes the active ingredients of therapy. Some clinicians argue that love, both in and out of therapy, is necessary for the development of individuals — that we simply don't develop except through all kinds of love. Others — although not many others — believe that erotic tension runs through therapy and prompts both doctor and patient to pay attention to each other. Is the new generation of female clinicians buying these ideas? And with their greater focus on intimacy, do they hope to restore the old doctor-patient closeness but without the wrong kinds of love barging in?

It seems to me that any book on psychotherapy can either deepen the divisions that already exist between doctor and patient, clinician and managed care company, male and female, fear and love, or it can search for reconciliations — not for compromises necessarily, but for an understanding or a story that makes sense of what is going on for everyone. This is not easy. Some readers will confuse my desire to understand what happens when doctor and patient are strongly attracted to each other with approval of such liaisons, and others will be so certain that men are always abusive or women always hysterical that they will have difficulty imagining a story that can respect the feelings of both.

"Reconciliation?" asked a woman who described herself as a survivor of clergy sexual abuse. "I can't imagine what a reconciliation between a victim and abuser would sound like unless one of them gave in."

What indeed? A story is told about the remains of Saint Nicholas, who, among other wonderful things, was the patron saint of sailors. Thus, centuries ago, when Italian mariners heard that Saint Nicholas's tomb, in what is now Turkey, was about to be desecrated by Muslims, they took his remains to the seaport of Bari and had a church built over the new grave. The structure was beautiful, full of dazzling embellishments that twined and twisted around apse and nave. However, it was later discovered that North African craftsmen had subtly worked Arabic letters into the decorations that read, "There is no God but Allah, and Mohammed is His prophet." Tear it out, the citizens cried. Plans were made to do just that, but as the design and the underlying construction of the church were studied in detail, it became apparent that the two were so intimately joined that the letters could not be removed without ruining the building. At last it was decided that the contradiction was going to have to remain, and that the unusual and altogether mysterious beauty of the church itself constituted an unexpected reconciliation.

This is not a perfect analogy for my story of sex, love, and psychotherapy, and I wonder if the citizens of Bari removed centuries of grime from the church as they studied the possibility of removing the Arabic letters. If they did, I could say I am in favor of removing the dirt, but I think that removing love itself — the privacy, the affection, the attraction, even the holding and comforting of the disconsolate — can only damage the very structure of therapy.

So I am after a story about men and women that overarches both troubled love and exploitation, that makes sense of the longing and the sadness of both doctor and patient without excusing one or babying the other. If such a story can be found for certain cases, I think the reconciliation will be discovered to lie in the unexpected merit of ambiguity — in the capacity of the human heart to bear and profit from the great and contradictory feelings it encounters.

"To be human is to be confused, distraught, in pain, in love, unable to decide what is right and what is wrong," wrote a Sufi poet many centuries ago.

Here are a few examples of that common confusion, taken from consulting rooms, hospitals, and offices, from wherever therapist and client sit across from each other, earnestly attempting to love and not love, to draw closer by the hour and also remain apart.

I

A HISTORY OF
SEXUAL ENCOUNTERS
IN PSYCHOTHERAPY

God is love — I dare say. But what a mischievous devil
Love is!

— Samuel Butler

At least since the 1880s, when Eugen Bleuler made the surprising discovery that even the sickest patients could sometimes be revitalized if a personal relationship were developed with them, it has been assumed that some form of mutually respectful affection is essential to serious psychotherapy. We now know that powerful bonds develop among people who share any intense emotional experience — a hotel fire, a rite of passage, a hijacking, serious therapy — but when men first set themselves up as scientific healers of the mind, it was not at all clear just what the relationship between doctor and patient ought to be or what it would be if left to develop naturally. In this section I present examples of the kinds of intimacy that have developed in various therapeutic settings over the last hundred years. Individually, these stories chronicle events in particular lives; together they illustrate our progressive attempts to define the proper relationship between the leader and the led.

In the early years of psychoanalysis, Freud had a great deal to say about doctor-patient intimacy. When his friend Josef Breuer first used the "talking cure" on the passionately hysterical Anna O., Freud was on hand to witness Breuer's distressing emotional involvement. So was Breuer's wife. After nearly losing his marriage over a long and dramatic treatment that culminated in Anna's going through the motions of giving birth to an imaginary child fathered by Breuer, the esteemed physician noted with irritation "that it was impossible . . . to treat a case of that kind without bringing his [the doctor's] activities and mode of life completely to an end. I vowed at the time I would *not* go through such an ordeal again."

Freud commiserated with Breuer's ordeal, but he saw no way of circumventing the possibility or even probability of intense attraction. In fact, after treating neurotic patients in Vienna, Freud came to believe that love was essential to his new method of psychoanalysis — but not *real* love, not love that involved the analyst. In his opinion, a patient would not "make the effort" or would not "listen when we submit our translation [interpretation] to him" unless he or she had transferred old longings and desires onto the analyst. In other words, when patients fell in love and thought that the love they felt was for their analyst, Freud called it a transference or transference love. "Essentially," he continued, "one might say, the cure is effected by love." Of course this posed certain dangers. Freud realized that to the extent that analysis is driven by the patient's transference love for the doctor and made possible by the doctor's deep yet unexpressed concern for the patient, psychoanalysts would always risk being "slandered and scorched by the love with which we operate — such are the perils of our trade." Freud further admitted that he himself had occasionally mistaken transference love for the real thing and come "very close to [an indiscretion] a number of times and had a narrow escape." Of his disciples, Carl Jung, Sandor Ferenczi, Otto Gross, Oskar Pfister, and Ernest Jones, among others, also came very close to it a number of times — and did not escape. Even for analysts who managed to stay in their chairs, erotic love posed a delicate problem. In these early days of psychoanalysis, most people were shocked by the idea that sexual longings and fantasies were discussed with young female patients at all, much less made the focus of treatment. Critics condemned the new treatment as "morally dangerous" and labeled its more flamboyant practitioners "pigs."

Thus in the first fifty years of psychoanalysis it was gradually recognized that love as well as sexual attraction was bound to hover dangerously near the couch. Controlled by the analyst who followed Freud's "rule of abstinence" and sought to resemble a blank screen, these essential longings energized the treatment and inspired remarkable insights into the workings of the human psyche. Less controlled by analysts who disliked this unnaturally cold and superior position and preferred a more egalitarian approach, the analysis became more humane — and the attraction more dangerous. Wilhelm Reich gave back rubs as part of his treatment. Ernest Jones was blackmailed by a former patient, Wilhelm

Stekel continually seduced patients, and the Swiss minister and analyst Oskar Pfister, undeterred by the triple prohibition of marriage, ministry, and professionalism, became enamored of a patient. As Freud learned of these goings-on, he was afraid. Such uncontrolled passion would damage the profession's reputation. It would also sabotage the therapy itself *and* hurt patients. He wrote a long letter to his favorite disciple, Ferenczi, urging him *not to kiss.*

When the talking cure crossed the Atlantic — driven in part by the expulsion of Jewish analysts from Europe before World War II — the very concept of "the perils of our trade" began to change as psychoanalysis took on some of the emotional caution characteristic of Americans. Although expatriate analysts like Otto Rank still cavorted in Harlem dance halls with desperately free spirits like Anaïs Nin, Americans in general were uncomfortable with the adoring dependence that neurotic women seemed to develop on their doctors, especially when the subject under discussion was sexual attraction. James Jackson Putnam, who first put Freudian doctrines to work in the New World, complained that the undercurrent of desire that bore therapy along was simply "an evil which must be accepted." (He also altered the seat of his daughter's bicycle so she would not be unduly stimulated.) Another American psychiatrist burned a book of Freud's because it was "filthy." This prudery, as Freud called it, did not stifle yearning for long, however, and in the 1940s, '50s, and '60s, new methods of therapy encouraged the doctor to take a more active, personal role and prompted techniques that variously offered support, insight, drama, wrestling, and sex. World-renowned figures such as Wilhelm Reich, Karen Horney, and Fritz Perls as well as barely remembered analysts from Manhattan to Los Angeles became sexually intimate with patients, who increasingly came from all walks of life, not just the upper class. In Europe too, the new, less formal approach to analysis led to some curious interactions. Melanie Klein, who believed that emotional disturbances could be traced all the way back to infancy, analyzed one of her male patients on her hotel bed while on vacation, and the beloved pediatrician-turned-analyst, Donald Winnicott, held his patients' hands, fed them biscuits, and opined that "probably there are times when a psychotic patient needs physical holding."

At the same time, new schools of psychological thought were beginning to proliferate, and nonmedical training programs created a new profession called clinical psychology. Each new therapeutic school re-defined its goals and techniques, and each encouraged a slightly differ-ent kind of doctor-patient interaction. Now, in addition to lying on couches, patients gathered in groups, sat in hot tubs, and went for walks with their increasingly accessible therapists. No longer cultivating a blank and neutral demeanor, men like Fritz Perls hugged, held, tackled, and screamed at their clients. Robert Lindner, author of *The Fifty-Min-ute Hour,* made emergency house calls, even to a single woman's house at night. And female analysts reported doing a lot of reanalyses of women who had been seduced by previous male analysts.

When self-enhancement movements such as those sponsored by the Esalen Institute in California gathered momentum, sexual intimacy briefly moved from its position as a peril to an active ingredient — an adjunct — of treatment. In those hip and flower-powered years when emotional health seemed primarily a matter of letting it all hang out, charismatic therapists like William Schutz "liberated" their followers by sleeping with them in the perhaps naive expectation that good sex would release and repair their emotional problems and lead directly to health. The most notorious of these loose cannons was a Dr. McCartney, who boasted that in forty years of practice he had treated more than fifteen hundred women, 30 percent of whom sat on his lap and kissed him and 10 percent of whom found it "necessary" to undress, fondle, or have in-tercourse.

Both the early laissez-faire attitude imported from Europe and this brief period of permissiveness turned a sharp corner in the 1970s, when society's thinking about doctor-patient affairs headed in an altogether different direction. For one thing, sexuality had moved from its central position as *the* underlying cause of most neuroses to being one of several causes of emotional distress. The drive for sexual union and all it repre-sented didn't seem as powerful a motivator anymore, and doctors en-couraged their patients to discuss other feelings. For another, both love and sex were being reevaluated in light of the women's movement, and Cupid was losing his credibility as the innocent bearer of happiness. Was it possible, some women began to ask, that love was also a chain that shackled them to the roles of mother and housewife? What then of therapy and therapists — that helpful process whereby kindly men calmed rebellious women and enabled them to return to their positions in the home? Could it be, they wondered, that therapy was sexist and therapists potential enemies?

Reignited by the women's movement, the old turn-of-the-century complaint that some therapies were dangerous and some therapists pigs took on broader meaning and was voiced with greater urgency. This time, professional organizations responded. In hopes of avoiding strict regulation by the state, such groups as the American Psychological Association issued codes of ethics that formally banned sexual intimacy between therapist and client and then between therapist and former client. A few years later, state regulations put teeth into these bans. Not surprisingly, the stories told about intimacy in therapy also changed. There were no more stories of celebrated analysts falling in love with patients. No more tales of dumpy little psychiatrists the shape of penguins holding schizophrenic charges on their laps and feeding them mashed potatoes to calm them down. And especially no more stories of nude volleyball games on the therapist's ranch. Instead, the standard account of powerful attraction in therapy became the imbroglio — the horrifying story of a vulnerable young woman going to a male therapist for help and receiving coercive propositions and sex instead. In little more than a single decade, all attraction in therapy was subsumed under this category and viewed as abuse. The examples that abound in both popular and scientific writings are part of the new literature of victimization and are emblematic of our day. *Betrayal* is a good example, as are *The Killing Cure* and *Sex in the Therapy Hour.*

Interestingly, some of the same groups who, in the name of greater equality for women, pushed for the regulation of doctor-patient relationships are now leaning tentatively in a different direction. Carter Heyward, a radical feminist and a professor at the Episcopal Divinity School, and Annie Rogers, an assistant professor at Harvard University and an active contributor to works on women's psychology, have both passionately and publicly criticized their personal experience in therapy. It was overregulated, rigid, and inflexible. It was rulebound. As patients, both Heyward and Rogers found themselves unable to explore — verbally — the mutual currents of love each felt in the therapeutic relationship. This is a new theme in doctor-patient relations, and women, more than men, are feeling their way toward a different form of intimacy, which may pose different dangers and promise different rewards. Finally, there still exist the hidden stories, the tales of therapist and client, clergy and parishioner, who insist they are in love. These stories are much less confident than they used to be. They are on the run.

Four years ago, at a workshop on sexual abuse among clergy, a lawyer presented the latest changes in the Episcopal Church's code of ethics. He told the audience that sexual relations of any kind between clergy and parishioners were henceforth forbidden. As many of the participants began mumbling to their neighbors, a silver-haired man in black clericals stood up.

"How many people here," the priest asked quietly, "are married to a parishioner? Will you stand?"

Amid the scraping and moving of chairs, some seventy-five men stood up, and the audience laughed with relief.

"Excuse me," broke in the lawyer. "This kind of thing happened under the old regulations, but it cannot happen any longer."

"Of course it will happen," said the priest kindly, as the room grew still. "We just won't talk about it anymore."

And we don't — not from the therapist's or the clergy's point of view. Officially banned, these apparently loving but possibly abusive relationships have disappeared into the shadows, where they cannot be seen or studied. Nevertheless, here is a sampling of all kinds of stories; each raises a question that needs to be pondered, not dismissed. Some accounts were written before doctor-patient liaisons were banned, some after. Most are private accounts — diaries, letters, guarded conversations — others are public statements of a grievance. Together, these stories may give us a clue to the nature of the love or lust that continues to be ignited between so many therapists and clients. We will not find in all the accounts the same flammable form of intimacy that drove Breuer out of the field and briefly flustered Freud. There is a variety of magnetism.

So let us start with Carl Jung. What did this brilliant and decidedly eccentric doctor find so irresistible in the young, pigtailed, and quite crazy Sabina Spielrein for the better part of fourteen years? And what did he mean to her?

1

Early Romantic Explosions

In view of the kind of matter we work with, it will
never be possible to avoid little laboratory explosions.

— *Sigmund Freud*

On a rainy afternoon in the fall of
1910, twenty-five-year-old Sabina Spielrein returned to her room in
Zurich to read for her courses in medical school. Torn between sobbing
and screaming with rage, the young woman stomped into her boardinghouse and made straight for her room and her diary. On the way she
passed a mirror.

"That couldn't be me," she wrote the next day, "that stony gray face
with the uncannily grim, burning black eyes staring out at me: it was a
powerful, baleful wolf that lurked there coldly in the depths and would
halt at nothing. 'What is it you want?' I asked myself in horror. Then I
saw all the lines in the room go crooked; everything became alien and
terrifying. 'The great chill is coming.'"

Spielrein did not lose her grip on reality this time — she went
straight to bed instead — but she knew without a doubt she was headed
for psychosis, for that horrifying state of mind that earlier in her life had
sent her howling through her home, beset by ineradicable visions of
human feces, and that had finally propelled her into Europe's best
asylum. She also knew that this particular episode was being triggered
by her analyst, colleague, and lover, Carl Jung. He had stood her up this
rainy autumn day, and when she reached his office, which was also his
home, "he could not even take the trouble to come downstairs and
apologize for having me travel all the way to Küssnacht in vain." The

following day she learned that her beloved Jung had been with his wife as she delivered a daughter.

~~~

Sabina Spielrein was Carl Jung's first psychoanalytic patient. In 1904, when she was nineteen, she had been admitted to the hospital where the thirty-year-old Jung worked as both clinician and researcher. Diagnosed as a "psychotic hysteric" — in other words, as a hysterical young woman whose symptoms were far worse than fainting spells and whose treatment required more than marriage — Spielrein was seen as both classic and unusual, a challenging subject on which to try a new word association test. Thus, as her delirium cleared largely of its own accord, Fräulein Spielrein began meeting with Dr. Jung every other day. There she sat in a chair, her bright peasant's dress falling in folds around her, her long, dark braids hanging down her back. The doctor sat behind her. While she gave her associations to a list of words and told stories from her troubled childhood in Russia, he wrote down what she said, noting especially any pauses or jumps in her associations.

After three months of this treatment, Jung believed he had discovered the cause of Spielrein's troubles — a cause that also expressed Jung's interest in the psychoanalytic thinking that a Professor Freud in Vienna was beginning to expound. Jung felt that Spielrein's preoccupation with feces and masturbation stemmed from spankings she had received as a child from her father. When she had been slapped on her bare behind, Jung believed that the young girl had been both humiliated and sexually stimulated. This created a muddle she could not solve. In her case, the frustration was so intense that she screamed uncontrollably and at times lost touch with reality. In later years, when something triggered memories of these beatings or of her father or even of a hand, Jung theorized that Spielrein was again pulled into a maelstrom of disgust, pleasure, and guilt and again reacted with a "screaming fit." These connections having been explained, Jung thought his patient would be cured once they figured out the chains of memories that triggered the screams. (Jung's method failed to unearth the startling fact that Spielrein's mother had kept her daughter completely innocent of the facts of life — even having a course in the girl's *Gymnasium* changed to eliminate all references to sexual reproduction.)

Jung also set out to educate the obviously bright young woman about hysteria and its symptoms, and toward this end he gave Spielrein his dissertation to read. A supposedly scientific evaluation of the séances he had attended with his cousin Helene, who acted as the medium, the dissertation expressed Jung's fascination with the mystical. Unerringly, Spielrein focused on the story between the lines and understood that Helene had developed a crush on Jung, which had both pleased and annoyed him. This intriguing predicament interested Spielrein far more than the séances themselves, and she began to compare Jung's treatment of Helene to his treatment of her. She noticed that with neither woman had Jung established "just the usual doctor-patient relationship." For example, shortly after Jung had assigned her to his hospital laboratory for "work therapy," he told Spielrein, "You must become a psychiatrist." When she described a dream she'd had about his wife, he sighed and admitted that marriage was difficult. And when she talked to him about his experiments, he suggested they go for a walk.

In a matter of months Jung and Spielrein became friends, which initially made them both noticeably happier and more productive. Jung received three promotions that year, and Spielrein, having done well as his assistant, enrolled in the medical school at the University of Zurich two months before leaving the asylum. At this point she was still an unusually naive schoolgirl, still extremely moody, and still fearful that she would not become the someone special that she hoped was her destiny. If on a Monday she felt "composed" and "reasonable," by Tuesday she would feel "destroyed" and "tortured." "May I not already be a hopeless case?" she would ask herself in one way or another almost every day. At the same time, her disturbing delusions were gone, and she had her screaming fits under control. Deemed well enough to leave the asylum, she embarked on the triple career of student, outpatient, and laboratory assistant. All three involved long, private talks with Jung. They saw each other daily and talked about their ambitions, their ancestors, their dreams and psychic experiences. They constantly surprised each other by supplying the very word the other had been searching for.

By 1908, three years after Spielrein had left the asylum, she and Jung had almost certainly become lovers. Returning to her boardinghouse from classes, she would look for Jung's calling card, which would provide the time and place of their next secret meeting. Thus, in addition to daily meetings at his office on the far side of the Zurich See and the occasional exchange of letters, the two would meet on the steep green hillsides outside the city or in some other quiet spot. Wherever they met, the now rapidly maturing Russian with her dark hair and eyes and the blond, charismatic doctor would throw themselves into discussions that simultaneously revealed the similarity of their temperaments and the intensity of their lonely yearning. Jung was particularly friendless at this time, for the one radically free spirit in whom he had confided, the analyst Otto Gross, had just left Zurich.

Gross had gotten into terrible trouble. He had given a patient who may have been his lover the poison she needed to commit suicide. He had fathered two children in a single year, one to his wife and one to someone else's wife, and he held group discussions where people took their clothes off. To protect him from retribution, his family committed him to the asylum where Jung worked. Jung was thrilled. Now he had one of the most spirited and experienced analysts in Europe to talk to. Doctor and patient quickly agreed to analyze each other, and they had been taking turns associating to words and interpreting dreams until, without warning, Gross hopped over the hospital fence and disappeared. Luckily for Jung, he was able to transfer some of his enthusiastic discussions about work and love to his friend Fräulein Spielrein.

"My dear," he wrote, "you cannot imagine how much it means to me to have the hopes of loving a person whom I must not condemn, and who does not condemn herself, to being smothered in the banality of habit." He had, he continued, become much more attached to her than he believed possible. This was doubly astonishing because "it is only with great difficulty that I can actually muster that belief in man's natural goodness which I so often proclaim."

Initially, the two seemed to have come together cautiously. For a time they had taken turns resisting each other's advances, for Jung did not want a scandal, and Spielrein did not want to ruin her chances of attracting a well-to-do husband. Yet she kept putting her fingers on precisely those topics dearest to Jung's heart. She claimed she had prophetic dreams: Jung was fascinated. She seemed to read his thoughts: he had been interested in this very phenomenon as a college student. She explained to him why Wagner was for her the most psychological composer: "Dr. Jung's eyes filled with tears. 'I will show you, I am just writing the very same thing.'" It seemed to both of them that they were soul-mates.

Sometime in this period Jung became Spielrein's "poet," as she termed it, "i.e., my beloved. Eventually he came to me and things went as they usually do with 'poetry.' He preached polygamy; his wife was supposed to have no objection, etc., etc."

In the literature of the time, "poetry" was a common metaphor for lovemaking, and although various historians have interpreted Spielrein's and Jung's "poetry" as "amorous intoxication," kissing and fondling, or sexual intercourse, it is clear from Spielrein's diary that at the very least there was an intoxicating amount of sighing, gazing, and holding, and that the effect of all this stimulation on her was riveting. When she played the piano in the evenings, she pretended Jung was listening, and when she worked on her dissertation, which supported many of his ideas, she thought of the project as "our little son, Siegfried." Spielrein sensed the power of Jung's imagination — its remarkable breadth, its daring — and when the two sat "in speechless ecstasy for hours," she felt secure in a private world of great richness. In love with Jung, she was smarter, stronger, and more beautiful. Standing before her mirror and admiring her "lovely and well developed" curves, she had to admit that everything in her life revolved around Jung — her hero, her teacher, her beloved . . . and her former doctor.

Not long after the two began composing "poetry," however, Jung got scared. Vacillating between playing the part of a sensitive, passionate lover whose "life means nothing to me without the joy of love, of tempestuous, eternally changing love," and a frightened doctor who needed to step back from his involvement, Jung reconsidered this risky relationship. When his wife gave birth to a longed-for son at the end of 1908, he found himself spinning out of control with anxiety. Surely Spielrein was going to choose this moment to go public with their affair. Now that he was corresponding with Freud and had been appointed editor of a new psychoanalytic journal, and now that he had the son and heir that Spielrein had dreamed she would someday give him herself, Jung became convinced that his life would collapse.

"I am looking for a person who can love without punishing, impris-oning and draining the other person," he wrote to her three days after the birth of Franz and one day after he had met with her and begged her to end the liaison. "Return to me, in this moment of my need, some of the love and guilt and altruism which I was able to give you at the time of your illness. Now," he added, "it is I who am ill."

In spite of Jung's mounting anxiety and Spielrein's anger at being discarded, the two continued to meet for more than a month, until Spielrein's mother received an anonymous warning that Jung was setting a match to her daughter's reputation. Caddishly, Jung answered Frau Spielrein's concern by saying that if she wanted him to treat her daughter properly, she should pay him for every one of their meetings.

"The doctor knows his limits and will never cross them," he wrote, "for he is *paid* for his troubles. That imposes the necessary restraints on him." At the same time, he hurriedly cut Spielrein's time back from one or more hours each day to a single hour per week. When she objected, he lectured her for being an insatiable, ungrateful woman. Stung by the condescending letters to her mother (which she read) and enraged by Jung's eagerness to discard their relationship of more than four years, Spielrein flew into one of her famous rages. Arriving at his home, knife in hand, she pushed her way into his office, scuffled with him, cut him — or possibly herself — then went tearing off again with a bloody hand. As she later confided to her diary, she attracted quite a crowd with her weeping and wailing. Jung was sure the scandal had begun.

Indeed, Spielrein was beside herself. For a time she left Zurich and went to the countryside. Then she returned, dropped most of her courses, and let her mother and father take care of her. Eventually she tried to confront Jung in person. She appeared at one of his lectures, turned white, and fled. Finally she made a desperate attempt to hold on to her love — not to hold on to Jung himself, but to resurrect her picture of him as a loving and wonderful healer. If she could do this, her affair would maintain its ambivalent status as a relationship with a gifted but difficult man. If not, then the entanglement was one big, long mistake. Spielrein explained all this in several letters, one of which was a detailed, twenty-page description of the affair. She sent them to a stranger, to the one man whom she believed treasured Jung as much as she did — Sigmund Freud.

"Dear Professor Freud," she began her third letter, "Please forgive me for disturbing you again. . . . You imagine that I have turned to you so that you may mediate between Dr. Jung and myself? Yes, but there was no quarrel between us! *My dearest wish is that I may part from him in love.*

"I . . . would like to part from Dr. Jung completely and go my own way. But I can do that only to the extent that I am free to love him: if I either forgive him everything or murder him."

The remainder of the letter made it clear that she felt more like killing than forgiving. Out poured all her fears — "he was using me for his first experiment," he is "a complete no-good" — and out poured memories of Jung's vicious parting shots — "wretched no-good," he had called her. "Let Siegfried fall." "A kiss without consequences costs 10 francs." She complained bitterly to Freud of her "faithless lover" and, to make her position absolutely clear, sent him copies of the letters Jung had written to her mother, his notes to her, and bits she had copied from his diary.

"Just think, Professor Freud," she wrote, "when he [Jung] handed me his diary, he said, hoarsely, 'only my wife has read this . . . and you.'"

It took Spielrein the better part of a month to write this passionate, disorganized account of her affair, but when at last it was mailed off to Freud, she apparently felt better. Turning Jung in to the authorities had lifted a lot of weight from her chest, and she began refocusing her attention on her studies. For his part, Freud passed most of the information Spielrein gave him straight back to Jung, and the two had a couple of condescending chuckles at her expense. Jung told Freud that "my test case," as he called Spielrein, had set out to seduce him just as "Gross' notions flitted about a bit too much in my head."

Freud responded in a companionable manner. Only the strain of his work and "the fact that I was ten years older than yourself when I came to psychoanalysis, have saved me from similar experiences," he wrote. "They help us to develop the thick skin we need and to dominate 'countertransference,' which is after all a permanent problem for us."

Spielrein, meanwhile, was struggling to survive upheavals that didn't feel like "little laboratory explosions" to her. Believing that Freud understood and sympathized with both Jung and herself, she found the courage to confront Jung and propose a truce. In exchange for her silence, Jung agreed to write to her parents and Freud and to admit to "a piece of knavery." In other words, Jung retracted the rumor he had been spreading that Spielrein's recent distress was merely the recurrence of her old illness. It was instead, he admitted, the natural reaction of a woman leaving an unhappy love affair.

Spielrein took the next year to pull herself together and finish a dissertation that centered on a woman not altogether different from herself. She probably gained considerable insight into her own difficulties from the case — an occurrence so common among clinicians that they have a saying: "If you wish to feel better, go into therapy. If you wish to get better, become a therapist." However it was accomplished, Spielrein was growing up. In six years, she had gone from a screaming psychotic girl to a young woman about to graduate from medical school, but a year after she left Jung, a different problem arose. No one was reading her dissertation. Eugen Bleuler, her university adviser and an expert on schizophrenia, was not comfortable with Spielrein's interest in analyzing her patients' sexual fantasies. Thus, as the months passed and Spielrein received no response to her work, she began to doubt her conclusions. Her insecurities returned, and by August 1910 she was frantic.

> Despair gave me courage. I ran to my friend, with whom I had not wanted to speak for a long time. For a good while I found no words, until I was finally able to tell him of my desperate situation and ask him to read my dissertation, if for no other reason than that he figures in it. . . .
>
> The most important outcome of our discussion was that we both loved each other fervently again. My friend said that we would always have to be careful not to fall in love again; we would always be dangerous to each other. He admitted to me that so far he knew no female who could replace me. It was as if he had a necklace in which all his other admirers were — pearls, and I — the medallion. At the beginning he was annoyed that I had not sent my paper to him long before, that I did not trust him, etc. Then he became more and more intense. At the end he pressed my hands to his heart several times and said this should mark the beginning of a new era.

The new era bore a striking resemblance to the old one. Again Spielrein burned for Jung, and again her moods and self-esteem were tightly tied to his words. If one summer afternoon she walked down the warm cobblestone streets of Zurich in private raptures, the next day she asked herself, "So why am I filled with agitation again? Why this pain?" Her nights were particularly dreadful.

"Two bad nights," she wrote in her diary. "My love overwhelmed me with a mad glow." She described how she lay in bed imagining herself struggling in Jung's arms, resisting violently. In her mind's eye, she could see him pulling her to his chest as repeatedly she tried to push away. Again and again this scene played over in her mind. Suddenly, she acquiesced. Swooning with love, she clung to his lips and let him kiss "every one of my little fingers."

"So how am I supposed to withstand this savage force?" she asked herself in the middle of a night "so wonderful, so treacherously warm," but her reason did not answer. Instead, the incestuously entwined streams of memory and imagination carried her through scenes of love-making — Jung tenderly embracing her, she pregnant with his son, Emma Jung divorcing her husband, she herself being driven out, the wholesome Emma being seduced by a Frenchman. She remained sleepless 'til dawn.

Spielrein found herself so distracted by her reunion with Jung that she feared her concentration would fail and she would bungle her exams. Although happy to be reunited with the one man she had ever loved, all the original problems remained. Nevertheless, Spielrein gradually found a stance she could maintain. Investing most of her energy in an attempt to find a position halfway between Freud's more intellectual and Jung's more emotional theories, she remained attentive to Jung but no longer one of his possessions. In fact, some four months into "the new era" Spielrein moved to Vienna, where she sat in on Freud's Wednesday evening gatherings and referred to herself as his pupil.

For a year or so Spielrein, Jung, and Freud bickered among themselves as ambitious colleagues often do. When Jung read Spielrein's papers, for example, he would write to her expressing modest praise, then send a letter to Freud criticizing her work as "heavily overweighted with her own complexes." Equally duplicitous, Freud would pleasantly agree with Jung while urging Spielrein to dump "as so much trash your infantile dreams of the Germanic champion and hero." Jung meanwhile complained to Spielrein that Freud "ascribes to a complex everything I do that does not fit the framework of his life."

After a year in the spiteful atmosphere of the Viennese psychoanalytic circle, Spielrein was convinced that neither Freud nor Jung nor the Wednesday evening analysts took her work seriously. In April 1912 she stopped trying to focus their attention on her ideas for reconciling the Freudian and Jungian philosophies and moved to Berlin. There she met Paul Scheftel, a Jewish physician about whom little is known. At the same time, for reasons both theoretical and personal, Freud and Jung broke what was supposed to have been the closest relationship in the select circle of psychoanalysts.

"I propose that we abandon our personal relationship entirely," Freud wrote to Jung after a long period of tension.

"I accede to your wish . . . for I never thrust my friendship on anyone," Jung responded. "You yourself are the best judge of what this moment means to you. 'The rest is silence.'"

Thus by 1913, when Sabina Spielrein was twenty-eight years old, she and Jung and Freud were going their separate ways — and discovering what each had lost. Freud moved another step away from the open collaboration he had tried to establish with his fellow analysts and increasingly worried about loyalty and allegiance. Later he became deeply depressed. For Jung, the loss of what were arguably the two most important relationships of his life was more painful still. Without Freud's insisting on intellectual honesty and daring and without Spielrein's encouraging the intensely emotional and imaginative side of his nature, Jung slipped from the delicately balanced position he had occupied. No longer able to hold himself between mind and emotion, male and female, past and present, Christianity and Judaism, his productive state of ambivalent yearning collapsed, landing him in a cul-de-sac. He suffered through an extended period of nightmares and morbid waking fantasies. At first he was able to distract himself from sadness and guilt in part by lecturing in America. Later, the lines in *his* room went crooked, and he had periods of barely controllable psychosis.

When Freud and Jung parted company, Spielrein was pregnant and already unhappy with her marriage. Although she occasionally wrote to both men, there is no record of her being close to either again. She told Freud that she still longed for Jung, which, of course, irked Freud considerably; at the same time, she sent her dreams and a few musical compositions to Jung, who answered her letters sporadically. After giving birth to a daughter, Spielrein wrote for psychoanalytic publications and also turned to music in a haphazard way. No matter what she did, however, she remained troubled by her ambivalent desire for Jung and, symbolically, for Siegfried, the great hero and son she had longed to give him. During her pregnancy, she had become convinced that her confusion over Siegfried was making her sick and would actually harm her unborn child. Although this hadn't happened, she was still concerned. Finally, in 1919 she asked Jung for advice on how to make sense of these lingering feelings.

"I sincerely want to learn how to accept Siegfried in the right way," she wrote, going on to describe a conversation she'd had with Freud nearly ten years earlier on the same subject. Stung by the news that Spielrein had shared their secret fantasies with Freud, Jung replied with a bitter, sarcastic letter. He equated Freud's work with darkness and said that anyone who went around telling secrets was just as bad. Although Jung said he couldn't tell Spielrein how to deal with her mixed feelings toward him, it is clear he wanted her affection and respect.

"I have lit in you a new light which you should protect," he wrote, adding that "this cannot be told to outsiders. . . ."

We have no record of how Spielrein responded to Jung's outburst, but five months later she received a very different kind of letter that suggested Jung too was at an age when he wanted to figure out what they had meant to each other.

Only with the passage of time do the patterns of a life become distinguishable, and it is in or after middle age that certain encounters stand out as inspiration, turning point, or missed opportunity. As Jung looked back, he increasingly saw Spielrein as all three. She was a light or a star that had, in combination with other influences, turned him toward the mystical complexities of the psyche and then held him on that course. Even her loss had generated a sad power of its own — an energy kindled more readily by loneliness than by satisfaction.

"The love of S. for J.," he wrote, "made the latter aware of something he had previously only vaguely suspected, that is, of a power in the unconscious that shapes one's destiny, a power which later led him to things of greatest importance. The relationship had to be 'sublimated' because otherwise it would have led him to delusion and madness. . . . Occasionally one must be unworthy, simply in order to be able to continue living."

Here, at last, was a full admission — two, actually. First, Spielrein had accomplished what she had so ardently hoped for. She had been Jung's inspiration and muse. She had been as important to him and his work as he had been to hers.

"Whatever the specific contributions of Spielrein or Jung to the Jungian system," wrote Bruno Bettelheim, "Jung asserts . . . that it was in their love affair that the system itself originated."

And second, Jung acknowledged again that he had been a cad, unworthy. It was he, not she-the-former-patient, not she-the-young-or-frivolous-woman, who had sacrificed their love in order to go on with his life.

Toward the end of the life that Jung had so often and so ruthlessly preserved, he described the discovery of the unconscious force that Spielrein's love had inspired. He said that he had become aware of a woman's voice in his head that expressed a point of view different from his own male point of view. He called this feminine force his anima, and it is now widely believed that Spielrein was this force.

"She had become a living figure within my mind," he wrote.

And he had become a "soul-mate," as Spielrein termed this ongoing and deeply spiritual aspect of their relationship.

At first, the presence of this anima or "ghost," which apparently had a mind of her own and was not merely a way of thinking that Jung could call on at will, annoyed him. However, late in his life he reported turning to her in times of trouble. He also turned to stones for comfort, and as he grew old he spent more and more time at his rural retreat, building stone towers and learning to carve stones. These remain as expressions of his last preoccupations. The stone carvings that represent the anima include a Russian bear with a Latin inscription *"Ursa movet molem,"* which Jung told a Swiss colleague symbolized the Russian bear getting the ball rolling. A second plaque shows a mare with the inscription "May the light arise which I have born in my body." A third in the anima series was not finished or destroyed.

There is no record of correspondence between Jung and Spielrein after 1919. After spending a few years in Geneva, where she used obser-vations of her daughter for papers on child development and became Jean Piaget's training analyst, Spielrein returned to Russia — first to Moscow and then to her home in Rostov-on-Don. In both places she worked as an analyst and teacher until Stalin came to power and psycho-analysis went into hiding. At some point she had a second daughter, and it is rumored that her husband returned to her after a long absence with a daughter from another woman. He died in 1938. With the approach of World War II, Spielrein's life, like many of those around her, took a tragic turn. Two of her three brothers were reportedly killed for political reasons, and when the Nazis occupied her town in 1941, she, her daughters, and the rest of the city's Jews were said to have been taken into a synagogue and shot. However, there is no official notice of her death.

For nearly forty years, Spielrein's only "headstone" was the thirty papers she had published and the often disguised references to her that Jung made both in his memoirs and in his carvings. With the publication of the Freud-Jung correspondence in 1974, Spielrein became known in her roles as a patient and a danger, but nothing was revealed of her personal life. Then, in 1977, a carton of letters and diaries was discovered in the basement of the Palais Wilson in Geneva, where Spielrein had worked. Apparently she left the box behind when she moved to Russia. Miraculously, the papers were not thrown out but sent to a Jungian analyst in Italy who had written on Spielrein and who quickly began a more extensive work. By this improbable series of events, Sabina Spielrein became the subject of *A Secret Symmetry* by Aldo Carotenuto. Through it she has emerged from the synagogue in Rostov-on-Don to take her place as a psychoanalyst in her own right and as the patient, colleague, and lover of Freud's "crown prince," Carl Jung.

~~~

The Jung-Spielrein affair raises all the common questions associated with erotic intimacy in therapy. Here I will mention only two. First, how can a woman make sense of an experience that seems to combine great affection with mean-spirited abuse? Had Spielrein been callously abused? Involved in a troubled love affair? Or both? Her evolving answer, of which we know only a little, was inevitably shaped by the cultural expectations of her day. This leads us to the second question, namely: In what ways and to what extent do cultural forces shape the stories of doctor-patient entanglements?

As is usually the case, critics are divided about the Jung-Spielrein relationship. Some judge Spielrein's treatment to have been unorthodox and inspired. Others consider it outrageously unethical. Yet they largely agree that Jung's intense interest in Spielrein drew her out of her psychosis, and her intense interest in Jung led him to a deep and unusual understanding of the psyche.

"Profound changes took place in both doctor and patient," wrote Ethel Person, a psychoanalyst and author of a book on love, "and must be largely attributed to the transformational power of love." Or, in the same vein, "We ought to ask ourselves," the celebrated analyst Bruno Bettelheim wrote, "what convincing evidence do we have that the same result would have been achieved if Jung had behaved toward her in the way we must expect a conscientious therapist to behave toward his patient? However questionable Jung's behavior was from a moral point of view — however unorthodox, even disreputable, it may have been — somehow it met the prime obligation of the therapist toward his patient: to cure her. True, Spielrein paid a very high price."

Subsequent critics have angrily called this a transparent excuse. Jung was known to have used women all his life — he had a forty-year affair with Antonia Wolff, another former patient turned analyst, and in his sixties he eased her out in favor of Ruth Bailey. In *Against Therapy*, Jeffrey Masson comes out strongly against Jung. He deems Jung's behavior toward Spielrein inexcusable, and believes that Spielrein got better in spite of, not because of, Jung.

If we allow Spielrein herself to be the judge, her letters and her continued desire to remain in contact with Jung suggest that the relationship organized her life for better as well as for worse. It gave her a purpose. Initially, she fell in love with a charismatic doctor, and later, became an able psychoanalyst and writer. Although the periods of passionate harmony with Jung were woven into her anger at his cavalier treatment of her, Spielrein seems to say in her diary that Jung was the man she loved most in her life. No other man ever drew from her, or matched, the full range of her powerful emotions and insightful thinking. Spielrein expected great things from herself at a time in history when women often measured success in terms of their collaboration with or inspiration of a man. These expectations, personal and cultural, may have combined with Spielrein's memories of walks and conversations and embraces to lead her to believe that there was more troubled love in their relationship than abuse. Maybe. All we know for sure is that she never stopped thinking about him. Although we must be cautious not to impose our own view of the world on her story, a case can just as easily be made for calling the relationship more exploitive than helpful. In either case, however, I think it is fair to say that Spielrein's long relationship with Jung danced crazily over both the warm and cool regions of the therapy wheel and involved both people at vulnerable moments of their lives as well as when they were more secure. The meaning of the relationship changed over time for both of them, and, like other affairs of the heart, it cannot be judged solely by the way it ended.

~~~

As Freud was receiving letters from Spielrein complaining that Jung was a faithless lover and cad, he was also getting letters from his Hungarian disciple Sandor Ferenczi, hinting that a married patient was becoming uncommonly important to him.

"My personal well-being (psychic) was good . . . ," the thirty-six-year-old bachelor wrote in October 1909, "as long as it was possible to keep frequent company with Frau Isolde. (I will call her that, which was also her name in one of my dreams.)" A few days later, Ferenczi admitted that the relationship was further advanced than he had intimated. "Evidently I have [found] *too much* in her," he wrote, "lover, friend, mother, and, in scientific matters, a pupil. . . . So, I have everything that can be distributed by nature between the two sexes combined in a single person."

Freud was not at all pleased. For one thing, the new discipline of psychoanalysis was regularly coming under fire as morally dangerous and it did not need another scandal; for another, Ferenczi was a favorite of his. A charming, quick-witted neurologist and would-be analyst from Budapest, Ferenczi had traveled to Vienna in 1908 to meet the man whose discoveries he could not get out of his head. The two men were drawn to each other immediately — Freud impressed by the younger man's readiness to speculate imaginatively on every conceivable topic, Ferenczi steadied by the professor's intellectual strength and integrity. Within a matter of months, Freud had invited Ferenczi to drop in on him during his summer vacation, and within a year the two began what became a long and revealing correspondence. At the same time Freud undertook a catch-as-catch-can analysis of Ferenczi, which proceeded both in their correspondence and whenever the two were together. Freud had high hopes for him, and he did not want his analysis or his career derailed by a dangerous love affair.

"When . . . I first learned of the relationship," Freud later wrote to Gizella Pálos (alias Frau Isolde, Frau S., and Frau G.), "I made a face and made it very clear to him that I wished something else for him."

Ferenczi tried to comply. He told himself that he needed a younger woman so that he could start a family. Analyzing his feelings toward his mother, he worried that the affair with Pálos was mixed up with old loves and hates. He even tried to have a fling with "a thirty-year-old divorced woman (not a patient)," but failed. "I am unshakably fixated on Frau G.," he wrote. And later, "she has proved herself to be a true life's companion."

Soon Freud himself agreed. When he met Frau Pálos, he was as delighted as Ferenczi by her wit, good sense, and intelligence. A naturally empathic person, she wanted to become an analyst, the kind who paid at least as much attention to healing as to learning. In spite of the risks involved, Freud could see that Ferenczi now "possessed incomparably more than what he had renounced. Since then," he wrote to Pálos, "not a word or a gesture has issued from me that could have weakened his attachment to you." And so the affair proceeded, thoroughly aired and analyzed by Ferenczi and quietly tolerated by Freud.

Quite abruptly, however, Ferenczi fell madly in love with his patient's daughter, Elma. He had taken her into analysis because she was depressed and inhibited — not good traits for a young woman of marriageable age — and within four or five months he admitted to Freud that he was smitten. Perhaps, he suggested, he should marry Elma and keep her mother as a friend. For a month the entire family was in an uproar, and letters flew between Budapest and Vienna as everyone wrote to everyone else. Finally, on December 30, 1911, Ferenczi wrote that "the — certainly positive — decision about my marriage to Elma will probably not be long in coming." Indeed, the already completed plan was put before Elma's father, who sputtered a bit, then reminded Elma that she had called off an earlier engagement. "At that," wrote Ferenczi on New Year's Day, "to my amazement, certain doubts crept into *Elma's* mind. That made me suspicious."

Finally realizing that he should be treating Elma, not marrying her, Ferenczi begged Freud to rescue him by taking the young woman into treatment. Thus Elma went to Vienna to be analyzed by Freud, and Ferenczi gradually found his way back to Gizella Pálos.

To Ferenczi's consternation, Elma soon returned from Vienna, feeling confused and betrayed. Encouraged and then dropped by Ferenczi, obviously in a muddle with her mother (who had not admitted that she was Ferenczi's lover), and let down by Freud, who passed the details of her analysis on to her former fiancé and mother, Elma belonged nowhere. Eventually she was shunted into a marriage of convenience, which ended unhappily, and the volatile yet indecisive Ferenczi married Pálos, who by this time had become an analyst herself.

Although never presented as a glorious chapter in the early annals of psychoanalysis, Ferenczi's personal struggles with love and erotic attraction led him to a series of insights that significantly changed the practice of psychotherapy. Ferenczi had first tried to copy Freud. Using the standard technique of frustration, he had remained totally detached from his patients. He sat behind them during analysis, revealed nothing of himself, and adhered to the "rule of abstinence," which meant he did not touch them, not even to shake their hands. This was supposed to frustrate their desire for a real relationship and force them to create an imaginary one in which they guessed at the analyst's responses. In other words, in the absence of real feedback, patients imagined what the analyst was thinking about them and behaved in accordance with these imagined responses. And what did patients imagine their analyst was thinking? Freud had realized that their guesses were shaped by the way they had been treated in the past, especially by their parents. Not only did patients expect from the analyst the same responses they were used to receiving, but they also responded to the imaginary feedback the same ways they had always responded. And these were, after all, the ways that had caused them pain and had brought them to analysis. In simplest terms, forcing a patient to jump to conclusions gave the analyst a map of her problems.

Useful as this technique was in Freud's hands — and it was immensely useful — it was abhorrent to Ferenczi. Identifying so easily with his patients' loneliness and dejection, he longed to make up for their unhappy childhoods and to show them how restorative a good relationship could be. Moreover, as he treated patients over long periods of time, he began to suspect that in successful analyses a realistic connection (as opposed to an imaginary or transference relationship) was established between analyst and patient *even when the frustration technique was used.* "Patients at some level are actually acutely aware of all our real feelings and thoughts," Ferenczi maintained.

"I tried to pursue the Freudian technique of frustration honestly and sincerely," he wrote in a diary he kept during the last several years of his life. "Following its failure I tried permissiveness and relaxation, again an exaggeration. In the wake of these two defeats, I am working humanely and naturally . . . on the acquisition of knowledge that will allow me to help." Noting that Gizella Pálos, now Mrs. Ferenczi, felt the same way, he let her express his deepest sentiments. "Mrs. Ferenczi felt, and rightly so, attracted to the essence of psycho-analysis — trauma and reconstruction — but repelled by all analysts for the way they make use of it. . . . She longs for an analyst who will be analytically as gifted as she is, who will be concerned above all with truth, but who will not only be scientifically true but also truthful regarding people."

How to be truthful regarding people: Ferenczi came at this problem from a dozen different directions and modified his technique with each discovery. For example, in 1926 he crossed the Atlantic to give a series of lectures in New York City and en route became miserably seasick. He began thinking of pain in context and how some of his delusional patients tried to alter or control their pain by radically changing its context — by flying out into the universe or dancing among the stars. Aha, thought Ferenczi, I am seasick because I am insisting on dragging my old context — terra firma — out to sea. If, by an effort of will, I become this boat, I will get better. So Ferenczi strenuously imagined himself merging with the boat, and his seasickness disappeared. Immediately he became fascinated by autosuggestion. How does it work? Do Christian Science beliefs produce physical cures? Always looking and asking, he wondered if psychic healers knew something he didn't know.

In this manner, Ferenczi happily whacked his way through the unexplored jungle of human desire and frustration, taking each insight *ad absurdum*, he liked to say, then falling back to a moderate and informed position. None of these exaggerations, however, was as dangerous as his experiments with indulgence. During this period his aim was to remain deeply relaxed in the patient's presence and let her do almost anything she wanted. In one case, this led to a kind of group analysis at a patient's hotel and included the patient — a woman the size of an elephant — her female companion, two monkeys, three dogs, and several cats. In another case, it led him to hold two- and three-hour sessions seven days a week and to take the patient with him on vacation. In the most celebrated case, it involved letting himself be kissed and cuddled by the strangely brilliant American analyst-in-training, Clara Thompson — and this one brought down the wrath of Freud. Unlike the jolly letters the professor had sent to Jung twenty years earlier about the Spielrein affair, Freud's response to Ferenczi had real anger beneath the surface. Kissing and snuggling were going to destroy psychoanalysis from the inside by attracting silly practitioners as well as from the outside by ruining its reputation.

> You have not made a secret of the fact that you kiss your patients and let them kiss you. . . .
>
> Now picture what will be the result of publishing your technique. . . . A number of independent thinkers in matters of technique will say to themselves: Why stop at a kiss? Certainly one gets further if one adopts "pawing" as well, which after all doesn't make a baby. And then bolder ones will come along who will go further, to peeping and showing — and soon we shall have accepted in the technique of analysis the whole repertoire of demiviergerie and petting parties, resulting in an enormous increase of interest in psychoanalysis among both analysts and patients. The new adherent, however, will easily claim too much of this interest for himself . . . and God the Father Ferenczi, gazing at the lively scene he has created, will perhaps say to himself: Maybe after all I should have halted in my technique of motherly affection *before* the kiss.

"And then you are to hear from the brutal fatherly side an admonition . . . ," Freud continued in a more serious tone. "According to my recollection a tendency to sexual play with patients was not completely alien to you in preanalytic times, so that the new technique could well be linked to an old error. That is why I spoke in my last letter of a new puberty."

Ferenczi was stung, not by Freud's objection to kissing, which he expected, but by his mentor's lack of faith in him. As he saw it, being indulgent was not seducing his patients, as other analysts had been known to do; it was seriously asking the basic question: "What helps?" It seemed to Ferenczi that Freud increasingly disregarded this question in favor of learning about neuroses and advancing the political fortunes of psychoanalysis.

To Freud he wrote:

Your fear that I might develop into a second Stekel [a well-known womanizer] is, I believe, unfounded. "Sins of youth," mistakes, once they have been overcome and analytically worked through, can even make one wiser and more prudent than people who have never experienced such storms.

And to his diary he confided:

I tend to think that originally Freud really did believe in analysis; he followed Breuer with enthusiasm and worked passionately, devotedly, on the curing of neurotics (if necessary spending hours lying on the floor next to a person in a hysterical crisis). He must have been first shaken and then disenchanted, however, by certain experiences, rather like Breuer when his patient had a relapse and when the problem of countertransference [the analyst's feelings toward the patient] opened up before him like an abyss.

. . . Freud no longer loves his patients. . . . He still remains attached to analysis intellectually, but not emotionally.

Ferenczi was especially worried that such a stance could not be assumed without condescension. It seemed to him that Freud's therapeutic technique was becoming less and less personal until the doctor was left "levitating like some kind of divinity above the poor patient, [who is] reduced to the status of a mere child." Worse, the transference, or imaginary relationship that the patient has formed in the absence of feedback and that constitutes the map of her problems, "is artificially provoked by this kind of behavior." In other words, in his effort to remain objective and safe from the "unbearable upheaval" of real relationships, Ferenczi believed that Freud may have created an artificial situation that evoked artificial responses from patient as well as doctor. What kind of recovery could that promote?

Although Ferenczi never broke off his relationship with Freud, he increasingly took the position that patients are sometimes confused by the hypocrisy of their analysts. If a patient doesn't fit your way of working, Ferenczi told his students, probably thinking of his own analysis with Freud, change your technique.

Thus in the last several years of his life Ferenczi experimented with "mutual analysis," whereby analyst and patient literally took turns on the couch. This was not an extension of his indulgence technique, however, which he had come to realize mixed real life into analysis too thoroughly. He could not let his patients believe that they could be cured simply by staying with the kind doctor. Recovery required more than tenderness, and being an analyst required not only self-control but the willingness to kill off the fantasy that the patient could rest forever in his love. He had to admit that "the hangman's work is inevitable." So back came the boundaries and discipline. In mutual analysis the doctor retained some authority, but the process worked toward mutual respect, equality, and independence. The technique had some daunting problems, Ferenczi admitted, one being confidentiality and another the anxiety he felt as he put himself "in the care and control of a madman," but it had some surprising advantages as well. The recovery was "no longer based on authority," and the patient was no longer shocked by the analyst's imperfections. In fact, Ferenczi thought that no matter how hard an analyst tried, he was bound to repeat the same mistakes that parents and lovers had already committed, to the detriment of the patient. Unlike these other people, however, the analyst admitted his inability to understand perfectly and to help effectively. He said he was sorry. At the last, Ferenczi wondered if successful analysis did not lie in mutual forgiveness.

The kindly, bespectacled Ferenczi, who admitted that he made mistakes because he could not bear to see patients suffer, died in 1933 of pernicious anemia. His diary remained discreetly unpublished during Freud's lifetime and was then delayed further by political squabbles among analysts. It finally appeared in English in 1988; his correspondence with Freud came out still later. One result is that sixty years after his death, Ferenczi has become popular with feminist therapists and theorists, some of whom see in him "the mother" of psychotherapy.

Ferenczi's marriage to Gizella Pálos, his flirtation with Elma, and his cuddling with Clara Thompson have a different flavor from Jung's relationships. Although both men helped as well as hurt the women they were attracted to — and in Elma's case the hurt vastly outweighed the help — Ferenczi's bumblings have about them a more earnest and compassionate air than Jung's. Rather than using a series of women to steady himself, learn about women, and offer affection, Ferenczi seemed mostly involved in mending the broken. He acquired the reputation of dealing with the sickest patients, those whom other analysts had given up on, and he would do anything, including make mistakes, to alleviate their suffering. If Jung's affairs represented a brilliant man's weakness, Ferenczi's kisses were a kind man's mistakes — at least in the case of Elma. His contented marriage to Pálos apparently represents a successful doctor–former patient relationship.

~~~

Jung's and Ferenczi's different styles of indiscretion did not exhaust the possibilities, and Freud continued to receive news of romantic explosions. Not only did patients tattle on their therapists who were his disciples — the prolific Otto Rank was too often "dazzled" by love, Victor Tausk had been engaged to marry a patient before he killed himself, Sandor Rado's third wife was a patient, and Wilhelm Reich believed sexual orgasm to be the key to personal and social freedom — but Freud also learned second hand about a second generation of analysts who were wrestling with the powerful attraction that the talking cure induced. A student of Ferenczi's had just gotten a banker's daughter pregnant — for the second time. Karen Horney was having an adulterous affair with the much younger Erich Fromm, who was still married to his former analyst, Frieda Fromm-Reichman. And Friedrich Perls (later known as Fritz) was listening attentively to Reich explain how fear gets locked in a person's muscles and can be liberated in treatment by a back rub. Nor were these indiscretions and experiments going on solely in Vienna. Horney was in Berlin, Rank in Paris, Perls on his way to South Africa. The new discipline of psychoanalysis was taking hold all over the world — and taking its problems with it. As might be expected, one of its more extravagant affairs occurred in April in Paris, in the City of Light. And this time two respected analysts, both writers, teachers, and members of prestigious psychoanalytic societies, seemed to have been taken for a ride.

For the writer, dancer, and seductress extraordinaire Anaïs (Ah-nah-ees) Nin, "life only became real when I wrote about it." So write she did. Starting the first of a hundred and fifty volumes of private journals at the age of eleven, Nin created an amazing series of portraits of herself, her times, and her shockingly erotic dreams. The first to admit that she tinkered creatively with the truth — "I always play roles to appear more powerful, more impressive than I feel" — she dramatized her way through a life that began inauspiciously with a sexually abusive father, a broken family, and a nomadic childhood. When her father, who took nude pictures of her as a youngster and later had an affair with her, abandoned his family for another woman, his wife and their three children moved first to Barcelona and then to Manhattan. There Nin lived with relatives until she turned twenty and married a wealthy American, Hugh Guiler, who took a position with a bank in Paris. In this bustling city, the home of a great group of bohemians, expatriate artists, surrealists, and composers, Nin metamorphosed from a shy, Catholic wife into an exotic enchantress. She took dancing lessons and had costumes made for her. She decorated a home on the outskirts of Paris to resemble a Middle Eastern palace. When she met Henry Miller in 1931, she bought a white beret and embarked with him on the passionate life of the uninhibited, unrestrained, and unrecognized artist.

Second only to her reputation as a diarist, Nin is known for the long and tumultuous affair she carried on with Miller during the years he wrote *Tropic of Cancer* and later. The two read each other's journals, drank together in small cafés, wrote introductions for each other's novels, and came together like cats. "I rush to my passion, Henry, last night, and we indulge in such an orgiastic fucking that I do not wish to awaken from it. And we laugh together — he says obscene words which I repeat. Afterward, lying in bed, we talk gravely about Dandieu's book on Proust."

Sexual activity uncorked Nin like a bottle of champagne. The stories, songs, and paintings, the dances, decorating, and entertaining, once stifled inside her now came boiling to the surface in a rush of manic energy. In a single day she would eat breakfast in a satin gown and give orders to the gardener as Mrs. Guiler, peel potatoes, edit, make love, and take walks as "Mrs. Miller," then copy over her diary, and take a dancing lesson all as Anaïs, and finally entertain guests in the evening as all three people in one. No matter which role she was playing, however, she stood at center stage. At the very least, she was acting for her diary. Occasionally all this activity exhausted her, and she went to bed in a cold and loveless mood that terrified her. She felt, but could not yet formulate, the destructive pattern that lay beneath her breathtakingly ornamental surface. There was a hidden cost for the power she enjoyed when on display.

In one of these pensive moments, Nin decided to seek the advice of a psychoanalyst. Perhaps, she thought, he could help her to understand, and fix, Miller's childlike dependence on her — and his continued attraction to "little whores." Thus on a warm spring day in April, when Paris cast a spell of tender green leaves over willing inhabitants, Nin knocked on the door of Dr. René Allendy, a founding member of the Paris Psychoanalytic Society, a writer, and a professor at the Sorbonne. Moments later, Nin found herself seated in a heavy armchair in a heavily draped office. Behind her, she could hear the forty-three-year-old Allendy scratching intermittently on a notepad. Very quickly he noted her seductiveness and suggested that she lacked self-confidence. He suspected that early in life she had associated — and confused — sex with affection. Being a Freudian, Allendy fit Nin's life into the Oedipal drama and told her that she must have wanted to win her father away from her mother at a very young age.

Nin was fascinated by Allendy's interpretations and even more intrigued by his way of thinking. The focus on sexuality and the primitive drive for pleasure fit perfectly with the themes of her diary — her life. Dressing more provocatively for each of her sessions, the twenty-nine-year-old Nin soon began describing for Allendy her personal insecurities. For example, she was afraid that her breasts were too small, and she insisted on rising from the armchair, confronting the doctor, and unbuttoning her blouse, then her bra. In her diary, she recalled his saying "lovely . . . well-shaped" in what she thought was a softer, deeper voice. She further challenged Allendy by telling him that she could not achieve orgasm, although in her diary she records many with Miller. When Miller cheated on her soon after, she confided to her diary that in revenge, she would now seduce Allendy. Since the analyst had already predicted that Nin would suffer the common feeling of being abandoned when analysis ended, a kind of preemptive revenge was directed toward him as well. In late summer, therefore, Nin marched into Allendy's office and announced that analysis was over. To her delight, he asked for a good-bye kiss but, to her annoyance, only brushed her lips lightly. Going a step further, Nin went to a clinic, had cosmetic surgery performed on her nose, then called her husband, Miller, and Allendy and told them all that she was in the hospital, having overdosed on cocaine. Each man rushed to help in his way, and Allendy took her back into analysis. He realized that she was toying with the treatment, however, and insisted on completing the analysis before a different relationship began. At the same time, he agreed to analyze Nin's husband in an effort to cure his passivity.

By the following winter, Allendy may have lost his grip on the treatment. According to Nin, they took turns sitting in the armchair and telling each other how wildly they desired each other's love — and then they kissed. According to Allendy, he analyzed her erotic wishes and that was all.

In Nin's version, "Today we kissed madly, madly. He was frenzied to let me go, repeating he must cure Hugh *vite, vite,* so that he can see me, be with me. And each time during the rest of the afternoon that I remembered his closeness I grew dizzy."

Some ten months after Allendy began the analysis it was formally completed, and Nin marked the event by inviting him to the house and giving him a lavish aquarium. Because she had accepted an informal position as his research assistant, the two would continue to see each other. He expected a passionate affair. She expected to torment him. Believing him "enslaved," she began speaking openly about her passion for Miller. Allendy was indeed jealous. "He reproaches me for playing with him. For ceasing to want him as soon as he became my slave. He begins to bite me, to caress me wildly. He sweeps me off my feet. We lie on the floor. . . . He misunderstands me completely. Every word he says is wrong. All the better. . . . The core of me is untouched."

Having gained both the reassurance that she was irresistible — and a moment of revenge — Nin was finished with Allendy. Although the two eventually met twice in a hotel, she was unmoved, and it was quickly over.

Before Nin broke off all relations with Allendy, she and her husband attended several dinner parties at his house, meeting such notables as Antonin Artaud, the French poet, actor, and founder of the "Theater of Cruelty," and Otto Rank, a Viennese psychoanalyst, a friend and collaborator of Ferenczi's, and the author of *Art and Artists.*

"The book I wanted to write," maintained Nin, who immediately began comparing the short and rather funny-looking Rank, with his passion for the creative spirit, with the dapper but less animated Allendy. When Rank said that the artist creates himself through his work, Nin knew that he was the perfect analyst — for Miller — and insisted that he make an appointment with Rank. The two met for an hour or so but, in view of Miller's lack of interest in being analyzed, Rank became his friend rather than doctor. Feeling left out, Nin impulsively called on Rank the next time she walked down his street. He answered the door himself.

Nin knew she had a way of ignoring the imperfections of any man she met and focusing on his most endearing or attractive feature. Although Rank was short, with dark skin and "homely teeth," Nin locked onto his deep, brown eyes, "large, dark, fiery." Magnified by glasses, they seemed to look out on the world with both a half-mocking curiosity and a passionate interest. Rank gave her an appointment.

Otto Rank was a good match for Anaïs Nin. Quick and intelligent, he loved to match wits with the most brilliant and creative people he could find. His interests were also similar to hers. Not only was he fascinated by art and artists, but he had written on Don Juan, a character that Nin felt held the key to an understanding of both herself and her father. Rank had joined Freud's group when he was twenty-one and had soon become one of his cleverest "sons." By the time he turned forty, however, he was convinced that the Oedipal drama did not explain everyone's troubles. When he showed Freud his book *The Trauma of Birth,* a whole series of disagreements came to the surface, and Rank, like many before and after him, was expelled from the inner circle. Moving to Paris in 1926 with his wife and daughter, Rank reestablished a practice but was not happy. Forty-two years old and at the height of his career, he could not make much money in a Catholic country that was wary of analysis. In addition, he was beginning to feel that psychoanalysis was bourgeois. In his eyes, most treatments reduced people to a normal and rather dull level rather than helping them to make productive — meaning artistic — use of their conflicts. By 1933, when he met Nin, Rank was seeing only a handful of patients and was planning to move to the United States.

Nin began analysis with Rank in November 1933, and each made a shrewd move that got treatment off to a promising start. Rank asked Nin to leave her diary with him so that she would not analyze the analysis and thus remain outside the process, and she agreed. Although her diary outlined plans for lying to Rank to appear more interesting and clearly indicated that she was going to him "for the sport of it, not to solve, but to aggrandize, dramatize my conflicts," she handed over the notebook. "Immediately I knew that we talk the same language," Nin recalled later. "We understood each other with half phrases." Rank also insisted that Nin temporarily move out of her husband's house and live on her own so that she would have time to untangle her thoughts. Nin loved the idea, but she made sure that Miller had a room next door.

Supposedly deprived of her props, Nin settled down to listen to Rank's interpretations of her exhilarating and exhausting preoccupation with sex. Noting that having lots of sex doesn't change a neurotic child into a woman, Rank supposedly told her that she was a child, a wife, and a mistress — but not yet a woman. Nin loved the sound of that, although when she realized that Rank's ideal woman fit the conventional stereotype of the 1930s — a person who yearned for a man rather than for her own art — she lost interest in that form of womanhood. But it didn't matter much what Rank said. With remarkable sensitivity toward her own inner workings, Nin realized that it was "the *presence* of Rank the man which imparts the wisdom he gives." Not what he said, not what he prompted her to remember, but primarily, said Nin, his enthusiasm, his warmth, his being-in-the-room "defeats the past."

Rank skillfully led Nin toward an understanding of herself until an unexpected conflict all but forced the young woman to change her analysis back into a deafening diversion. She had become pregnant by Miller in March, but because she had been told she could never conceive, she did not believe it for nearly two months. In May she admitted that she was with child. Her husband, thinking it was his, was thrilled. So were her relatives. Miller was less thrilled. Nin realized two things: first, she felt and looked simply wonderful. She was making a baby. She was going to be a woman after all. However, she also believed that if she kept this child it would displace her as the pampered darling in her husband's eyes. Equally distressing, it would displace Miller in her own eyes, for in many ways he was Nin's project or child. So it seemed that the price of becoming a mother was losing a "father" *and* a lover. Did she want to be a woman that badly? Or did she want to be a princess, an artist, and a part-time mother and lover to artists? Her mind said, "Artist!" Nature, her husband, and social expectations ganged up on her to shout just as loudly, "Woman!"

In the face of this conflict, exacerbated as it was by the lack of safe abortions, Nin launched herself into a new affair, distracting herself with a passion so fiery it made her physically ill. Although she had done the same thing with Allendy, using her involvement with him to distract her from decisions that Miller's infidelities should have forced on her, she did not see the pattern. Nor did Rank. On May 19, she told her diary that she wanted Rank as a companion in this time of trouble. Less than a week later, she thought she might be falling in love with him. Two days after that she announced, "I will not be haunted. I will kiss Rank. *Et tout s'évanouira — tout fondra,*" she added. All will evaporate — all melt away.

"On Tuesday I decided to become an analyst," she wrote in her diary. "I fussed and fretted to obtain my new hyacinth blue dress from the cleaner. I would go to Rank the next day in my new dress because he was going to kiss me. I went to sleep full of dreams, energies, desires, I got up vibrant, courageous, impulsive. I rushed to Rank." Slender and beautiful in her slippery silk dress, Nin left her chair in Rank's office, knelt before her doctor, "and offered my mouth." He held her for a moment, then asked her to come back and talk about her work. Nin didn't get the kiss, but she knew from the embrace that she had gotten Rank.

> Oh God, I know no joy as great as the moment of rushing into a new love, no ecstasy like that of a new love. I swim in the sky; I float; my body is full of flowers, flowers with fingers giving me acute, acute caresses, sparks, jewels, quivers of joy, dizziness, such dizziness. Music inside of one, drunkenness. Only closing the eyes and remembering, and the hunger, the hunger for more, more, the great hunger, the voracious hunger, and thirst.

When Nin returned to Rank's office the next day the two were "mowed down by the same desire." They kissed. They embraced. They reached for each other roughly. And they talked. This new turn of events was enough to keep Nin's mind occupied, but not for long.

Three months pregnant, Nin went to a *sage femme,* who gave her quinine and other concoctions intended to abort the child. With each treatment, the need to reinforce the image of herself as artist and lover increased.

June 6, 1934

After dreaming all night of an orgy with Henry, I went to him and found him depressed and desirous. He had refused other times to resort to perverse ways of love, but today, after much teasing . . . he forgot himself and I swallowed his sperm for the first time.

I had to powder myself quickly afterward to arrive in time at Rank's.

Half-stretched on the couch we talked, and all the magic continued. He said, "You are an unknown woman for me. Everything I knew before about you I have forgotten, or it does not serve me. . . ."

. . . Suddenly he kissed me, kissed me voraciously. And he made me lie under him and we kissed until we forgot ourselves again, but he knew we had to stop, yet we couldn't, and in our drunkenness I found myself drinking his sperm, too. And he threw himself over me and whispered, wildly, in my hair: "You! You! You!" It was like a cry of surprise, of worship, of joy, of ecstasy.

I came away with the manuscript of one of his books, and I saw Henry again. I said to Henry, "A woman should be nourished with nothing but sperm." And we talked psychoanalysis. And Henry said, "Get independent soon so we can begin our new life soon, soon."

When Nin caught herself beginning to seduce a fourth man and wondering if she should "go to Jung now and get another scalp," she was brought up short by what she thought of as her diabolical compulsion: "not love, but revenge, or love and revenge always mixed." She believed that she betrayed men because they were treacherous. Her father had left her and the rest of the family, Henry Miller had left his second wife for Nin, Allendy and a dozen others had betrayed their wives, and now Rank was ready to break his vows. She, too, would love and betray them all.

"Will Rank be another victim, or do I love him?" she wrote in her diary. ". . . Oh, God, there is absolute confusion in me. I don't know what I am. I carry a demon in me, I feel that. Two truths, always."

After this "moment of darkness," Nin threw herself into her dream-world with Rank with, if possible, even more passion and excitement. She wrote out a ten-page summary of the effect that his theories had on her; he was pleased to be understood so directly and unintellectually. She began to criticize her father as cruel, her husband as mean, and Miller as exploitive. Rank agreed. She encouraged him to indulge the voracious appetite he had for living — a responsiveness he had always postponed. He told Nin that he did not want to live an "unused" life.

"I have found love — I have found love, love, equal love!" crowed Nin at the end of June. Having desperately blasted herself into orbit, she was astonished and delighted to find that Rank, "white with passion," was out among the galaxies ahead of her. He matched her suicidal passion, risk for risk. "Love overwhelms him, hurts him as it does me." Mysterious forces shoved him bodily across the room and into her arms. He was no longer able to walk next to her without clutching her. "YOU!" he shouted. "YOU!" The room spun for both of them, but when they made plans to consummate their love, they both lost so much sleep that they got physically sick and had to scrap the rendezvous. Finally, in mid-July, they met in Nin's house while her husband was away. The passionate Rank was, alas, "too swift." *And* he snored.

When Nin's fetus began to kick and move, she awoke from her dream of passion and realized that she was going to be a mother if she didn't act fast. Finding a doctor who was willing to induce labor prematurely, Nin sent a message to Rank that she was dying, then went through several days of painful contractions attended by husband and lovers. The baby was born dead. Nin was, if anything, less thoughtful after the abortion than before. Rather than returning in her diary to the painful dilemma presented by the pregnancy — the feeling of being trapped by her own and others' neediness — she excused herself from questions of responsibility in silly ways. Nature had shaped her body for passion only, she wrote. Destiny called her for art, not motherhood. Her love for Henry required that she not commit to anything else. After the delivery, she wrote, "the doctor came, examined me, could not believe his eyes. I was intact, as if nothing had ever happened to me." Poor Nin was right; nothing had.

When Nin was fully recovered, Rank announced that he was moving to New York, alone, and wanted her with him. Nin told him she would go but admitted to her diary that she was undecided. Nevertheless, Nin began stitching together her most audacious set of prevarications. To her husband she said she was going to New York to study psychoanalysis for two months and would then meet him in Manhattan and visit his family. To Henry Miller she said she was going to New York, not alone, but with her husband. And to Rank she wrote that she was leaving the others behind forever and joining him. He was ecstatic. "*I* am dying now," he wrote to her, echoing her summons when she was in labor. "Come to my rescue."

Nin arrived in New York right after Thanksgiving and in December started working for Rank. During the day, while he saw wealthy patients, she read his manuscripts and kept his books — tasks she found increasingly boring. At night she took him to Harlem and taught him to dance. She adored Manhattan. He adored Nin. They adored each other. But in less than two months the affair was over.

When Rank learned that both Hugh Guiler and Henry Miller were due to arrive in New York in January, he realized that he would never have a lasting relationship with Nin. He asked for his letters back and planned a lecture tour in California. He would leave as they arrived. Nin did not stop him. Feeling stifled by both Rank and psychoanalysis, she danced away from the liaison, maintaining that she escaped from theory into poetry. Again she counted herself lucky to be unmoved, writing, "The core of me is untouched."

In a last grand and comic gesture, Rank turned over his patients to Nin while he was out of town. They exhausted her. Six hours a day of listening was more difficult than she had imagined. Perhaps she was not cut out to be an analyst. On the verge of giving up her new career, Nin attended a conference on Long Island. Seated among therapists with name tags pinned to their chests, she found herself listening to the sound of the surf outside the heavily curtained windows. "I'm not an analyst," she said to herself. "I'm a writer." Immediately she booked passage back to France.

Nin saw Rank once more during his lifetime. She was in New York again in 1936 and saw him in his office for an hour. He looked good. He had a new assistant (whom he later married) and was planning to move to the West Coast, as his unconventional practices were not welcome in eastern psychoanalytic circles. In 1940 Nin again tried to call on Rank but learned he had died the year before. In her diary she wondered if she had properly told him of the considerable influence he had exerted on her. Indeed, memories of Rank remained, and his thoughtful presence appeared as the Voice and the Lie Detector in two of her stories. Nin liked to say that Rank had loved her the way she had loved Henry Miller, with impetuous generosity and tender concern. But then she would change her mind and say something else.

Nin's affairs with Allendy and Rank raise the delicate question of responsibility. Although, as we will see, the rules that now control doctor-patient and doctor–former patient relationships state that a patient is never at fault for starting an erotic liaison nor can a patient ever give true consent, it is hard not to feel that in Nin's case the exploitation was mutual. This is a common confusion. Although Nin admitted to exaggerating, to making up scenes for her diaries (one critic called them "liaries"), and to using men in malicious, premeditated ways, these were all expressions of her problems. It seems clear that she was repeating an old and destructive pattern by having sex with her former analysts — a pattern both men would have done better to resist if they wanted to change rather than reinforce her habits. In other words, it doesn't matter how exploitive, obnoxious, or seductive a patient is: no bad habit justifies turning therapy into an affair. It is preferable to refer a poorly matched patient to another analyst or terminate with one who is insincere. As Nin herself kept saying, no one could resist her and no one could help her.

Nin's affairs raise another question: Who gets to tell the story of what happened? The search for the "true account" of doctor-patient dealings has become the most important and controversial part of the current movement to clean up therapy. Although it might seem that Nin purposely misled her readers, in a modern context each of her stories would be considered to contain part of the truth. If she maintained that

Rank's touch was seductive, then that's what she felt — seduced. As the director of an institution that rehabilitates doctors said recently, "It's a case of nontherapeutic touch if the patient didn't feel it was therapeutic." However, if this is the case, what are we to make of Nin's statements that Rank exerted no influence at all on her or that he helped her? Are those true, too? In Nin's time, the doctor told the story of what happened between him and his patient, and he was usually believed. Now others have that power — sometimes the patient, sometimes the subsequent doctor, and increasingly the lawyer.

Finally, it seems clear — in spite of Nin's writings — that the two relationships affected her differently. She and Allendy used each other and threw each other away. She and Rank fascinated and respected each other. For a time, at least, Rank believed he had met his perfect mate and companion in Nin. This she did not forget.

~~~

Although we have looked at only a bare sampling of doctor-patient relationships — Jung and Spielrein, Ferenczi with both Pálos and her daughter, Nin with Rank and Allendy, and a few others in passing — it is tempting to search for generalities in light of what we know today. We could say, for example, that most of the doctors so far described seem to have been successful, married men in middle age who were attracted to women who were young, single, and intelligent. But among the doctors we have observed, Ferenczi wasn't married, his student who got the banker's daughter pregnant wasn't famous or married, Jung wasn't middle-aged, and Frieda Fromm-Reichman wasn't a man. The same unpredictable variety is found among patients. So we will need many, many more stories before we can generalize. At this point it is clear only that there is variety, there is surprise — variety that increased as psychotherapy expanded in the 1950s and '60s, and surprise that is nowhere exceeded by the improbable story of a slender young Jewish woman and a giant blob of a therapist in Nazi-occupied Amsterdam.

2

Variety and Surprise

Love affairs between therapists and patients don't always come out one way or the other. It depends on
what the affair means and on the strengths of the two
people.

— *Max Day*

In 1941, the same year that Sabina
Spielrein died in Russia and Henry Miller and his Greenwich Village
friends began exploring Eastern mysticism in California, a twenty-
seven-year-old Dutch girl attended a recital in Nazi-occupied Amsterdam, where she met a huge mound of a man who was both an amateur
singer and a therapist who had been analyzed and guided by Carl Jung.
Etty Hillesum was a bright, neurotic young woman who had moved
from the countryside to Amsterdam to continue her education. Already
holding a law degree but wishing to perfect her Russian, she found a
room in a boardinghouse overlooking the Museumplein, the city's main
square, where she could live, study, and tutor a few private students.
There she lived, in exchange first for housekeeping, then for sexual
intimacies with her landlord, a sixty-two-year-old widower.

On a winter's evening in January 1941, Hillesum walked dreamily
around the huge skating rink that was set up every year in the middle of
the square. Passing between the imposing Rijksmuseum on one side and
the columned concert hall on the other, she made her way to the home
of a friend where her brother and a few other musicians were perform-
ing. Sitting with several companions, Hillesum was surprised to see a
new face — in fact, a huge new presence.

The singer she didn't recognize was Julius Spier, a fifty-four-year-old German who had moved to the Netherlands in 1939 to live with his sister. Many years earlier, he had held positions as a bank manager, publisher, and entrepreneur before meeting Jung. During analysis, Jung persuaded him to take his talent for seeing into people and his hobby of reading palms seriously and urged him to embark on a career as a psychochirologist, a reader of palm prints. As Spier began to see patients week after week, he gradually became a therapist as well as a reader. He was also reputed to be a womanizer, and in 1935 he was divorced from his non-Jewish wife, with whom he had two children. When he met Etty Hillesum, he was renting an apartment four streets and two bridges away from her boardinghouse, supporting himself with a modest practice and writing letters to his twenty-five-year-old fiancée in London.

If his background was unusual, Spier's physical appearance was downright strange. An enormously fat man, he apparently had a body like a bull's topped with a huge, craggy head barely covered by a thinning shag of silvery hair. His jowly face was dominated by a lower lip that protruded like a shelf and quivered when he became emotional. With huge, paddle-like hands fanning the air as he sang, he reminded Hillesum of either "an ugly, ancient goblin" or an entire landscape, rough and gray and wintry, or then again he looked like "a stout, good-natured, biscuit-loving uncle." By the end of the evening, Hillesum and her girlfriends had decided that "the chamber with the warm voice" had a "magical personality." In other words, he was a thoroughly dangerous man.

Hillesum had good reason to be wary of a charming palm reader. Raised in a chaotic family with a radically unstable mother and a distant father, each of the children seemed to have inherited some aspect of the family fragility, which made them exceptionally vulnerable to outside influence. Hillesum's moody, musical brother became so distraught that he had to be institutionalized, her second brother threw himself into his medical studies with desperate zeal, and Hillesum herself was so depressed, anxious, and compulsive that she needed a two-hour nap every afternoon and a pound of aspirin every month just to keep up with a light course of study. She felt that she had an eating disorder, a sleep disorder, and an inferiority complex. Although she didn't give them a name, she also suffered from what appear to be full-fledged panic attacks, with racing thoughts and heavy breathing. These alternated with "the feeling that everything was empty of meaning, the sense that life was unfulfilled." Almost daily, the color drained from Hillesum's world, and she was stopped in her tracks by a "leaden oppression." Especially when she had her monthly period, she alternated so rapidly and so violently between great expectations and abject misery, between yes and no, between try and give up, that her friends were amazed she did not rattle.

In spite of this inconstancy and the impressionable nature that went with it, Hillesum joined her friends in signing up for weekly meetings with the singing therapist. Her hope was that this great warm man would gather up all the jumbled and broken parts of her mind and put them in order. Like the earlier formulas she had tried to live by — "get rid of pathos," "don't anticipate," "avoid hatred" — Julius Spier represented a "plan" for attaining a calm and productive life. Also like earlier formulas, Spier's therapy initiated an immediate rush of hope followed by dismal disappointment.

Some six weeks into treatment, Hillesum admitted to herself how deeply she distrusted Spier's apparently straightforward, but actually manipulative, technique. His habit of wrestling his clients to the floor and lying on top of them particularly confused her. In her diary she wrote:

When we wrestled the first time it was an enjoyable contest and though it was a little unexpected I immediately "caught on": I realized it was all part of the treatment. And that's indeed what it was, for when it was all over he stated very matter-of-factly, "Body and soul are one." I was, of course, erotically aroused by then, but he was being so businesslike that I quickly recovered. And when we sat down and faced each other, he said, "Now look, I hope this doesn't excite you, because I keep touching you everywhere," and by demonstration he put his hands out and touched my breast, then my arms and shoulders. I thought something like, "Well, my friend, you ought to know just how 'excitable' I am, because I told you so myself, but all right, it's decent of you to discuss it so openly," and I recovered a little. Then he added that I mustn't fall in love with him, and that he always said this at the beginning. Well, it was fair enough, but I felt a bit uncomfortable about it.

But the second time we wrestled, things were quite different. Then he too showed passion. And when at one point he lay groaning on top of me, for just a brief moment, and made the oldest convulsive movement in the world, then the lowest of thoughts rose up in me like a miasma from a swamp, something like: "a funny way of treating patients, you have, you get your pleasure out of it and you get paid for it as well even if it's just a pittance."

But the way his hands reached for me during the fight, the way he nipped my ear and held my face in his great hand, all drove me completely mad. I could sense the skilled and fascinating lover behind all these gestures. Yet I also thought it exceedingly mean of him to abuse his position. In the end my rebelliousness died down and there was a sense of closeness between us, and more personal contact than we may ever have again. But while we were still lying on the floor he said, "I don't want to have a relationship with you." And he added, "I must tell you honestly, I find you very attractive." And then he said something about similar temperaments. . . . Then he told me a bit about his life. He talked and I listened, all surrender, and now and then he put his hand very tenderly on my face. And that's how I went home, with the most conflicting feelings, rebellious ones because I thought he was mean, and tender ones, overflowing with human kindness and warmth. And all the while I was overwhelmed by erotic fantasies brought on by the guileful movements of his hands. For a few days I could do nothing but think of him. Though you couldn't really call it thinking, it was more like a sort of physical endurance test he was subjecting me to. His great supple body threatened me from all sides, it was on top of me, under me, everywhere, it threatened to crush me, I was quite unable to work and thought in horror, my God, what have I let myself in for; I went to this man for psychological treatment to get some insight into myself and now this, it's worse than anything I've ever known.

Hillesum and Spier were quickly locked in an unequal battle of wills. Struggle as she would not to be taken over, she found herself continually distracted. She wanted to own the man, see him all the time, ingest him. He became the drug she couldn't live without, and the depth of her dependency appalled her. Even when she managed to hate him for the torment he stirred up, she found herself wondering compulsively what part of him belonged to her, what, if anything, was left over after he poured out his affection to six patients a day, his fiancée, an old flame, and a former wife. All five girls who had signed on as patients after the musical soirée, she noted balefully, had tremendous crushes on the corpulent Herr Spier. Was he taking advantage of their loneliness, too? Although she didn't call it abuse, she recognized the exploitation.

As Hillesum was struggling to regain her equilibrium, Spier was apparently struggling to remain faithful to his fiancée. He had been successful in this awkward endeavor for almost two full years and said he was determined to continue. Yet Hillesum was such a challenge. When he felt sufficiently in control of his emotions, he'd risk pulling her to him at the end of a session just to feel a woman in his arms in these sad times and to receive the jolt she always delivered in spite of herself. If he bent close to her, she was the one of all his patients who would casually brush his enormous lower lip with her soft mouth. She would rest in his arms.

In spite of this explosive situation, which was extremely trying for both of them, Spier hired Hillesum as his assistant. They began meeting several evenings a week in his apartment, where they worked on opposite sides of a small desk. In this way the two tortured themselves by becoming companions as well as therapist and client. Hillesum grew familiar with the photo of his fiancée Spier kept on his bureau. Spier knew about Han, her loving landlord. She saw the rug beside his bed where he prayed, his Bible, his pajamas. He grew accustomed to the smell of her lilac soap. As living conditions deteriorated in Amsterdam, they increasingly consoled each other with a hug or a clinch. Hillesum noted, "A quick wrestle, threw him on the divan, nearly killed him, and then we were ready to get down to hard work."

In part, but only in part, this closer association benefited Hillesum. Gradually she adopted portions of the regime he had developed over the years to contain a similarly unruly temperament. She set aside certain times to walk and to read poetry. She adopted Spier's deep breathing exercises and tried to incorporate gymnastics into her schedule. She was fascinated by his philosophy, too, and began reading the works of Freud.

"You cannot heal disturbed people without love," she recalled Spier's saying, and she began to understand that one of the most powerful tools in his therapy was his ability to see each patient as he or she could be — *would be* — without the superficial storm and fuss. Once Spier caught a person's flavor, so to speak, he described the wonderful individual each could be. As Hillesum noted, once patients identified with the picture he drew of them, "they know what to do."

At the same time, the growing intimacy between doctor and patient increased all Hillesum's ambivalent yearnings and eventually precipitated a crisis. Spier had "laid bare the man in him so suddenly, not waiting until I asked him to throw away the psychologist's mask," that he not only lost authority in her eyes, but also jerked her violently from the protected position of patient into the vulnerable role of a theoretically equal — but actually much younger, less experienced, and less powerful — adult. It was too much. All the contradictions that characterized Hillesum's troubled attitude toward her own adulthood — she would be a great writer, she was a silly dreamer, she wanted a husband, she couldn't possibly devote herself to one man, life is wonderful, life is meaningless — rose in a tidal wave of emotion. One evening she returned from Spier's apartment shaking uncontrollably. Shutting herself in the unheated bathroom, she stripped and threw cold water all over her body. Still she shook, unable even to name much less control the conflict that gripped her.

Hillesum felt "Mortal fear in every fibre. Complete collapse. Lack of self-confidence. Aversion. Panic."

Abruptly she felt herself forced to her knees. Blue with cold, she knelt naked on the coco matting on the bathroom floor and out of her chattering mouth came a prayer. She heard herself telling God that she would resist no longer. She understood now that she was not an island, not a sanctuary-in-the-making, but a battlefield on which the problems of the times were being fought, both those of love and those of genocide and war. From now on, she told God, she would be a willing battlefield. Let the fight rage on.

Hillesum's conversation with God in the bathroom did not immediately change her feelings toward Spier or toward the war. For a few months more she alternated between wanting to forget him and to love him. She still waited tensely for his phone calls in the evening, still agonized over the absence of a letter from him on the rare occasions she left town to visit her parents, and still carried pictures of him in her head. "Does he kneel before he takes his dentures out or afterwards?" she wondered. When she saw women "give him a look of total devotion," she still believed the lecherous old bull was "skimming the cream." And yet there were moments and then hours when she was content with this impossible situation. To her diary she confided:

> Something has happened to me and I don't know if it's just a passing mood or something crucial. It is as if I had been pulled back abruptly to my roots, and had become a little more self-reliant and independent. Last night, cycling through cold, dark Lairesse Straat — if only I could repeat everything I babbled out then! Something like this:
>
> "God, take me by Your hand, I shall follow You dutifully, and not resist too much. I shall evade none of the tempests life has in store for me, I shall try to face it all as best I can. But now and then grant me a short respite. I shall never again assume, in my innocence, that any peace that comes my way will be eternal. I shall accept all the inevitable tumult and struggle. . . . I shall follow wherever Your hand leads me and shall try not to be afraid."

"Sometimes," she added, "I think that my life is only just beginning. That the real difficulties are still to come, although at times I feel that I have struggled through so many already. I shall study and try to comprehend. I shall allow myself to become thoroughly perplexed."

Something was also happening to Spier. Although in some ways he seemed to be aging before Hillesum's eyes, he was also becoming more patient and content. Hillesum's girlfriends no longer talked of having crushes on him. One confided that she was waiting for God to give her a man of her own, hopefully soon. Hillesum no longer felt jealous.

A year after the two met, Hillesum and Spier became lovers. Rumors were circulating through the city that all Jews would be deported to concentration camps, and everyone in their circle had already lost friends to the Nazis and to suicide. Every day further rationing and restrictions were imposed on the Jews. Every night they listened to broadcasts from Britain that made it increasingly clear that "our impending destruction and annihilation" were being planned. Under these circumstances, there were "hardly any accidental relationships left," Hillesum noted. "There are no wasted and boring minutes any longer."

> Last night, when I bicycled over to see S. I was filled with a warm, intense longing for spring. And as I rode dreamily along, over the

asphalt of Lairessestraat, looking forward to seeing him, I suddenly felt the caress of balmy spring air. Yes, I thought, that's how it should be. Why shouldn't one feel an immense, tender ecstasy of love for the spring, or for all humanity? And one can befriend the winter, too, or a town or a country . . . a wine-red beech tree. . . .

And so I came to him. The small bedroom held a glimmer of light from his study and when I walked in I saw that his bed had been turned down and above it a heavy-laden spray of orchids had been hung to spread its fragrance. On the little table beside his pillow stood daffodils — so yellow, so poignantly yellow and young. The turned-down bed, the orchids, the daffodils — there was no need to lie down in that bed; even as I stood in that dimly lit room it was as if I had had a whole night of loving. And there he was sitting at his small desk, and I thought again how much his head resembled some grey, weather-beaten, age-old landscape.

. . . Was it only fourteen days ago that I had been so wild and wanton, pulling him towards me, bringing him down on top of me and later feeling so unhappy that I could barely go on living? And was it only a week ago that I slid into his arms and was still unhappy somehow because something about it seemed so forced?

No doubt these ports of call were necessary in order to reach these calm waters, this intimacy, this cherishing and valuing of each other. A night like this lingers as large as life in one's memory. And not many such nights may be needed for the feeling that life is rich and full of love.

As vast fields of tulips bloom in Amsterdam, in sun or rain, peacetime or wartime, so Etty and Julius presented their new love to each other and to the world. "In a flush of spring fever" this mountainous man bought his love yellow bell flowers and daffodils, then fragrant orchids and tulips whose small red buds and tiny white ones were "so tight, so inaccessible, so incredibly dear." He marveled at the changes he saw in her — such mounting happiness — and in the new feelings of dedication and trust he felt in himself. He wanted her to see him without his teeth.

In the afternoons the two walked together hand in hand along the quiet canals, wearing the gold stars that marked them as Jews and that kept them off public transportation and out of certain streets. In the evenings they scrounged some bread, a little honey, perhaps a bottle of wine, and met with friends for music and poetry. One evening Julius read Rilke's poetry — to Etty's surprise, the very work she had begun to read on her own — and his great lower lip quivered. "And I am touched by the fact that at that moment he looks as if he is about to burst into tears," she wrote. "And I would gladly weep in unison with him."

And laugh. With her "beloved, dearly beloved . . . priceless, private psychological university," Etty found that so many things made her happy and so many things connected her to a kind of energy and enthusiasm she had never experienced before. She read the Gospels and called the change a spiritual awakening. She wrestled with Julius and called it ripening "into a genuine and adult human being. A bit more every day." Whatever it was, she daily exchanged large portions of neurotic anxiety for a joy so radiant that it startled her friends and for "a vast and fruitful loneliness" that she knew would sustain her forever.

> I feel so sure of myself and not the least afraid and somehow so triumphant and unbreakable, and so full of love and confidence. And whenever even the smallest vacillation, the tiniest fear should beset you, I shall be there to support you. An old dress, a couple of sandwiches, a little bit of sun and now and then a kindly glance at each other. One hand is all we need to caress. And a little work. And our work can be done anywhere, wherever there is a human being, be he only a camp guard. I am coming over to your place right now. I have put on a beauty of a new pink wool blouse, and I have washed myself from top to toe with lilac soap.
>
> I once quietly bemoaned the fact that there is so little space for our physical love in your two small rooms, and no chance of going elsewhere because of all those notices and prohibitions. And now it seems a veritable paradise of promise and freedom.

As this curious relationship moved with the speed of an armored division from casual exploitation through love to devotion, much of the rest of life moved in the opposite direction. Having been forced to turn in their bicycles, Jews now walked wherever they needed to go. They trudged along the streets they were allowed to use, stood in food lines for rapidly diminishing supplies, and daily grew more exhausted. Julius had begun suffering intense pains in his head that worried him, and Etty, never robust, knew she'd be dead in three days if sent to a camp. Yet they walked together to the doctor's office, to the nearly empty stores, and to the Jewish Council to be interviewed by Germans. In another time they might have been considered an increasingly mad pair — he still engaged to a dark-haired, melancholic young woman in London, she still sleeping with her landlord — but in this period of insanity they were accepted by their friends as a devoted couple who miraculously saw goodness amid increasing pain.

"A few months ago," Etty wrote,

I was in two minds as to how to choose, when it came to it, between this sunny verandah, my untroubled studies and Han's faithful eyes on the one hand, and a concentration or some other camp where I could share my troubles with S. Now all that has ceased to matter. . . . I know now that I shall follow S. wherever he goes and share his sorrows. And that, I believe, is because I have grown so much less dependent on him and so am able to tie my life to his, without feeling that I am sacrificing mine.

That must sound paradoxical, but it is the only wisdom there is between a man and a woman. And this too: a few months ago, I was perhaps frightened that our dream would go sour on us in a life so full of care and pain. Yet somewhere inside me I now feel so at one with myself, and also with him, that the outer reality can do little damage to that bond. And as the emphasis shifts increasingly towards the inner life, so one grows less and less dependent on circumstances.

Increasingly secure in her new strength and independence and anxious to put these qualities to work for other people, Etty decided to leave Julius. She had answered two closely related questions that had deeply disturbed her: Could she commit herself unreservedly to another? Could she commit her life to God? She believed that in showing her how to love, Julius had placed her hand in God's, and now she was ready to carry on both her partner's and God's work in a wider and more demanding arena. Kneeling again on the coco matting in the bathroom, Etty reassured God that He would not be left alone. In this time of hatred and hopelessness, she would bind herself to Him and share his sorrows too. She would remind everyone she encountered of His abiding goodness. The following day she volunteered to work at Westerbork, a transit camp where Jews were held before their deportation to Auschwitz.

"I do not wish to be exempted from the fate of my people," she stated simply.

Etty's friends were horrified. They pleaded with her to go into hiding, and more than one family offered to take her in. But Etty, the battlefield, chose Westerbork, and Julius understood that his part in her accelerating life was over. "My whole being has become one great prayer for him," she wrote. Then she gave him her diary to read and left on a transport.

From August 1942 to September 1943, Etty worked at Westerbork and became "the thinking heart of the barracks." For most of this time she was allowed to visit Amsterdam once a month to pick up medicine for the camp's hospital. She was also sent home whenever she became seriously ill, which was often. Thus in September 1942 she was in Amsterdam on medical leave, sitting at Julius's bedside, when he died. "God and I have been left together," she wrote in her diary, although for the rest of her brief life she continued to talk to both God and Julius every night.

Exactly one year later, Etty, one brother, and her parents were placed on a train to Auschwitz. She died there on November 30 at the age of twenty-nine.

~~~

What a remarkable woman. What a strange and touching relationship. In the two years they spent together, Spier changed from a womanizer and certainly an insensitive, self-centered, unethical therapist to a devoted partner and supporter of Hillesum's. Although he started by crushing her under him, he ended by holding her the way a setting holds a diamond. Introducing her to the world, he let her shine on her own even as he approached death and may have wanted her for himself. But Hillesum made the greater change. Within a year of meeting Spier, she left behind a debilitating array of nervous disorders and settled down to give herself to the world with tender affection. Rippling outward like rings from a tremendous splash, Hillesum's love of life encompassed everything. No person was too fat, too angry, or too foreign to love, not even a Nazi. No tree was too bare or twisted to be admired. No friend too silly. No aspect of herself too ridiculous — at last. "You cannot heal disturbed people without love," Spier had told her. In a disturbed time, Hillesum took that injunction to the limit.

Hillesum's diaries, like Spielrein's, lay unread for several decades until they came to the attention of a man who essentially made it his career to get them published. His first task was to decipher the documents, so messy was her handwriting, and his second was to find a publisher who was not scared off by Hillesum's avant-garde life or by a comparison of her reminiscences to Anne Frank's. After many rejections, the diaries were published in Holland and soon after in the rest of the world.

So here again is a story of transparent abuse and improbable devotion, one that illustrates particularly well the way some doctor-patient relationships change course. Although Hillesum was initially drawn into the orbit of Spier's desire — into his shortsighted attempt to satisfy his own longings — the story didn't end there. She not only got better, she also gained a remarkable degree of independence. She became the equal of her "beloved psychological university" and hand in hand with him made the poignant discovery that life, even a very short life, can be "rich and full of love."

~~~

Before crossing the Atlantic to see what kinds of relationships developed between doctors and patients in America, let us briefly visit the Zurich of the 1950s, where analysts from all over the world gathered to study at the Carl Gustave Jung Institute. Sensitized to the seductive dangers of intense psychotherapy by Jung himself, the training analysts at the institute talked openly of the attractions that developed in therapy. They realized that a lonely therapist is a vulnerable one, and they tried to prevent the kind of self-centered grappling that Spier initially indulged in by giving each of the trainees a great deal of support and attention.

Typically, students at the institute attended classes in a big house in the center of town and at the same time entered into treatment with both a male and a female analyst. These men and women had offices throughout the city — usually in their own apartments — and charged a modest fee. It was important for any student who was serious about becoming an analyst to experience trusting and confiding in both a man and a woman. In addition, students were encouraged to wander off alone to paint or write and to gather in groups to talk of myths, dreams, and fairy tales. Although the young men and women came and went irregularly, many spent four or more years in Zurich and soon got to know everyone in the analytic community. Before Jung's death in 1961, the institute was often described as a family.

Lillian arrived in Zurich from her home in Atlanta, Georgia, in the spring of 1955. A vivacious and truly beautiful girl with a southern drawl and a trunkful of dancing dresses, she had recently suffered an unhappy love affair that left her badly shaken. Attending classes with the awful feeling that she would never recover, the normally outgoing young woman "hibernated" for a full two years. During this time she attended lectures, spent afternoons writing in a journal or walking alone in mountain forests, and entered analysis. Twice a week she would take the trolley to either Dr. Meier's or Dr. Frye's apartment, and there she gradually came back to life.

In those years the director of studies was James Hillman, and as Lillian began to participate in the activities of the institute, she sometimes accompanied him to his office where they would light a potbellied stove and work on dreams. On certain holidays, especially around Christmas, the institute would put on dances. Then laughing analysts and chattering students waltzed and jitterbugged through the night. Dr. Meier was there with his wife, and Lillian danced with her analyst, danced with the director of studies, and danced with her fellow students. Once she wore a saffron yellow sarong with a beautiful lei, and one of the professors — a woman — chased her around the dance floor calling loudly, "Fräulein, Fräulein, zat iss not a gostume, zat iss *you!*" Thus work and play, solitude and camaraderie, wove in and out of Lillian's days in Zurich. She was amazed at how "human" everyone was and how delightfully rowdy. She was also amazed at how well she took to the material.

One of the topics that regularly came up among the students was love. Lillian from Atlanta fell passionately in love with Norbert from

Australia. Lillian's girlfriend fell in love with her analyst, and occasionally a student who had passed the oral exams and was seeing patients fell in love with one of them.

> I remember a fellow student telling Dr. Meier that he was becoming involved with a patient and wanted to make love to her. "No," was the answer. "But Dr. Meier, Professor Jung made love to a former patient," the student said. "But *you* are not Dr. Jung."

You see our analysts held us to a high standard of conduct where sexual attraction to patients was concerned. Because we were expected to learn everything from our own material, it was hoped that we would face many, many dilemmas during our training and learn what they felt like. Loving someone you cannot possibly have is a common situation after all. For some of my friends, this experience first came with patients. For me, with Norbert.

Norbert had come to Zurich for a single academic year, but after he met Lillian he wanted to stay. The two sat in class together and went to coffeehouses. They danced. They ate fondue. They walked together in the mountains, retelling myths and tales and working on interpretations. She told him of Acis and Galatea, and how the two were parted by the Cyclops. He told her of Orpheus and Eurydice, how they lived together — but briefly. Apollo and Daphne, Ceyx and Halcyone, Cupid and Psyche — the old stories twined around their heads like wildflowers as they trudged through the hills. "Which myth or fairy tale are we living at the moment?" one of them would ask. And the other would show how the ancient story illuminated the workings of the unconscious. Forty years later, memories of the lush high pastures still bring to Lillian's mind the sound of Norbert's voice. "Norbert was my animus, and I was his anima," recalled Lillian, referring to Jung's discovery with Spielrein of a female presence — the anima — in men, and a male presence — the animus — in women. It is the Jungian way of saying that two people are soulmates.

As spring rolled around again and icy streams came racing off the glaciers bound for the Zurich Sea, Dr. Meier and Dr. Frye, who were also Norbert's analysts, encouraged the couple to say good-bye. Neither analyst believed that Norbert should abandon his life in Australia. At first Lillian was confused and unhappy. She was already beginning to cry at the thought of losing her lover, and as had happened before, she was sure that months of misery lay ahead for them both. Yet her analysts encouraged her to talk, just as they had encouraged the young man who had fallen in love with his patient to talk. They wanted to hear about the good parts of the relationship, the reasons she had for loving Norbert, and, most important, they wanted her to find these loved qualities within herself.

Norbert and Lillian cried for three weeks and then parted. To her surprise, she did not slide into loneliness and depression. Instead, she was sad and victorious.

The traits she had seen in Norbert and believed were his alone — his confidence and easygoing affection — she realized were also hers. As they said at the institute, she was withdrawing her "projections" and settling the admired attributes comfortably inside herself. They had been there all the time, she discovered.

"I wasn't too lonely when Norbert left," she said, thinking back. "I feel the essence of him is mine forever."

And did this sad, victorious way of parting work for everyone? When being or remaining together was not the wisest course, did everyone at the institute fare as well as Lillian?

"Oh, no," she said lightly. "There were students who slipped and had affairs with patients, although not many. It was hurtful when they did. It disrupted 'the family' and divided us into camps. I remember one scandal that was particularly bad or rather unusually public. Some students thought it should be handled one way, some another. After Jung died, in came rules and laws to cover these situations. Certain books were even locked up. The family atmosphere disappeared."

Lillian returned to the United States and, homesick for the warmth and kindness of her analysts, entered treatment with a doctor trained in America. The two were equally shocked by the different pictures of analysis each of them held. Lillian found the American version dry and without soul. Perhaps, she thought, it was because her analyst practiced alone, without a community to support and contain the doctor-patient relationships. Having to do everything himself — all the experimenting and all the regulating — he was cautious in the extreme. "In Zurich I had this perfectly wonderful purple dress," Lillian recalled. "It had a skirt built in layers like a flamenco costume. It was banded in red ribbon, and when I danced it flew out all over. My American analyst was shocked when I told him how everyone at the institute danced."

~~~

Although the institute's easy incorporation of dancing and attraction never crossed the Atlantic and its effective training methods are still largely ignored, many analysts did head west, and by the end of World War II the center of psychoanalysis had shifted from Europe to the United States. Hundreds of expatriate analysts were offering their services both as therapists and teachers, especially in New York City. At the same time, new kinds of psychotherapies were being developed by practitioners called clinical psychologists. Large numbers of these men (and a few women) had been trained during the war to test soldiers and sailors for emotional stability and to treat returning veterans. Unlike most analysts and all psychiatrists, clinical psychologists did not attend medical school but were trained partly as scientists to do research and partly as practitioners. The scientific part of their training put them in touch with experimental work on language, thinking, and behavior, and each of these fields was a source of new therapeutic techniques. In addition, systems of philosophy from ancient Eastern mysticism to modern existentialism were also being mined for new ideas. Such writings suggested alternate ways of approaching emotional problems that were now variously traced to human nature, industrialization, the loss of religious faith, or two world wars.

Many of these new ideas came together at Esalen, a little hot springs resort on the Big Sur coast in California. As one of the homes of the human potential movement, with an exhilarating sense of opportunity and an emphasis on immediate personal and social change, Esalen became the most famous growth center in the country.

Today the beauty of the Big Sur coast is taken for granted, but in the 1950s and '60s, when those who launched the human potential movement were discovering California, the wild Pacific shoreline was an astonishing surprise. When Aldous Huxley, Abraham Maslow, Alan Watts, Fritz Perls, Carl Rogers, Rollo May, Anaïs Nin, R. D. Laing, among others, left behind the battered cities of Europe or the growing congestion of the East Coast and saw the Santa Lucia Mountains heaving themselves straight up out of the cold Pacific into the warm sunlight, it was almost impossible not to entertain new ideas. There was such an immediacy to the scenery in California and to life itself there. "It's happening right now, baby," was a common expression, and even psychotherapy began to reflect this enchantment with the present moment.

According to Michael Murphy and Richard Price, the Stanford graduates who decided to turn the rundown resort into a gathering place for thinkers, Esalen went through several phases. Initially, the main draw was lectures — lectures on anything that could open your eyes, from Eastern philosophy and meditation through scientific research to peyote mushrooms as a method of enlightenment. In the mid-1960s this was followed by a more active, hands-on approach, and the encounter group became the mainstay of Esalen's offerings. At the same time, Gestalt therapy and body work became popular routes to what was increasingly called self-realization. Fritz Perls, the author of *Gestalt Therapy*, was in residence, as were teachers of yoga and Tai Chi Chuan. Perls could be seen wandering about the grounds in coveralls and beads, while down by the open-air hot tubs Ida Rolf could be seen Rolfing. Eventually the lectures and the learning took a back seat to a kind of pampered self-preoccupation, and Esalen went through a difficult time of turmoil and indecision. At present the institute is a calm and only mildly experimental center where people go both to investigate and to indulge their holistic selves.

What set Esalen apart from other sites where psychotherapists gathered — Vienna, Zurich, and New York, for example — was its remarkable eclecticism, its physical isolation, and its frank experimentation with drugs and sex. Not only was occasional intimacy between therapist and client benignly tolerated, but casual sex was actually encouraged for a number of years. The philosophy behind this "treatment" stemmed from the belief that in modern, industrial countries, human beings rarely confront each other candidly. But remedies were being discovered. Both psychodrama, with its spontaneous and often surprising reenactments of a person's life, and sensitivity training, with its honest feedback from group members, offered rare moments of real contact among people — even strangers. "Let go!" and "Act out!" became the preferred antidote to dehumanization. "Don't live in your head." At Esalen, hundreds of encounter groups were organized to give participants refreshing jolts of candor and reality. Some meetings were brief, others stretched over weeks, but all were believed to represent an exhilarating shortcut to self-knowledge, a kind of drugless high in the service of self-actualization. Urged to take chances by expressing themselves with a directness heretofore unimagined, members earnestly sought "real encounters" with one another. Sometimes these were fist-fights, sometimes conversations, and sometimes sex.

The best known leader of Esalen's encounter groups and the man who more than any other promoted sex as an adjunct to therapy was William Schutz, a social psychologist who had taught at Harvard. On his arrival in California, Schutz first worked in a mental hospital but found the thinking there inflexible. In 1967 he moved to Esalen and loved it. He ran hundreds of encounter groups, and his methods became so popular that he organized national tours. As the Flying Circus, he and his students led encounter groups in cities across the country.

Schutz was candid about his frequent affairs with members of his groups. In fact, in the name of honesty, he would announce these relationships as soon as they began. He encouraged the women and the smaller numbers of men in his groups to take personal risks in order to expand their capacity to feel and to free themselves from the arbitrary restrictions of conventional morality. Schutz was all for responsibility too, but in a form that today seems somewhat self-serving and unrealistic. "You choose your life," he liked to say, meaning that we unknowingly want everything that happens to us. Thus, if a woman felt abused or abandoned when the encounter group ended, he would remind her that she had chosen the experience and now she could choose what it meant to her — joy or pain. Schutz, with an unbounded belief in the power of mind over matter, even maintained that "the laws of nature only function if we want them to."

Schutz was by no means the only therapist to treat his encounter groups like a giant dating pool. Some leaders of est, Arica, and psychosynthesis preached and practiced the benefits of casual sex, as did some independent gurus. How these encounters affected the women involved is difficult to say because few left records. Perhaps because the affairs rarely developed into long-term relationships, neither therapist nor client seemed inspired to say or write much about them. A few brief accounts of general disillusionment with group leaders found their way into print, but there are almost no detailed, personal tales like Spielrein's or Hillesum's. Nor are there extensive, secondhand examinations of these casual couplings. Opposition to sex in encounter groups briefly gained a toehold in the 1970s, when the Women's Studies Program was established at Esalen. The group was forced to disband when it tried to become an autonomous unit within Esalen.

An exception to the statement that therapists who routinely encouraged clients to have sex with them didn't form relationships worth remembering is Fritz Perls, whose unconventional affair with Marty Fromm is documented by both participants. This relationship shows better than most the dangers of a particular kind of talent and of particular kinds of loneliness. It also points up the differences between Europe and America and between pre– and post–World War II thinking.

In 1893, on the outskirts of Berlin, Fritz Perls was born into a modern Jewish family that was not a particularly happy one. Fitting neither into the Orthodox Jewish community nor into the world of Protestant Germans, the family was uncomfortably adrift. Nor was there a sense of security at home, for Perls's parents were not well suited to each other. Under these conditions, Perls became restless and rebellious. He skipped in and out of school and as a teenager tried to become an actor and a director. The sensitivity he developed for body language during this period later became an important part of his therapeutic technique. World War I broke out just as Perls, changing his plans yet again, started medical school, and he was pulled out of classes to serve in the trenches as a medic. Given the most dangerous and miserable jobs, as German Jews often were, he saw more than his share of the horrors caused by gassing and hand-to-hand combat. Once, on a furlough, he attended a performance of *The Marriage of Figaro*. He was so appalled by the discrepancies between the elegant opera house and the bloody trenches that he fled from the theater, sobbing. When the Great War was over, his closest friend was dead and his own belief in a safe and just world destroyed. Like many others of his generation, he emerged deeply cynical about the nature of man.

Although Perls completed his medical degree, he became increasingly restless and distraught. He finally entered psychoanalysis with

Karen Horney but did not find relief. After he had tried several other analysts, Horney said that the only person who could help him was the renegade analyst Wilhelm Reich. Perls went to see this man, who had already been blackballed by his Freudian colleagues for his unorthodox theories on sex and society, and found the fit perfect. Because Reich believed that the social oppression he saw all around him was a powerful force in a person's life, he paid more attention to his patients' present problems than to their childhoods. He also thought that every neurosis took up residence in the body as well as the mind, so noticing posture and body language were important parts of his treatment. He prescribed breathing exercises and massage — two elements that later became parts of some therapies. Furthermore, Reich believed that the greatest release of all was the sexual orgasm. Although he did not openly advocate sex with patients, he did think they ought to fantasize freely about their desires — including their dreams involving the analyst. All this fit very nicely into the fears and interests of the young Perls. Since boyhood, he once said, he had been preoccupied with sex.

In 1933 both Reich and Perls fled Germany, the former moving to Scandinavia, the latter to South Africa. There Perls practiced a conventional form of psychoanalysis for more than a decade and led an ordinary life with a wife and children. Again, political upheavals drove him out, and in 1946 a demoralized Perls arrived in New York City. His marriage was unworkable, he had lost a lucrative practice, and he was friendless. Luckily, he met Clara Thompson and Erich Fromm, who helped him find patients, although they never accepted him wholeheartedly into their professional circle. This was at least partly due to his growing reputation as a womanizer.

For several years Perls worked as an analyst and wrote a book on Gestalt therapy. (*Gestalt* means "whole," and Gestalt psychologists try to deal with whole persons and whole experiences, not bits and pieces.) His book emphasized the importance of recognizing the urges a person feels from moment to moment and understanding how the drive to satisfy these urges may influence behavior. Perls wanted to counteract the forces that were persuading his patients to hide both aggression and erotic desire under a veneer of politeness — a strategy that he believed led to emotional numbness, duplicity, and ulcers. Although he publicized his new methods extensively, his fortunes did not rise. Rather, his spirits and health declined together. In 1956 he left his family and moved to Miami, where he intended to work a few hours a day until his heart gave out.

The sixty-three-year-old Perls lived the life of a disappointed hermit. He rented a cheap apartment, ate his meals out, and became increasingly critical of and distant from other therapists in the area. He ran one group a week and saw a few private patients. Even sex was no longer an outlet, for he feared it would trigger a heart attack. After two years of this existence, the scruffy old Perls met the beautiful thirty-two-year-old Marty Fromm at a social function. She began attending his group irregularly, then entered individual therapy when her six-year-old daughter became so unruly that she could not be sent to school.

In an interview with Martin Shepard, who was writing a biography of Perls, Fromm described herself as a mixed-up and destructive woman living a life of superficial elegance: "I was frigid and vicious, ugly, sharp, sarcastic, hateful, turned everyone off yet had no way of doing anything other than what I was doing. I was filled with a great deal of personal despair that was never shared with anyone." Constantly concerned with how her family appeared to the neighbors, Fromm was furious that her daughter had exposed the misery between her and her husband. She was sure everyone thought that her husband was sweet and she was a bitch.

Therapy helped. Although Fromm cried through session after session, at least she was able to talk about her troubles. At the end of each session — three a week — Perls gave her a big hug.

Fromm knew that he kissed everybody, and she assumed that his bear hugs gave everyone a feeling of great warmth and comfort. "But suddenly," she recalled, "it became very much of a man/male kiss. I got out of there one day and drove home absolutely dazed. I was very nasty when he did that. I looked at him and said, 'I need a therapist, not a lover,' and stomped out of the room."

That night Fromm had a very obvious sexy dream about Fritz, which compared him to her husband. She returned to therapy the next day but wouldn't look Perls in the eye. Reluctantly, she related her dream and revealed that her husband was a perfectly dreadful lover.

That evening Fromm decided she would take Perls as a lover. "I was much sterner then," she recalled, "and came into the next session with my diaphragm. After the session, when Fritz kissed me, he was suddenly over me but we were fully clothed and never fucked. I think he was testing me. A session or two later, we were intimate."

Fromm was still the patient in all respects — and the maid and the "wife." She was cooking for him, taking care of his laundry, and inviting him to parties. In return, she was introduced to sex.

> What we did for each other sexually was absolute sheer magic. Fritz came to Miami to die. His heart was bad. . . . He was worried about his heart pounding. Yet there was enough sex, attraction, magnetism, excitement and magic that made it another world type of sexual existence together. For I was dead and absolutely frigid and not going to let myself get all excited if all I could have were my husband's twenty-nine-second touches. Fritz was similarly fearful of getting excited. . . . He was sixty-five when we met. Yet our sexuality was just amazing.

So Perls played the part of Pygmalion and wished Fromm into the woman of his dreams, which is to say that he introduced her to many different kinds of sex, some involving other people. He wanted her to experience every variation. "And he wanted to be the manipulator and puppeteer who was pulling my strings," said Fromm later. Throughout this education, Perls insisted that he was doing all this for his lover. Later Fromm realized that "Fritz didn't do anything for me. What he was doing was for himself. I was young and beautiful and I provided lots of access to lots of scenes Fritz wanted. So I did as much for him . . . as he did for me."

One of the things Perls did for Fromm was to convince her that she was no dummy. She soon went back to school, first to complete her undergraduate degree and then to earn a master's degree in psychology. Eventually she taught the subject at a community college. One of the things Fromm did for Perls was to criticize him and his theories. She told him when he was being selfish or slovenly or inconsistent. He didn't like to hear these things, but no one else would tell him. He was as friendless as she.

About six months after Perls and Fromm had become lovers, Perls received the kind of offer he'd been waiting for: he was invited to become a training psychiatrist at a large mental hospital in Ohio. When he saw

Fromm, he announced he was moving. She had a fit. "I screamed and cried and ranted and raved. 'How could you do this to me? . . . You're letting me down.'"

Although Perls's abrupt good-bye fit his philosophy perfectly, it did not feel like good Gestalt therapy to Fromm. It felt like rejection and abandonment. Still treating Perls as "the official psychiatrist" with the answers, however, she tried to convince herself that an independent and totally uncommitted life was a sign of maturity. She repeated all the right words — "I'm not responsible for you. I don't owe you anything. Good-bye." — but she had terrible doubts.

Nine months later, Perls returned from Ohio. To his surprise, he had been unable to live happily without Fromm. He moved into a sunny apartment on the beach just five minutes from her house, and the two enjoyed a kind of honeymoon for nearly six months. Perls was amazed at how fond he had become of her. Yet, as he began to experience several new medical problems, the sixty-seven-year-old was distressed to discover that he needed to rely on another person. Dependence, like commitment, had no place in his scheme of things. Rejecting both yet obviously needing reliable support, Perls found himself increasingly confused. Against his will, he grew possessive of Fromm, then jealous, and finally literally psychotic. During this time he relentlessly sent Fromm a double message: "You do your thing, and I'll do mine" *and* "How dare you leave me alone?" The stress on her was considerable, and the self-confidence she had gained in the first year or so of therapy began to erode. As Perls demanded that she pay more and more attention to him, Fromm felt like shouting, "ME ME ME. I PATIENT." It did not help that Perls was regularly tripping on LSD. "Well, Marty," she remembered his saying at this time, "you're certainly a lot less crazy than I imagined and I'm certainly a lot more crazy than I imagined."

Their crisis came to a head when Perls went into the hospital for two surgeries in a single month. He became convinced that Fromm was having an affair with a student of his, and in spite of his philosophy of noncommitment, he couldn't stand the possibility that she was in love with someone else. He called Fromm and said, "Make a choice." "Okay," she said, "I choose you." And so they started all over again in (dare it be said) a somewhat more conventional manner. They tried to trust each other, and they almost succeeded. When Perls got an offer to move to

California and try again to launch a Gestalt institute, he talked it over with Fromm, and when the two agreed he should go, he gave her a good-bye present: a trip to Europe, the land of his early memories.

Fromm was enchanted. "We ended up on very good terms. Because Fritz's final gift to me was that last summer in Europe. We had five marvelous weeks together, as marvelous as the previous winter had been horrid. We ended up so close and loving and attuned and sexually alive with each other that parting from him in New York was at a very high point in our relationship."

"Fritz was a very good therapist for me in the beginning," Fromm said many years later. He helped with her daughter, her friends, and her career. He gave her confidence. But he was not such a good therapist, she thought, the year he became jealous and psychotic. His message that every person needed to take responsibility for his or her own life was a fine one, but from Fromm's point of view "he certainly wasn't a model. So what I created of myself is me. . . . I did that alone."

In his autobiography, *In and Out of the Garbage Pail*, published nine years after Perls had moved west, he included a long open letter to Fromm. It is full of compliments that he immediately retracts. He adored her looks; she shouldn't have had her nose reshaped. He loved her forthrightness; "cruel honesty," he called it. "I was so proud to show you real beauty [in Italy], as if I owned it and to help you overcome your mediocre taste in art." Even the sex that he likened to poetry cost him dearly in spasms of jealousy and possessiveness. As he was fond of saying, "In this life you don't get something for nothing."

But at the very end of the letter, Perls let down his guard. Perhaps mellowed by age or by the three thousand miles separating the lovers, he seems to have come down unequivocally on the side of gratitude: "I survived those operations. I survived our separation. I survived our final fights and reconciliation. I am here and you are there. It feels good and solid whenever we meet again. Thank you for being the most important person in my life."

Although Perls continued to seek brief sexual encounters in his final eight years, he never again formed a liaison that could actually be called a relationship. Installing himself at Esalen, he took on everyone as a patient in his group therapy sessions and trained hundreds in the art of fast, intense therapy. He was known as an irascible, insulting old man who shuffled around in dirty coveralls, smoked constantly, and saw further into a person in two minutes than anyone else. The year before he died, he left California to open his own institute, but his health failed and he was hospitalized. His estranged wife arrived, as did a number of friends, who reported that Perls's last words were directed to a nurse. "Don't tell me what to do," he growled, then died.

Now, some twenty-five years later, Fritz Perls is recognized as the founder and most important proponent of Gestalt therapy. Arrogant and lonely in equal measure, he seems the very picture of the therapist most likely to ignore conventional ethics. The radical instability and repeated disappointments that he suffered throughout his formative years gave to his inspired rebelliousness a cynical twist. His willingness to experiment led him to devise therapeutic techniques altogether different from analysis, but the bitterness he felt gave to some of these experiments a shortsighted and self-centered focus. In addition to being outside his profession, Perls was disappointed in it. He was convinced that conventional therapies wasted time, and he was angry that conventional therapists did not acknowledge his innovations. This was an explosive combination. Especially when the disgruntled iconoclast was friendless, without family, scientifically isolated, and ill, as he had been in Miami and California, he used patients for comfort, for life rafts. That his practice coincided with the sexual revolution, when so many people threw off social and personal restrictions, assured him of partners. Nor were his colleagues likely to object, for they were doing the same thing. Perls contributed a great deal to the exploding field of psychotherapy, but a lifetime of personal unhappiness made it difficult for him to form or appreciate a loving, stable, and mutually respectful relationship. In its absence, he used a lot of people to stay afloat. Marty Fromm was certainly one of them, and she makes it clear that, for her, their relationship was both exploitive and productive.

~~~

Sexual freedom, so visible at Esalen but alive in other places as well, did not generally promote the same kinds of relationships between doctor and patient as middle-class morality had previously allowed. The brief sexual encounters that group leaders like William Schutz enjoyed or that are described by Martin Shepard in *The Love Cure* or that were cultivated by charismatic gurus at private retreats do not sound like Jung's attraction to Spielrein or even Rank's obsession with Nin. Not that womanizers had not been present among early psychoanalysts and not that love affairs did not occur during the sexual revolution, but as the pendulum swung toward instant gratification, casual sexual encounters gained tremendous popularity. Clinicians were now frank about their short-term desires. Perls would have been the first to admit that physical desire, not committed love, motivated his liaisons. Such encounters as blossomed during the Summer of Love developed between people who knew little about each other. They were likely to be self-centered affairs — brief interludes designed to satisfy the therapist's immediate desires with little thought for how the experience would affect his partner. If she said yes, the reasoning went, it must be good for her too. By contrast, the longer and more complex relationships embarked on by Jung, Ferenczi, and Spier, for example, occurred when a doctor identified with "a kindred soul" and could not control his desire to act on his feelings. Overinvolved and without boundaries — which, after all, is a passable description of being in love — these men believed in their hearts that their affection would help far more than it would harm. This distinction between fleeting desire and inappropriate or off-limits love appears again and again. It is important to appreciate the different settings, feelings, outcomes, and remedies that are associated with each.

Although by the early 1970s these two basic plots were familiar, the women who had been drawn into sexual relationships with present or former therapists had only one story to tell. Unless they were forcibly raped, the common assumption was that they must have agreed to the affair, short or long. Thus any regrets were their own fault. No matter what they felt, the only complaint that was considered legitimate for them to voice afterward was self-reproach. When doctor-patient sex was officially banned, however, first by professional organizations and then by state licensing boards, a second story came pouring out of a thousand mouths. It told of subtle forms of coercion, profound confusion, self-doubt, anger, and years and years of silent pain.

3

Recent Intimacies

> Regardless of what position an individual takes on this issue, it is evident that erotic contacts do take place, and that they are more prevalent than the professional community would like to acknowledge.
>
> — *B. J. Taylor and N. N. Wagner*

The time is now 1977, and the American Psychological Association has just adopted a code of ethics stating that "sexual intimacies with clients are unethical." It is a scant four years behind the American Psychiatric Association and a few years ahead of other professional groups that represent many kinds of psychotherapists. Thus, in the late 1970s, the relationships that people like Spier and Hillesum, Ferenczi and Pálos, Rank and Nin, Perls and Marty Fromm, had publicly enjoyed were banned.

"We wish to stress that these behaviors are no longer acceptable," proclaimed representatives of the new era. While three quarters of a century of experimentation, self-indulgence, and occasional romance came to an official end, the affairs themselves did not. They continued, but with changes. The most noticeable difference was that the chroniclers became women. No therapist now dared to describe techniques like Milton Erickson's provocative directives — undress here in the office, or go home and look at your "fur" — nor could they write to colleagues about "little laboratory explosions." But the consumer could, and the right to tell the story of erotic dealings and of other ethically suspect practices now passed from doctor to patient. Accounts poured in at an astonishing rate. In newspapers and magazines, in exposés and documentaries, in textbooks and professional journals, the big news became sexual abuse by therapists. Gathering momentum in the 1980s, a tide of pain and anger surged forward from hundreds, then thousands, of women.

"It is a rape," said Susan Radonsky, a librarian who won a civil settlement from her former psychiatrist. "It's a power thing, and I was powerless to say no to him."

"He is a predator," said a former patient of an elderly analyst who settled five sexual malpractice lawsuits for a million dollars.

"I'm left with a picture of the good man that hurt me," wrote Carolyn Bates in *Sex in the Therapy Hour.*

By 1990 this bitter tide was still rising. A new kind of complaint was appearing: allegations of propositioning, fondling, and erotic hugging — a kind of toying with the patient, it seemed, that often went on for years. Men charged female therapists with leading them on, gay clients charged gay therapists with propositioning them, women sought divorces — and damages — from their therapists-turned-husbands, parishioners blew the whistle on suggestive hugging by clergy, and spiritual masters at yoga centers were sued for having sex with devotees. No school of therapy was exempt from this flood of complaints and reevaluations, no group or profession, no word or gesture. The definition of sexual abuse and harassment expanded like a deep breath, and women who had long been silent charged that "depending on how we process the abuse, how our psyche copes, a few kisses can be as traumatic and damaging as outright rape and are just as abusive." "Yes!" said therapists as they organized groups across the country to support women who stepped forward with their stories. "No!" said others, including some rape-at-gunpoint victims, a different group of therapists, and a fairly large chunk of the general public.

"Let's face it," said a woman who feels she lost more than twenty years of her life to a seductive, self-centered therapist, "if you haven't gone through it, you don't get it." Get it or not, the new concern for sexual misconduct that gathered force in the 1980s has called into question our very definitions of abuse, responsibility, power, and justice.

As for the stories that emerged in these confusing years, there is a much wider selection than before. Although published accounts are virtually all told from the woman's or client's point of view and involve accusations that have taken years to formulate, unpublished stories from ongoing or newly terminated relationships give a broader, more varied sense of the struggle. Among these tentative accounts are stories that range from horrifying abuse all the way to what the British call "inappropriate relationships" — decent interactions that take place in the wrong setting. There are also some strange and strangely poignant tales, like one I heard from a profoundly mentally ill woman who believes she has "slept in a double bed between the minister and the angels." Because this woman lives in her fantasies so much of the time, there is little chance that the basis of her story will ever be known. Given the wide variety of stories being told — or discreetly whispered — let us begin with a brief sample of current accounts before turning to surveys that will give us an idea of the size of the problem today. Later, more complex tales will flesh out the sketches of this quintessentially modern dilemma.

~~~

On a questionnaire, a fifty-seven-year-old, married clinician wrote that she had been having sexual relations with a schizophrenic man who was also her patient. She said she was trying to offer him a second chance — "a corrective emotional experience," it is often called — to progress from an "infantile stage to [an] adult over a period of years." Having consulted with her former analyst, who apparently supported the plan, she felt this was a reasonable course of action. However, she was forced to keep the relationship secret, and this led to its demise. It was "too much trouble — I'm an open person, and the secretiveness was not to my liking."

~~~

A sixty-four-year-old professor of psychiatry who left his wife of many years to marry a patient did not stroll away so easily. After he lost a thirty-one-year-old son in a sailing accident, he began having an affair with a woman the same age who suffered from a severe dissociative disorder. When she became pregnant, he divorced his wife and married the younger woman. A few years later, after the birth of a son, the second wife decided that she had been taken advantage of. She is now seeking a divorce and a huge civil settlement.

~~~

"This is an unexciting story," began another woman, now sixty-seven years old, who fell in love with her European psychiatrist in New York

City some twenty years ago. "We grew to be such good friends during therapy that we decided to get married. Have been ever since."

And was there opposition to the marriage? "I don't think so," she said, "although my husband thought he should see his analyst before he formally proposed." Unfortunately, the analyst was in Hungary, and the meeting did not take place until ten years after the couple was married: "We met the analyst and his wife in Vienna, and then we all went out for dinner."

~~~

From my own practice comes an account of two boisterous women, Mimi and Rhonda, who had been living together for five years before seeking counseling for their quarrels over money. They found a lesbian therapist who quickly included the two in her social life. The couple was invited for coffee after each session and urged to attend a support group in which the smartly dressed therapist functioned as hostess. "She was very vain about her hair," Mimi remembered. "She was always scooping it off the back of her neck and letting it fall around her shoulders." As time went on, the therapist took a dislike to Mimi and her sharply observant ways and began excluding her from the sessions. Mimi believed the therapist was trying to break up the relationship and seduce Rhonda. "The doctor," as they refer to her, insisted that Rhonda spend the night on her couch when the roads were icy, and she coerced her into spying on a former girlfriend.

"Can't you see what's going on?" Mimi would scream. "She's controlling you! She's breaking us up!"

"You're jealous!" shouted Rhonda. "You don't trust anybody."

Although the two women left therapy before "the doctor" climbed in bed with Rhonda, they did not escape before losing the trust they had in each other and in therapy.

~~~

A different predicament faced Mr. Anderson, a young man who was encouraged to go into the ministry by a rector who "answered my theological questions and established my faith." When Anderson was ordained, he went to work for his mentor in a rapidly growing church of "signs and wonders" that was establishing itself as a breakaway denomination. It was an exciting time. Some six months into the job, however,

Anderson was asked to provide counseling for his boss, whose marriage was faltering. In the impossible position of therapist, friend, colleague, *and* employee, Anderson gradually discovered that his client was not only falling out of love with his uncommonly spiritual wife but also falling in love with a down-to-earth high school girl whom he had been counseling.

"'What I am doing is so unacceptable,' he would say to me," Anderson recalled. "'I can't tell you, but. . . .' One afternoon he brought a radio to a diner where we had coffee, and *played* it! I mean right at the table, like . . . like a high school kid. 'Listen to this song,' he'd say, closing his eyes. 'It's so cool. Don't you love the part where the guitar comes in?'"

Before Anderson's eyes, his boss gradually slipped backward into a carefree, happy adolescence that, in fact, he had never experienced. This grown man with his radio had discovered youthful, impetuous love with a girl his daughter's age. "It's about being alive," he said over and over again. "It's too good, too genuine to let go." Two months into therapy, the rector started wearing blue jeans. Three months, and all he talked about were the chances he'd taken in life — the dramatic longshots. He had taken risks that had led to missionary work in India. More risks, and a church was established on the West Coast. The work saved thousands of souls, he believed, and he described himself as "a man who is willing to do what God wants me to do — without fear." Four months into therapy, he and his girlfriend disappeared.

"Such a mess," moaned Anderson. "Such a mess." He sighed. "I think the missing link in our understanding of therapist and clergy affairs is that they're so powerfully real to these men. They're not just running off to be devious or to get back at someone. They're alive and in love — kidding themselves that the love will prosper — but wholeheartedly in love.

"So now," he continued, "the girl needs help, the rector needs help, his wife and children need support, the parish is hurt and confused, and I'm mixed up. How can someone so intelligent and caring, so personally helpful to me and thousands of others, and so . . . well, so *devout*, how can he just run off like that? Can I trust what he taught me?"

~~~

And finally, an example of what is pejoratively called a "bughouse romance." When a counselor fell in love with a woman living in an apartment complex for the mentally ill, he began slipping into her apartment after work and spending the night. This went on, undiscovered, for nearly six months, until the man became acutely ill and had to be rushed to the hospital by ambulance from his lover's apartment. He lost his job and, unfortunately, the use of his legs, but when the shouting and the tumult died down, his girlfriend quietly rejoined him. They live now in his apartment for the physically disabled.*

~~~

My informal survey could go on and on, but at this point I wish only to note one thing: variety. As in earlier decades, therapists run off with younger women, gays seduce gays, and women become erotically involved with male clients. In all cases the therapy is over — gone — and in most cases the new, erotic relationship brings no contentment. But the experiences are not all the same.

Before 1977, there was almost no information on the number of therapists who were sexually involved with their clients. Although several attempts had been made to launch surveys, they had been energetically discouraged. The funds needed to ask embarrassing questions of thousands of clinicians were not forthcoming from granting agencies or universities, and if that was not enough to dissuade investigators, they were threatened with expulsion from their professional organizations. Nevertheless, several studies were carried out — but scientific journals refused to publish them. Especially in psychiatry and psychology, it was widely feared that any confirmation of sexual misconduct would diminish the reputation of Dr. Wonderful.

The well-known team of William Masters and Virginia Johnson, the authors of *Human Sexual Inadequacy*, were among the first to blow the whistle on their colleagues. Working with eight hundred people with sexual problems, they found to their surprise that "a sizable number" had been sexually involved with a therapist. Stating that "if only 25 percent of

---

* Stories such as the last one are not often heard, partly because the people involved rarely have money or power. They bring fewer lawsuits and attract less publicity. In addition, mental health aides are not licensed and thus are not affected by professional codes of ethics. Although aides can give or withhold a large number of favors and have more influence on their charges than doctors generally imagine, they are regulated only by their employers' policies. Given this combination of closeness and influence on the one hand and lack of visibility and regulation on the other, relationships of all kinds develop but rarely surface.

these specific reports are correct, there is still an overwhelming issue confronting professionals in this field," Masters and Johnson went on to compare these encounters with rape. The majority of the stories they heard came from young women who felt they had been used and discarded by middle-age men. Feminist clinicians were outraged. No longer in a mood to protect the reputations of such colleagues, they threw their considerable weight behind the languishing surveys, and the presses began to roll. Hundreds, then thousands, of clinicians were polled as a major survey was launched almost every year in the 1980s.

The results of the surveys were startling, although not easy to interpret. An early one, launched just *before* sexual relations were specifically prohibited and answered by a surprisingly large proportion of psychologists, found that nearly 8 percent of therapists admitted to making "erotic contact" with patients. Some 85 percent of these contacts were made by males. A far larger study of psychiatrists revealed that 7 percent of male doctors and 3 percent of female doctors admitted to some form of what by now were sexual violations. Although this particular survey was mailed to 5,574 doctors, only a quarter returned the form, leading the authors to wonder whether their figures represented the field as a whole or only those doctors who answered. When still another survey asked psychologists if they had ever had sexual relationships with *former* clients, 11 percent checked "yes." Four percent of clergymen checked "yes" when asked about relationships with parishioners. And among social workers, finally polled in 1989, 4 percent of males and no females admitted to erotic contact or intercourse — low numbers, but not surprising for a field dominated by women and concentrated in clinics and hospitals rather than private offices.

In one of the rare investigations of ethical complaints against female clinicians — psychiatrists, in this case — it was found that over a five-year period only 30 complaints were received against women by the American Psychiatric Association. During the same period, 259 were filed against men. More than half the cases against the women were dismissed, and of those that remained, eight involved unethical sexual liaisons. Six involved doctors who had become entangled with a female client, and two involved male clients. (Male patients are unlikely to report sexual relationships with their doctors; on all surveys this number is considered grossly underreported.) Fewer of the complaints against male psychiatrists were dismissed, and in cases of sexual involvement, almost all the entanglements were heterosexual.

At first glance, it seemed that these surveys were suggesting that, on average, some 6 percent of clinicians began a sexual relationship at some time in his or her career. This does not mean that 6 percent of practitioners across the country are carrying on with a client right now, nor does "sexual contact" necessarily mean intercourse. What the surveys can tell us is that in the course of a thirty- or forty-year career, six clinicians of every hundred have slipped across the line to express love or lust to, usually, a former client. This estimate is undoubtedly low. It takes into account neither repeated seductions nor the bias toward underreporting that has distorted all self-reports of punishable behavior.* To correct the first problem, at least two surveys asked psychotherapists how many unethical contacts he or she had ever made. Two thirds of the respondents on one survey indicated that sex with a patient was a one-time occurrence. But four fifths of the respondents on the other survey admitted to more than one relationship. Unfortunately, there is no way of knowing which gives the truer picture. And how true is any picture drawn by people asked to report their own bad behavior? Jeffrey Masson has pointed out that asking clinicians how often they are unethical is like asking *un*convicted rapists how many are guilty.

"The profession itself is obviously not keen on doing sophisticated research in the field." If it were, Masson continued, its members would launch national surveys of clients, not therapists. But this technique would encounter a different bias. As noted earlier, even biased numbers are missing from hospitals and residential homes, although we know that aides and counselors become involved with their charges. Anecdotal information has been gathered, but no large surveys run. "When the

---

* Attempts to establish the prevalence of adultery illustrate the problems of self-reporting. When married women of child-bearing age are asked if they have had extramarital sex, the numbers are typically low. However, when genetic studies are performed in which the blood types of mother, father, and newborn are tested, it is found that as many as 30 percent of the babies have blood group substances belonging to a man other than the supposed father. Even this figure is bound to be low, as all intercourse does not lead to conception. "Obviously we are on shaky ground if we expect an honest answer when we ask people their attitudes about extramarital sex," wrote Jared Diamond in *The Third Chimpanzee.* (Harper Perennial, 1992, p. 86) The same is true of doctor-patient liaisons.

subject of a survey is sex," wrote a demographer, "it is never clear which respondents are telling the truth, which are lying, which are talking, and which are silent."

So how can we tell how many of our country's roughly 1.2 million clinicians and clergy cross ethical boundaries to kiss, hold, seduce, or ensnare their patients and former patients? Unfortunately, there is no way to estimate the number with any certainty. However, since "life is the art of drawing sufficient conclusions from insufficient premises," as Samuel Butler asserted, it comes as no surprise to find social scientists, the media, politicians, victimized women, and aggrieved clinicians all making speculations. At one extreme, social scientists have insisted that "the true base rate of sexual misconduct among psychologists is not known" and that "one *cannot* learn the percentage of sexually involved therapists from these studies except in the most general terms" (my emphasis). In other words, all we know with certainty is that between 1 and 12 percent of the clinicians who choose to answer questionnaires admit that they have engaged in unethical sexual behavior at least once. Most are male. At the other extreme are some feminists, who insist that 25 percent of all men, including therapists, are coercive and exploitive. So is it around 6 percent? Or 25 percent? This degree of uncertainty does not satisfy anyone, and although psychotherapists have learned repeatedly that statistics are more accurate than hunches when it comes to making estimates, it is not surprising that anecdotal information has been added to surveys in hopes of drawing a clearer picture of the problem.

A member of a board of examiners in New England feels that "there are two cases out there for every one we see." A feature article, "Psychiatrists and Sex Abuse," in the *Boston Globe* stated that experts believe the frequency of abuse is as high as 25 percent. The Episcopal bishop Barbara Harris was quoted as reporting that "between 14 and 25 percent of clergy are involved in sexual encounters with parishioners, staff members, or colleagues." And therapists who specialize in helping women who have become entangled shrug their shoulders at the question of how many and point to their waiting lists. Each of these unofficial sources of information suggests that more is going on than meets the surveyor's eye. My guess — and it is only that — is that roughly 10 percent of male clinicians have made love to a client or former client at some time during their career but that a much larger number have kissed and fondled. I think the figure for women is closer to 5 percent.

What does the average clinician think of all this misconduct? In a savvy move to assess support for ethical codes, professional organizations launched surveys to measure therapists' attitudes. What did social workers, for example, think about sex with patients?

"I am so ashamed of social workers who engage in erotic experiences with their clients that I have dropped my professional practice and am exploring new careers," wrote one. "This is sick and contaminating behavior!" "What I do is none of your g-d business."

Another national survey, conducted more than ten years after sex with patients was specifically banned, revealed that a full 98 percent of respondents felt that sex was "always inappropriate" in therapy. However, when it came to sleeping with former clients — that is, terminating therapy and then acting on physical attraction — almost 30 percent of the doctors thought that it was "sometimes acceptable." Shared among them was the belief that ethical considerations regulated therapy but common sense guided everything else. As one respondent stated, "If you fall in love, end the therapy. At that point there are no rules."

Others suggested that a potential couple should allow at least six months to elapse before acting on their desires. In the meantime, the patient should see another therapist. The majority of respondents — 70 percent — thought sex with former patients would only lead to trouble, however, and an even larger majority — 96 percent — thought that professional organizations should take an active role in making sure that this kind of trouble did not occur.

So why do sexual intimacies continue among persons who say they are against them? We have a group of professions whose members are united in condemning sex between therapists and their current clients — 98 percent say it is wrong — yet among the 1.2 million or so individuals out there who offer advice in consulting rooms, hospitals, clinics, churches, prisons, and halfway houses, many more than 2 percent enter into erotic relations. Are psychotherapists insincere in their protestations? Naive in estimating the force of doctor-patient attraction? Unaware that their actions are being construed as erotic? I doubt the answers to these questions are going to come from surveys, so let us turn to a couple of actual cases. Perhaps they will show us where the reasoning that begins "I shouldn't do this" breaks down or how a counselor can truly believe that his kisses are seen as nothing more than supportive extras.

~~~

Katherine was always introduced as the daughter of a bishop. Now forty-four, a divorced mother of one, and an active advocate for women who have been sexually exploited by the clergy, her interest in this topic grew from personal experience. After tolerating an uncomfortably silent childhood in a household where good manners kept all negative feelings tucked away, Katherine "the Goody Two-shoes" left home to become Katherine "the mousewife." When being a dutiful wife to a cold, self-centered husband led to despair, however, she sought counseling from an Episcopal minister, who gave her unexpected forms of encouragement.

"He was a terrific hugger," Katherine remembered, and she frankly enjoyed the Reverend Mr. Blanford's big, teddy bear hugs until the day she and her son left the area and moved back to Long Island. "Just before leaving, I attended a vestry meeting to say good-bye," she said. "Mr. Blanford had encouraged me to join the vestry, and these were my friends. It was very teary." Afterward, she and the reverend went to his office for a personal farewell. She was crying, and he held her in one of his long and wonderful embraces. Then, to her astonishment, he kissed her. "And *what* a kiss!" she said. "It went on and on and on and *on*. My first reaction was, 'What's going on here?' Then, 'This is nice.'"

After this unexpectedly visceral good-bye, Katherine didn't see the Reverend Mr. Blanford for two years, until he and his wife came to Long Island, where they often vacationed. He called on her, and again a friendly hug became a clinch. This bittersweet pattern of summer kisses accompanied by endless fantasizing continued for another eight years. Once Katherine's son almost caught them. "Mom, were you kissing the minister?" he asked in amazement. "No," she lied, feeling terrible.

For no apparent reason, Katherine's life gradually began to unravel. She felt depressed, distracted, and fearful, and although she put new locks on the doors and windows and slept with the lights on, she became increasingly jumpy. She went into therapy to find out what was troubling her, but discussions of her childhood didn't make her feel any better.

One Sunday Katherine read an article in the newspaper on clergy abuse; she recognized herself as clearly as if the paper had been a mirror. She rushed the column to her therapist, who agreed. Here at last, she felt, was a way of talking that unlocked her heart. When she spoke about the "dirty secret" she shared with Mr. Blanford — the kisses and caresses, the lies and shame — feelings came pouring out on a flood of tears. Perhaps for the first time in her life, Katherine voiced her feelings of pain, anger, and confusion and was listened to sympathetically. "It was such a confirmation," Katherine said. "'I'm not crazy,' I could say at last. 'If what happened to me happened to anyone else, they'd be upset too. I'm not crazy.'"

Although still fearful that anyone who heard her speak from the heart would reject her as weak or wrong-headed, Katherine was ready to break a silence that had built up over a lifetime. Starting in the relative safety of her therapist's presence and progressing to her best friend and a group of women who met to talk of their sexual abuse, Katherine began telling her story over and over again. At first, she dismissed the degree to which the minister's affection had bothered her. "For a year I actually defended him. At group meetings I'd say, 'What happened to me wasn't so bad. I shouldn't complain.' 'But it's how you process the experience that counts,' the leader told us. She kept trying to drum that into our heads. A single pat on the fanny was monumental for one woman. She fell apart. Although none of us had been forced, we had all been raped emotionally or physically."

Of course, not everyone saw the experience as she did. "These things happen," a close male friend told her. "It sounds as if there was a lot of chemistry between you two. Put the incident behind you and get on with life."

"I thought he didn't get it because I wasn't explaining it right," Katherine said. "I didn't have the part about power imbalance down pat, so I took him to my therapist and let her explain. He *still* didn't get it. That pushed me back a lot." So did speaking at a clergy conference, where some ministers didn't think kissing and groping were as abusive as intercourse no matter how the experience was processed.

But Katherine kept speaking out, and three years later, taking what she thought would be the last steps on her journey, she wrote a booklet about recovery. She also arranged to see Mr. Blanford again. Although the minister's license to serve as a priest had been suspended while he underwent mandatory therapy and his counseling privileges were permanently revoked, Katherine wanted a personal apology, "closure." As she and her advocate approached the bishop's study, where they were to meet, Katherine could hear Mr. Blanford laughing with the bishop. "It sounded like a men's club," she said, "and I became very anxious." Indeed, the bishop's office was not her therapist's, and the two men sitting before her not her friends or group members. Instead of hearing Mr. Blanford apologize, long, unnerving silences punctuated the meeting. Twice he said, "I never meant to harm you," but that made no sense to Katherine. In fact, it only showed that he still didn't understand what he'd done. "There was no apology forthcoming from the abuser, and that left me feeling reabused, totally enraged, and nearly incapable of functioning," she said. "You see," she continued, "if his account of the relationship is true — if this married priest was expressing concern for me with his kissing and fondling — then my story of abuse is wrong." In fact, Katherine realized that if Mr. Blanford's version were right, it meant that she lacked the capacity to interpret what happened to her and respond appropriately. Conversely, if her account were true, then he was a weak and morally flawed individual.

How could these two stories be reconciled, which literally means reunited? "They won't be," said Katherine. "I've yet to hear of a case where that happened. The bishop told me that nine out of ten times victim and abuser never reconcile. Their interpretations are too different." In fact, Katherine said she cannot imagine what a reconciliation would sound like, and given the facts we have, it appears to be a clearcut case of an insensitive, self-absorbed man exploiting a vulnerable woman — a classic example of coldhearted abuse.

Yet, when Katherine talked about her recovery, both from the stifling silence of her childhood and from her guilt-ridden entanglement with the minister, a curious fact emerges. When she said, with gratitude, that she no longer had only two states of mind to choose between — anger and despair — and that her life contained longer and longer periods of pleasure, she ascribed these happy changes to the patience of compassionate listeners. "Above all," she said, "it is the people who have listened to me who have changed my life."

Could she recall who was at the head of this line, who liked her and believed in her first? Why, "Milton Blanford," she said without hesitation. "He gave me my first crack at being me. He did a lot of good stuff for me. Initially, he accepted me unconditionally and no one had before. I am who I am today, I'm the one who broke out of the family mold, because of Milton's encouragement. I'd say I have an inner sense of contentment now that I never had in my life."

This sounds like a strange thing for a woman to say about a cold-hearted abuser, but it is a surprisingly common part of a confusing picture. In subsequent chapters, other women will have more to say about making peace with therapists who both helped and hurt them, and we will see that Mr. Blanford's inability or unwillingness to admit his mistake makes appreciating his help and finding peace exceptionally difficult.

~~~

"I have spent a large part of my life waiting on situations that didn't quite work out," said Douglas, a twenty-seven-year-old who worked at a halfway house until he fell in love with a resident. "The minute I saw Jeannette I wanted to marry her — that kind of impact. She's very beautiful. Very bright. She wants to be loved and so do I. Her story is much like mine. But," he continued, " but . . . What I mean is I have no regrets, but the circumstances are impossible."

If two young, unmarried people are in love, what circumstances stand in their way? "Plenty," said Douglas. "I would never have believed things could get so complicated."

Douglas grew up with an unusual concern for the mentally ill. The youngest of five children, he had a sister who had lupus and a brother who was schizophrenic. ("Do you see that?" he said. "My sister *has* a physical illness, but my brother *is* his illness. I sensed that at the residence. The diagnosis becomes the life.") The five children grew up in the rolling foothills of the Berkshires, where centers for the arts such as Tanglewood and Jacob's Pillow pulled at Douglas's imagination. He became fascinated by mime and equally good at long-distance bicycle racing. Nevertheless, he followed his father's footsteps toward engineering. He majored in chemistry in college but didn't like it at all: "It took me an extra semester because my papers were always late. My parents were disappointed." Halfway through this exercise in frustration,

Douglas fell in love with a fellow student, and the two lived together for nearly three years. She wanted to marry, but he was unsure, and they parted bitterly after graduation.

When Douglas was twenty-five and sure of nothing except his dislike of chemical engineering, he moved to New York City, got a job in a halfway house, and started taking mime lessons. "I was free and happy," he said. "I felt I'd shaken off chemistry, my old girlfriend, a discouraging job, the old neighborhood, a brother I couldn't fix — all that stuff. I was light on my feet." His first "house" was a large, modern establishment in a nice neighborhood. He learned the ropes, and his willingness to tackle every part of the job prompted people to call him "the Energizer." Several months later, he moved to a modest house in Brooklyn. "I felt more comfortable there," he said. "It was a little less formal, but it was an on-the-go kinda place and a lot more interesting." And why was that? "Oh, there were a lot of great characters there. These guys were completely immersed in their difficult lives. The passion was still intact — and the suffering. I felt at home there. Also . . . well, I was able to help as I hadn't done with my brother. Before, I had tried hard to make him normal and it didn't work. Now I was simply trying to give them a boost — help them go in whatever direction they chose. My energy was really appreciated there."

It was in this second house that Douglas met Jeannette: he saw the red-haired twenty-four-year-old walk down a carpeted flight of stairs the first morning and *kablam!*, he was smitten. At this point, however, it did not occur to him to alter his usual way of working, so Jeannette, who still suffered from the phobias and eating disorder that had brought her to the house a year before, was simply added to his list of not-so-happy campers. With them Douglas went hiking in a bird sanctuary, cleaned up a nearby park, went bowling and roller-blading, gawked at the Christmas tree in Rockefeller Plaza, and hung out in front of F.A.O. Schwarz, watching motorized stuffed animals skate and twirl across a winter tableau. Douglas saw himself and Jeannette reflected in the window. Standing close to each other and superimposed on the sparkling fantasy land, they made a striking pair: each was just under six feet tall, each long and lean under layers of mufflers and mittens, and each leaning ever so slightly toward the other. Douglas was glad he had organized a bottle drive that raised enough money to permit them to rent a van so that Jeannette, still deathly afraid of subways, could accompany the group to Manhattan. It seemed the least Douglas could do for this lovely woman. Within two months of his arrival, Jeannette felt so much safer and more confident that she was spending twice as much time outside the house, and Douglas was in trouble.

It started when he took Jeannette to a mime show — alone. The next morning he learned from a fellow staff member that the director had "rumbled about boundaries." Nothing was said to Douglas directly, but he knew that his feelings for Jeannette were beginning to show. "I began to feel confused and much more vulnerable to criticism," he said. "I wasn't her advocate, and I *never* looked at her chart, yet I became very self-conscious. I knew I was treating her differently." Led naturally by his enthusiasm for characters, not to mention his easy familiarity with passion and suffering *and* his attraction to Jeannette, Douglas had unwittingly wandered into a position halfway between staff and resident. He lived like a counselor — came and went as he pleased, got paid, took classes — but he identified with the residents, his new family of misfits and eccentrics. This dual citizenship gave him an edge with the residents, for he could almost see through their eyes, but it handicapped him with the staff. He said, "I became so aware of the condescension that permeates the place. It's unconscious. Without thinking, they just 'know' that a mentally ill person is not as good at anything — across the board." Adding to this awkwardness, Douglas learned that one of the long-term residents had formed a relationship with Jeannette a year earlier. Douglas had particularly liked this man, but now found himself in the impossible position of being his replacement. All these complexities remained secret, however. No one said a word, least of all Douglas or Jeannette.

This situation continued for five months. Douglas sensed (correctly, as he later learned) that if he were to confide in the director, he would dismiss Douglas's love as ludicrous. Finally Douglas invited Jeannette for a walk, and along the littered periphery of Gramercy Park he declared his love. She accepted it — sort of. "She wasn't ready to say 'love,'" Douglas recalled, "but she wanted to go out with me." Both knew that dating was against the regulations, and they decided that one of them had to leave the house. Jeannette elected to move, and within a month she had found an apartment and a part-time job.

Douglas stayed on at the house for another six months, feeling worse and worse. He became painfully aware of which residents he touched — say, in a game of basketball — and which ones he made sure he never touched. He had thought he treated everyone the same, but now he knew better. As he and Jeannette began to date, he felt increasingly alive with her and increasingly cowardly at the house. He withdrew from the staff — "I thought they would all condemn me if they knew" — and from the residents — "I couldn't be spontaneous anymore. Pretty soon I couldn't touch anyone in *any* way. I said to myself, 'Now I'm failing again at work.'"

No longer feeling a part of the community where he had lived for more than a year, Douglas gave his notice. Still, the secrecy bothered him, and before he left, he announced at the residents' weekly meeting that he and Jeannette had struck up a friendship. "I kept it vague, but it was a reality check. I wanted to level with the residents especially. 'Yes, something was going on. You weren't crazy, not your imagination. It was real.' At the staff meeting immediately afterward the director said, 'I didn't appreciate you announcing that to the whole house. It should have been handled differently.'" Douglas agreed. "It" should have. He remembered hearing the director speak of "maintaining proper boundaries with *these* people," but no one talked of loving the residents, not romantically or platonically. Douglas would have had something to say about both feelings.

In retrospect, he wished someone had asked him, "Are you O.K.?" Instead, the director "hinted around" and said, "'You don't have sexual fantasies about *her*, do you?'" The message Douglas heard was that a sane person could not possibly love Jeannette. "I was offended by the question. I wanted to explain, but I didn't think they'd understand. They were so uncomfortable already that I just left." A friend told Douglas later that the staff had discussed possible actions but decided to do nothing, since no one knew if sex were involved and, anyway, Douglas had already resigned. Some months later, "I received a surprisingly good letter of reference."

Now the problem shifted. Not only was Douglas so uncomfortable as a counselor that he feared he would never work again in the field — no more engineering, no more counseling — but he and Jeannette were running into trouble. For one thing, he felt so guilty that he had violated her boundaries that he found himself taking responsibility for each of her bad moods and fears. "Perhaps our relationship is making it harder for her," he wondered. "Maybe I am thinking of myself too much." For another, the couple had no friends. The former residents Jeannette hung out with still saw Douglas as a counselor, and it was unthinkable that the couple should mix with his counselor friends.

Douglas decided to get personal therapy. But with whom? "Therapists will disapprove of me," he believed. "I think they've already made up their minds." In exasperation he gave up the idea. "I wish we could just *have* this relationship, like other people."

So Douglas redoubled his efforts to be sensitive to Jeannette's needs, especially her desire to go very slowly where sex was concerned. He sent her funny cards. He asked her opinion on everything. "I'd risked so much for this friendship . . . I mean, I'd put so much on the line by following my heart instead of the rules that I was *determined* to make it last. That wore me out. I kept trying, but the problems kept coming — just like an interracial marriage or a homosexual thing. You think to yourself, big parts of the world have got to change just to make room for this one little relationship." It sometimes seemed that one of those big parts of the world was Jeannette herself. "How can I even hope to steer it?" he asked. "I mean, sometimes I'm afraid she has such conflicts and fears that she won't be able to have a normal relationship. She has so many 'can'ts.' That's an awful thing to say," he added quickly, "but I think it."

At Easter, Douglas and Jeannette spent three days in the Berkshires — in separate beds. For once the relationship seemed easy. "We didn't get in one of those cycles where we're each holding back and trying to guess what the other is thinking. We talked all the way up the Taconic and all the way back. We've already told each other more than we've told anyone else in the world." Douglas said later that the two were not giving each other what they had expected to give — hugs and kisses — but were doing a lot of agreeing. "About loneliness. We were both *really* lonely, not just without a boyfriend or girlfriend. But alone in a more permanent way. I think we'd both grown up in homes where the people just couldn't get together even though they wanted to. Effort wasn't enough. We had both felt lonely right in the middle of the family. And we both had big expectations put on us that we couldn't meet. We agreed about that too."

The trip constituted a kind of breakthrough for Jeannette. It seemed to Douglas that she decided to "risk another round in the ring." She changed jobs, cut her long auburn hair short, and by June had enrolled in a writing course. She saw less and less of Douglas. "She's doing wonderful things, but I'm stuck," he said at the time. "Things have kinda reversed now, and I feel like I'm the patient. I'm the one in the hole, and she's moving ahead. I sent her a bon voyage card before she left for the writers' conference and signed it 'your forever friend and soulmate.' That's how I feel right now." And? "And I haven't heard back — naturally."

Douglas and Jeannette quietly broke up in the fall, and Douglas felt "kinda brokenhearted." For several months he drifted downward, struggling to reconcile the message he got from articles on "exploitive therapists" — that he must be dysfunctional and sadistic — with the compliments he received in his new job. As a part-time playground supervisor, he was again being praised as the nicest guy on the staff — but no longer as "the Energizer." He was depressed and gradually running out of steam. One evening he scared himself by having an attack of nerves curiously reminiscent of Jeannette's troubles. Was he crazy as well as bad? He called three therapists, made three appointments for interviews, and found one to his liking. "I told Bob right up front why I needed therapy," he said, "and he told me that once he referred a patient to a friend of his. They hit it off and now they're married. Bob considers it a good relationship. I felt such relief. You don't know."

Thus Douglas found an ally as he embarked on the difficult task of figuring out what had happened. Six months later he sounded different. He was completing a master's program in counseling that he'd begun earlier and was working at a home for the mentally retarded. He was out of debt and had joined a cycling club that regularly planned trips to Connecticut. "I have gained a completely new sense of the dedication needed to treat a patient," he said. "I think we should take a vow, like a priest — a vow of honor and service . . . and celibacy. I think there should be more support for counselors too, not just when they get in trouble, but right from the start and with someone who's sympathetic and understands that you can't boss your heart around." Douglas also had a new view of his relationship with Jeannette: "I idealized Jeannette, and I only wanted to see the beautiful, talented woman who appreciated me so much. I didn't want to see her unreadiness. I think I also had a completely unrealistic view of the kind of future we could make to-gether." And an unrealistic view of himself? "Yes," he said slowly. "I've lost some innocence, and I'm less split apart from myself. The good and the bad are kinda coming together. I would like to be a good friend of Jeannette's now — nothing more. But I don't want to think it's all been a mess."

One spring evening more than a year after the couple had split up, Jeannette came down to New York from the college where she was finally completing her undergraduate degree. At an off-Broadway per-formance of a mime troupe, she bumped into Douglas. "Big hug!" Douglas said. "Big smile! It was, oh! It was so wonderful to see her. No wonder I fell in love with her. She is terrific." The two managed to switch their tickets and sit together in the tiny theater. The next day Douglas sent Jeannette a "light, funny note. Not serious, but I think she'll get the point — I enjoyed seeing her." A month later he received a letter from Jeannette which said, among many other things, "thanks."

Douglas breathed a big sigh of relief. "We have had such an impact on each other's life. That's the way I see it now. Yes, it started as a rescue mission — *another* rescue mission — and that's not too good. But that wasn't the end of it. I gave her sincere and honest love — from the heart — and she cared about me too. We took an unexpected trip to . . . well, to a place that changed our minds about a lot of things. I'll never do it again, but I have no regrets."

Clearly Douglas did have regrets. Dating a resident from the house where he worked turned out to be a nightmare. However, the relation-ship itself seemed to push Jeannette into school and Douglas into ther-apy. Although both were vulnerable, inexperienced kids when they met, the relationship was marked with goodwill, and Jeannette consistently exercised her right to say no. As we will see in other cases, when a client feels the attraction is mutual, has control over its course, and is dealing with an unmarried therapist, she is far less likely to feel exploited.

~~~

Many questions have been raised in these opening chapters — most of them about the variety of intimate doctor-patient relationships that have developed over the years. Lasting less than a day or filling a life-time, leading to betrayal as well as tenderness, and bringing together men and women who are old and young, rich and poor, educated and self-taught, inspired and self-serving, the attraction that is dangerous to psychotherapy takes many different forms. And the stories we tell ourselves about these liaisons change as our culture changes.

Fifty or a hundred years ago, the Jungs, Spiers, Ferenczis, and Allendys of the world hired their special patient as an assistant, and the two quickly expanded the range of activities they undertook together. Now the Douglases go out for coffee and take walks, and the Blanfords encourage attractive parishioners to join the vestry and go on retreats. But in all such instances, the therapeutic relationship is braided into a larger, richer skein of shared experience. A friendship has begun. The possibility of intimacy approaches.

From the young woman's point of view, be she a Spielrein or a Katherine, it frequently seems at first that she has met the man of her dreams. Here is a kind and confident man, wise in the ways of the world, who is listening to her with great attentiveness. Like the keenly intuitive Jung, he sees into her, sees beyond the nervous laughter she uses to cover up her feelings, beyond even the feelings of depression and anxiety that she equates with failure, sees all the way into her heart, where she has stored an almost forgotten remnant of hope. That such a man should think she is wonderful is enough to restore her faith in life. She will get better, and not just better: she will become the special person with the unusual gifts that she had originally dreamed of being. Frequently she goes back to school to become a therapist, as Spielrein, Gizella Pálos, Nin, and Marty Fromm all did.

But two things are likely to happen. First, such a young woman often finds herself overpowered by her own response. Her constant fantasies of loving this man drown out all other thoughts. Initially, it is the pleasantest of miseries, but soon she feels overwhelmed — enslaved — and finds herself wishing for an affair that a short time before she would have considered immoral or inadequate. At the same time, she is likely to notice other women looking at her therapist adoringly, and she is faced with the question of what she can realistically hope for. Usually, the answer is "not much." She may fantasize, as Spielrein did, that a Frenchman will come along and whisk away the therapist's wife, but in reality, the love she feels for her doctor has no room to grow. Frustrated, the young woman tries to find a part of the therapist's life that is uniquely hers. She turns herself into his smartest assistant, his most attentive companion, his most daring lover — but this does not solve the underlying problems. As both Marty Fromm and Katherine discovered, the initial gains in confidence and self-knowledge begin to unravel. Sooner or later the frustration of being in a relationship that reveals itself to be a dead end forces a change. When therapist and patient part, as often happens, the result used to be called heartbreak. Now it is called abuse. Both are often true.

Yet even as the number and variety of relationships that have sprung up against the better judgment of clinicians during the past hundred years have become apparent, the ability to talk about the subject has all but disappeared. It has become a form of blasphemy to ask: Did all the good things the reverend did for Katherine's self-esteem evaporate with the first kiss? Or, as Chaucer asked in *The Canterbury Tales* after the greedy Pardonner has told an honest story about greed, can a moral lesson be learned from an immoral man? Equally unacceptable now is the question that Douglas's story raises: Can the therapist get hurt too or even instead?

Only one scenario is seen as politically correct today, and to talk or ask about anything else is considered vile and abusive. "It is alarming that the topic has become . . . undiscussible," stated two of the foremost commentators on doctor-patient intimacy, Thomas Gutheil and Glen Gabbard. "The unfortunate effect . . . is the creation of a . . . blind spot in the precise area where we desperately need to increase and expand our understanding."

How did serious considerations of the physical attraction that develops so often between doctor and patient get swept under the rug — again?

II

THE

CURRENT

SITUATION

Instead of loving a human being for his hunger, we love him as food for ourselves. We love like cannibals.

— *Simone Weil*

In state capitols, at weekend seminars, in graduate schools, in judges' chambers — wherever professional men and women gather to discuss doctor-patient sex — a politically correct version of this problem is trundled into the room and prepared for battle. Every therapist who becomes involved with a client or former client is sick, exploitive, and unreliable, this version states. Every client is an innocent being led into harm's way. Often no opposition at all is mounted against this horrifying picture, but curiously, it rarely prevents a fight. Hyperboles fly back and forth across the hotel ballroom. Faces turn red. Voices rise. Something or someone is on the march.

In this section, I would like to examine what might be called the life cycle of the doctor-patient sexual involvement. How do these entanglements start? What kinds of doctors become involved with what kinds of patients? Who gets hurt? And what is being done to repair the damage and prevent the abuse? Along the way I will pay special attention to what is considered to be the typical doctor-patient erotic involvement — a modern story of heartless exploitation — and ask how representative it really is. Like all emblematic stories, the politically correct version of doctor-patient liaisons took some time to settle out of a broader, more varied "literature" on male-female interactions. Thus, in the first published examinations of doctor-patient pairs, it was not clear whether the involvements were being shaped to fit the old love-makes-the-world-go-'round pattern or the new and still ill-defined men-are-out-to-exploit-women pattern. For example, in an article that reviewed "every available case of sex between therapists and clients" — all thirty-four of them — the authors concluded that "the results . . . ranged from being extremely devastating to one or both of the participants, to relationships that had positive influences upon the individuals' lives." They estimated that in seven instances, the sexual relationship was positive, for eleven couples it was mixed, and for sixteen pairs the experience was awful. They discussed power disguised as attraction, mismatched expectations, incest, adultery, but also the "genuine human relationship" that sometimes develops between therapist and client. They urged therapists not to take the risk, but included guidelines for transferring a client to another therapist and putting the relationship on a more equal footing if doctor and now former patient were determined to become a couple. Writing in a time of rapid social change, the authors urged their colleagues not to retreat to a knee-jerk reaction — "it is unethical and therefore unthinkable" — but to engage in the broadest possible discussion. Doctor-patient stories, they argued, fell into more than one category. Moreover, something important could be learned about how therapy works from these relationships.

In the same decade, 1965–1975, a radically different view of doctor-patient relationships was developing in two groups whose members argued not so much against complexity as in favor of dramatic simplicity. Early feminists, convinced that women were getting hurt in therapy far more often than was generally known, wanted this abuse forcefully brought to the public's attention. Complicated cases, they found, led to endless rumination, but simple, malicious ones akin to rape woke people up. Moreover, such stories of abuse fit the prevailing sexual stereotypes and were easy to believe. There was something seductively familiar, even intoxicatingly dreadful, in listening to a woman describe a psychiatrist who wheedled and whined until she agreed to come to sessions without underwear. Supposedly this would allow her to lie on his couch and get in touch with her sexual longing. Several sessions later, he forced himself on her. Such a disgustingly duplicitous story, feminists found, fit the expectations of many women. The ordinary experience of being female in America had prepared them for every single detail. Any woman who had tried unsuccessfully to fight off a "boyfriend" in the back seat of a car recognized lust disguised as charm, force disguised as passion, and the awful letdown that was almost sure to follow. Women everywhere had waited in vain for the phone calls that were supposed to come, and all had compulsively eaten their share of brownies at midnight as they berated themselves for "allowing" themselves to be overpowered. In hearing a patient describe forced sex with a therapist, most women were ready to augment her complaints with all the grievances they had personally suffered themselves. As with the common love story that these tales replaced, the listeners already knew the words.

Naturally, most clinicians did not want the negative publicity that these dramatic accounts engendered. However, a few agreed with the feminists. These practitioners believed that the reputation of their field was already being ruined by unscrupulous therapists. To draw attention to these emotional gangsters and at the same time to put as much distance as possible between them and their ethical colleagues, the horror story was the most useful account. It allowed good therapists to point with anger to the Don Juans without feeling implicated themselves.

Concern for the safety of women and the reputation of psychotherapy came together in Dr. Phyllis Chesler. In her popular book *Women and Madness,* she presented several vignettes that set the tone for future accounts. In one chapter, "Sex Between Patient and Therapist," Chesler's stories illustrated a single theme, pure exploitation. Take "Stephanie," for example. This young woman went into therapy because she was depressed. She had left her family of origin and its strife and alcoholism years before, had left a brief marriage, and was now alone with no friends. She found herself either sleeping or eating a great deal of the time. Initially, the doctor she went to saw her for only ten minutes at a time and gave her pills for depression, weight control — and birth control. He kissed her "crudely" at the end of every session, and when she told him this practice bothered her, he suggested she pretend to like it. After three months of his pestering, Stephanie agreed to lie down on the couch with him, hoping that he would be kinder to her if he got what he wanted. He wasn't. He hopped off after sex and went back to his typing. Now guilt and remorse piled on top of Stephanie's other problems. The doctor ignored her complaints, even when she swallowed a handful of sleeping pills, and gave her a job typing his letters instead. She realized she was being exploited, but every time she tried to leave, she would go back. Once, when she returned, the therapist said he didn't want to sleep with her anymore but asked her to type a book. Finally, during one session when the two were naked in his office, his doorbell rang and kept ringing for twenty minutes. Stephanie looked out the window and saw a girl standing at his door, crying. "That's me next year," she said to herself. Shortly after receiving this shock, Stephanie left treatment.

Other stories in the chapter have the same components. Each account involves a woman who has had a miserable childhood and a lonely adulthood. She lacks confidence and friends. She turns to an insensitive doctor, who is concerned only for himself. Receiving a few words of flattery that suggest the possibility of affection, the woman is quickly roped into serving the doctor's needs. It is a pattern she probably recognizes from childhood. When she gets worse instead of better, the doctor first prescribes pills, then criticizes her, and finally ends the relationship. Feeling guilty, angry, lonely, crazy, and abandoned, the patient goes through a crisis that may include an attempt — sometimes successful — at suicide. If she pulls through it, she finds herself unable to fight her abuser. Labeled neurotic, hysterical, or worse, she and her account of the fiasco are dismissed.

Chesler's stories appeared in 1972, and within five years the brand of callous exploitation they illustrated and that undoubtedly was occurring had become the accepted script for *all* doctor-patient intimacies. Complex interactions were increasingly ignored in popular literature or dismissed in professional articles with such vague and unverifiable statements as "those women were in denial" or "it can take years for the harm to surface." Clearly, the political need to protect women and level the therapeutic playing field for all consumers had become greater than the scientific need to document the intricacies of human behavior. Outwardly, the point was made that achieving social justice for more than half the population was more important than ensuring that every last doctor got a fair hearing. Inwardly, healers again backed away from looking squarely at the loaded relationships that often exist between therapist and doctor. As had happened in Mesmer's time and again in Freud's, any serious interest in the therapist-client bond was stuffed back in the closet. Tentative accounts of affection and attraction published in the late 1960s and early 1970s were replaced by *Betrayal, Men Who Rape,* and *A Killing Cure.*

In the next two chapters, I will examine several modern cases and see how they are supposed to work. Not only will we hear more stories from women whose lives have been disrupted by doctor-patient relationships, but we will also listen to a psychiatrist explain what it feels like to fall for a client — and act on it. Next I will present several stories that illustrate how the transference love that Freud spoke of, and that some people believe is always established in therapy, leads to an imbalance of power between doctor and patient. In each, I will ask which of our politically correct assertions are supported by the story or by research and which, while reflecting the feelings and expectations of the day, are not? The role that recovery groups now play for patients is of particular interest, for in the process of straightening out their confused stories, the group leaders actively shape the problem they are attempting to rectify.

The final two chapters in this section focus on attempts to control the incidence of doctor-patient sexual involvement and to repair the damage they cause. Chapter 6 examines the increased regulation found in the health care industry and in so many areas of our lives and that represents our attempt to maintain order as our traditions drop away. Although Americans are fond of responding to problems such as sexual abuse or terrorism with a cry for legislation, we do not give away our personal freedoms easily. However, they are being given away nonetheless. In the case of health care, new legislation seems motivated primarily by the rapid growth of the industry itself and by the privatization of former state facilities. Pressure from feminists and consumer rights activists also increases regulation. Frequently, clinicians oppose some of the new restrictions, partly for the loss of independence and, more important, for the resulting attenuation of the doctor-patient relationship.

One way of justifying the increasing control is to exaggerate the dangers that the new rules are supposed to prevent. Statements commonly made within the mental health system, for example, erroneously suggest that 10 percent of therapists sexually abuse clients and that 90 percent of these clients are severely harmed. Neither statement can be substantiated, yet both provide powerful impetus for the passage of legislation.

During the past ten years, we have seen regulations originally intended to protect children extended first to handicapped persons, then to senior citizens, and now to women. Apparently the portion of the population that is "vulnerable" and childlike is growing with amazing speed. Some clinicians argue that the next step is to recognize how many men are being sexually abused by their therapists. They will need regulations to protect them too, it is said.

Although the campaign to clean up psychotherapy has educated a generation of clients, making them better able to spot if not withstand unethical practices, the vehemence of the crusade has led to certain distortions. It has driven parts of the discussion underground, leaving us with an incomplete picture of doctor-patient liaisons to study, and, further, it has forced women into the narrow role of innocent victims — lambs. This position may provide a starting point for some patients, but "innocent victim" is not a role that is large enough or flexible enough to accommodate most women's feelings and actions. It puts them in a triply uncomfortable position: helpless vis-à-vis their unethical therapists, dependent on their new therapists, and silent on the subject of their own lust and desire.

In an odd turn, the new regulations sometimes protect the system at the patients' expense. I will argue that in at least four or five distinct ways, well-intentioned regulations take from the patients they are supposed to protect services, money, and moral support. In return, they offer a form of therapy that is more businesslike, more conventional both in technique and objectives, less risky, and less personal. One example of this sleight of hand is the common practice adopted by insurance companies of capping the amount they will pay for sexual malpractice suits. Although this limit is supposed to discourage doctors from becoming sexually involved with clients, its greater effect is to restrict the money available for helping victims.

A second example involves what is called parallel process or second-hand sadism, when clinicians pass on to their patients the anger and frustration they feel as restrictions on their practice rise and the pay dwindles. We do not always appreciate that with each new safeguard meant to protect patients, practitioners lose some of the right to use their own judgment. We are now required to call in social services when a mother slaps her son, even if it is the first incident we know of and even if we are sure the family will drop out of therapy if we turn them in. We may not balance the advantages and disadvantages and make our own decision. Such mandated responses have become so numerous that some clinicians feel like robots. Add to this that each loss of freedom is accompanied by an increase in paperwork and often a decline in real earnings, and it is not surprising that clinicians everywhere are worried and that many are disgruntled. What *is* surprising is that doctors are starting to take out their frustrations on patients. Could this lead to an increase rather than a decrease in certain kinds of sexual exploitation?

Many more examples of what are called the unintended consequences of regulations could be given; unfortunately, they all fit into a vicious cycle, which tends to perpetuate itself. As our relationships with teachers, doctors, therapists, and clergy become more regulated and thus more distant, our hunger for personal attention, which is already high in our society, seems to mount. With this increased loneliness and neediness comes an increased vulnerability to just the kind of exploitation we are trying to regulate away. As more abuse occurs, more regulations are put into effect, and the cycle continues. If this officially sanctioned retreat from the patient continues, the problem of troubled love may indeed dwindle as doctor-patient closeness disappears. There would then be fewer cases like those of Hillesum and Spier, Douglas and Jeannette. However, I believe that exploitive sex would remain or possibly rise as increasingly lonely women take their troubles to increasingly angry men. This would represent a very large unintended consequence, and one that more and more clinicians predict.

The last chapter in this section focuses on what happens to a woman when the erotic relationship with her therapist is finally over: What, if anything, restores her emotional well-being? We will listen to Barbara, who is weighing the advantages and disadvantages of turning her psychiatrist over to an ethics committee versus interpreting his seductive acts as affection. We will hear a therapist who runs groups for women who have been involved with therapists or clergy describe the typical steps that women like Barbara pass through.

Likewise, we will examine the methods used to train therapists in matters of attraction and to repair those who have crossed the line. Especially in the case of lovestruck therapists — clinicians who insist they are lovers, not exploiters — rehabilitation poses difficult questions. Regardless of what a therapist may say to get his license back, does he really want to be cured of the feeling that he loved his patient? An ancient Arab tale of passion dramatically examines the standard ways we have of "fixing" people who think they have fallen in love. And a marvelously eccentric collection of priests chime in with thoughts on reliable celibacy.

~~~

So who or what is on the march when doctor-patient sex is hotly debated in public — when, for example, an international conference organized by CHASTEN proclaims on posters and handouts in enormous red letters with an *X* running through them that "it's NEVER o.k."? Outraged women may be the most visible group behind "safe therapy" and the easiest to understand, but behind their insistence that therapists stay in their chairs and leave former patients alone forever lie many other social and economic interests. Less visible than most of these reasons is the need we all feel to turn away from the uncomfortable possibility that reason and right action may not be the best or only ingredients of processes as important as healing and teaching. How disturbing for a technologically sophisticated society to discover that a form of intimacy akin to love and closely allied to desire may lie at the heart of one person's ability to help another.

4

As Wolves Love Lambs

As wolves love lambs, so lovers love their loves.
— *Socrates*

An exquisite example of the seduction of an innocent by a professional heartbreaker is presented by Aldous Huxley in *The Devils of Loudun*. A biography of a seventeenth-century curé, the account both parallels and fills out the kind of stories we hear about doctors who abuse one woman after another. Like Jules Masserman of Chicago or Edward Daniels, formerly of the Boston Psychoanalytic Institute, both of whom left trails of devastation behind, Father Urbain Grandier occupied a unique position of power and respect in his community. Educated by the Jesuits and assigned to the prosperous town of Loudun, he was priest, counselor, and politician rolled into one. He was the holder of secrets and the arbiter of truth.

One of the women this powerful priest set out to seduce was the young, unmarried daughter of a friend. Accepting an offer to tutor Philippe Trincant, Grandier began visiting her household twice, then three times, then four times a week. There he sat, alone in the library with Philippe, giving her the more seductive passages of the ancients to translate — and waiting. He complimented her on her intelligence. He looked at her in a way that made her blush.

Huxley perceptively points out that "they sat in the same room, but not in the same universe." Grandier was a man of experience. He had toyed with and seduced women of all ages and stations. The inexperienced Philippe, however, inhabited a half-imaginary world of feelings and fantasies. She was experimenting with what D. H. Lawrence called "sex in the head." And Grandier was the perfect hero for her fantasies. He was handsome. He was educated far beyond the norm. He was kind. *And* he liked her. He focused his entire attention on her and called her clever. To her surprise and secret delight, Philippe began to enjoy moments of vague but violent longing for her priest. She knew it was a sin, but she could not bring herself either to stop or to confess to Grandier this attraction that made her feel so warm and vital. Instead, she prolonged her daydreams, much as patients commonly enjoy the fantasies they spin about their therapists.

Sensing her attraction, Grandier patiently fanned the flame until it seemed to Philippe that she, not he, was leading the two of them into a dangerous adventure. In several months the seduction was complete. For Grandier, the climax was slightly disappointing, but for Philippe it was disastrous in ways that were not immediately obvious.

The shift from fantasy to reality that Philippe had so earnestly wished for ushered in a great many feelings that she had not expected — feelings that also take patients seduced by therapists by surprise. For one, she abruptly felt alienated from the rest of her family. Although they did not know her secret, she realized that she now lived as an unworthy sinner in their midst. Moreover, she could no longer count on them for the sympathy and understanding she had taken for granted even a day before. Another surprise was the war of emotions that started in her own heart. She prayed for strength to resist temptation, but failed. She made vows, then broke them. She discovered the awful power of brutish desire in both Grandier and herself and she despaired. She no longer trusted herself and she no longer liked herself. Truly, she had lost her innocence. A short while later she lost her reputation as well: she was pregnant. When Grandier found out, he slid like an eel from lover back to priest. Buttoning his clothes, he blessed Philippe and was gone. She never saw him again alone except during confession, where he urged her to bear her cross with humility. By a curious but not uncommon logic, the more threatened Grandier felt by Philippe's pregnancy, the more he disliked her. Like many a therapist confronting a sobbing former lover, he did not conclude from her blotchy face and sagging posture that he had made a terrible mistake but, rather, that she had been ugly and not worth the trouble. Grandier denied any involvement. To enemies as well as friends, and even to himself, he said that the idea that he would bother with Philippe was preposterous.

Huxley's portrait of Grandier as an evil opportunist has obvious parallels to the psychotherapists who sneak and lie their way through the most sensational accounts of doctor-patient sex. He is not unlike the unnamed doctor who had sex with "Stephanie," fastened his pants, and went back to his typing. He is the villain in the movies and on television.

For many people, no further distinctions are made among kinds of clinicians or their motivations. Every professional who acts on a physical attraction with a client or former client is assumed to be irremediably bad, and whether the clinician is a man like William Schutz, who slept with members of his encounter groups, or a Ferenczi, who eventually married a patient, they are thrown in the same pile. Almost all offenders are repeat offenders, these lawyers and consumer advocates say. "They're power-hungry." "It's incest." "They should be castrated." When a case comes to court or reaches the newspapers, the doctor is almost sure to be cast as an evil, exploitive bastard — period.

Nevertheless, a few distinctions — a few shades of gray, if you will — are being introduced behind the scenes for both disciplinary purposes and research. Whether based on questions on a survey, examinations of unethical behavior made by boards of registration, or therapy administered as part of the rehabilitation of errant therapists, the general consensus among clinicians and investigators is that there are four different kinds of unethical therapists. Each is likely to become embroiled in a different kind of problem with a different kind of patient. Each is led into these liaisons for different reasons and must follow different routes if he is to emerge with a new philosophy.

Although emotional thugs get the most publicity, a more common type of errant therapist may be the lovestruck offender who starts a relationship with a former patient in the hope that it will last, then feels remorseful after he sees what he has done. Several lines of research suggest that such a person rarely repeats the experiment. Douglas and Frieda Fromm-Reichman fall into this category. Both swore they would never become involved with a patient again, even though no pressure was officially brought to bear on either one. Several clinicians I have interviewed have said the same thing. "I had one homosexual affair," said a thirty-eight-year-old psychologist, "and I am still ashamed. Patients are entirely off limits for me now." "We're not angels," said a psychiatrist in his forties, "but we learn. Inexperienced doctors make all kinds of mistakes — but hopefully only once." When these men and women are still in the relationship, however, their doubts are pushed aside by what sounds like, and may be, love. The doctor and his former patient want to be with each other all the time. They entwine their initials on the borders of their blotters. They buy books of poetry and talk of being soulmates. They stare into space when they ought to be working.

In the "scientific literature," all this talk of love is explained away. Lovestruck or lovesick therapists are compared to irresponsible, emotionally dependent people, they are called "alarmingly naive" in their belief that love can cure, and their true motives are simply asserted to be sick. The well-known psychiatrist Glen Gabbard maintains that "the sadistic wish to destroy is the perverse core of the lovesick . . . relationship." The lovestruck are also called "the most puzzling" because in them we see what looks like an uncomfortably close relationship between therapy and passion. Lovestruck therapists may not *say* that romantic love is closely related to good therapy, but they *act* as if it is. They seem to believe that a good therapeutic relationship is so intimate that occasional slips are to be expected.

Roughly one in ten or twelve lovestruck clinicians is a woman; an example is Dr. Norman, who to her dismay fell in love with a patient some years ago, not when she was in her twenties, but when she was "gray-haired and middle-aged." An articulate, soft-spoken woman who says she "favors suits" and looks like the president of an Ivy League college, Dr. Norman has recently settled into the private practice of psychiatry, a step she swore she would never take. She had expected to remain in hospitals, caring for the acutely ill, where she began her career more than thirty years ago. "About half my patients were experiencing their first breaks," she remembered, "and the other half were men and women who went in and out of the hospital every couple of years. I liked treating initial breakdowns, because I could still see so much of the functioning person. They hadn't yet adapted to being mentally ill. But I was also drawn to long-term care. I liked the feeling of being on call for patients whom I had known for eight or ten years."

In retrospect, Dr. Norman felt that her job may have demanded too much of her time and was one of the reasons she and her husband divorced when their only child entered college. Dr. Norman moved back east to be near family and again found a position in a small hospital. She bought a house, made friends, and within two or three years was beginning to feel at home. "And then one day — this is still hard to say — I fell in love with a patient. He was an attractive man my own age, and I felt a sense of kinship the moment he walked into the office. There was a surprising feeling of relief too. 'Oh, at last, here's a man who speaks my language.' I didn't see any problem at this point. It didn't occur to me that I'd ever act on the attraction, so I looked forward to our meetings."

No obvious ethical problems arose for several months. The two talked easily together and appreciated each other's company and philosophy. "We are both avid mystery readers," Dr. Norman said, "and even as he left the hospital we were planning to swap books. I'd done that with patients before."

Gradually, however, Dr. Norman found herself doing two things that she had not done before and that she did not immediately associate with her feelings of attraction. First, she began spending more time than usual with this patient. She didn't see him for more than an hour nor did she see him as an outpatient more than twice a month, but neither did she cut back his time to a half hour and then to fifteen minutes a month as she usually did with patients who were stable. Instead, she continued to meet him on Tuesday afternoons, when they discussed "everything under the sun." She learned, for example, that he had a cat named Sneaky Pie (Rita Mae Brown's famous feline sleuth), and he learned that she had once gone to England to get a book signed by P. D. James.

The second development was that she became increasingly critical of the mental health system, including her own part in it. "It became very awkward to write a discharge summary in the usual professional terms of a person I liked so much. I could state that he was a divorced, white, Irish Catholic male, but when it came to giving him a diagnosis and adding the usual vignettes about . . . oh about how he came to be hospitalized because he was 'abusing alcohol' or 'noncompliant with medication,' then I felt torn. At least in this case, the customary explanations seemed like formulas that were included to make the staff feel justified in using the usual, somewhat heavy-handed treatment. But when I liked a patient as much as this one and knew him as a person — I know that sounds odd, but I think we usually know the mentally ill only in their role as patients — then I began to realize how little of each life we were taking into account.

"When I read phrases in my patient's chart like 'denies excessive use of alcohol' and then found out he drinks one Sam Adams beer on Saturday nights and has for years, I thought, 'Why use the word *denies?* Why not trust the patient?' I thought I had confronted these dilemmas in medical school, but questions of respect and condescension returned. It was *not* refreshing. At the time I didn't feel I was reevaluating the field and my place in it, although now I think I was. It felt then as if I was sabotaging the hospital's policies just by being on this man's side. Emotionally I had joined forces with the enemy."

Was Dr. Norman simply picking holes in a system that wouldn't let her do what she wanted? Or did love for a patient force her to see the mental health system in a new way and confront practices she had ignored in the past? Either way, within six months of meeting the patient, Dr. Norman realized she was too fond of him. She thought about him frequently; she found herself buying a blue wool suit because he'd like the color. Once, when he told her that he was going to the town hall to get a dog license, she nearly went there at the same time.

"'What am I doing?' I asked myself, and the answer seemed to be that I was comforting myself with the affection that had grown between us. Thinking of this man was like holding a lucky stone in my pocket. Just thinking about him made me feel good. It also prompted me to reevaluate my personal life as well as professional dealings. I couldn't see where I wanted to go in either area, but it was clear by this time that this awkward, embarrassing, exciting situation was a big turning point. I remember thinking that it felt like I was living in a house that was being moved across town. Every day I found myself in a different position in regard to everything."

As Dr. Norman and her patient started sending each other reviews of new mysteries with notes attached, the forty-five-year-old psychiatrist tentatively reached out for help. A reserved and private person, she didn't talk with anyone but read articles on the harm that doctor-patient intimacy can cause.

"It was hard to read these articles and even harder to hear what they had to say," she admitted. "I wanted to argue with every word. I kept thinking about all the other kinds of mistakes doctors make, and I wanted to know why falling in love was any worse than abandoning a patient or giving him too much medication as a kind of punishment. I also began wondering why all the attention was focused on the morality of individual doctors rather than on hospitals. The rules said I couldn't terminate with this patient and start dating him, but there weren't any hard and fast rules that said my hospital had to let a patient stay when his insurance ran out, and there is no rule saying you can't close a chronic ward or a halfway house and scatter patients who have lived together for years to the four corners. In order to save money, we play havoc with patients' lives, but no one says that's unethical. But you get the point. Every time I tried to read about the damage that falling in love with a patient can do, I changed the subject."

Increasingly concerned for her patient and for her own reputation, Dr. Norman took a vacation to put the case in perspective. She told her patient that she was having a difficult time honoring the doctor-patient boundary, and they agreed not to be in contact while she was away. During this time, she found herself swinging back and forth between feeling that she could handle the situation and feeling that she couldn't and was, therefore, a terrible psychiatrist. "On some days the attraction would seem like such an ordinary mess, and I'd think, 'Well, every one of my colleagues has probably gone through something like this.' But other days, I felt awful. I distrusted the affection I felt for my patient. I distrusted my ability to treat people. I distrusted my self-control. And there was no one I could talk to without risking a great deal. The ethics made it clear that what I was already doing and thinking was wrong. Just by falling for this man I felt kicked out of the club."

Dr. Norman, usually so self-possessed, alternated with increasing force and discomfort between delight in her new relationship and alienation. She stepped away from friends as well as colleagues. "I felt like a foreigner." Finally, she took an obvious step, one she admitted she should have taken months before. She requested a consult. To ensure confidentiality, she went out of town. What had stopped her before?

"Knowing in advance what my colleague would say. Simple as that. And not just about my patient — about me. Any one of my male colleagues could walk into another doctor's office, describe a charming female patient, and expect the other man to smile and nod. In fact, a story is circulating in town right now about a psychiatrist who did just that. He wanted his colleague to cover for him while he attended a meeting — in Australia, I think it was — and he had to explain why this one patient needed such special care. *She had been living with him.* I don't think most doctors agree with this kind of treatment, but none of them would look at this man and say, 'You *what?* At your age, you *what?* And with a patient?' Women are supposed to be different. We are not supposed to be so strongly attracted to anyone that we do foolish things. It was bad enough that any decent supervisor would tell me that my affection was wrong and my actions unprofessional. But I was also sure he'd be shocked."

However, it was Dr. Norman herself who was the most thoroughly shocked. She realized later that the picture of her that was emerging — that of a professional woman panting after a patient and risking a precious career to do so — was seriously at odds with how she saw herself. She had, it seemed, a willful, self-centered, and passionate side that had to be acknowledged and accommodated: it was an unpleasant surprise.

The day Dr. Norman "accidentally" bumped into her patient at an antiques fair and had coffee with him, she called a doctor she had known on the West Coast and fled into consultation. "I can't remember how I broached the subject, but at one point I asked, 'Have you ever been dangerously attracted to a client?' Of course that told him that I was dangerously attracted to the man I was discussing, and it also told him that I wanted to find out how far I could trust him — the consultant. Did he know firsthand about attraction? Did he want to hear whatever confession I might be on the verge of making? I wasn't sure he wanted to get involved.

"I certainly remember his reply. 'It is a common problem among inexperienced therapists,' he said, and then went on to relate two or three anecdotes about how he had handled women who were attracted *to him!* They were wild stories too. One woman threw a rock with a love letter through his window; another came to her sessions with no underclothes on. I've heard that one from half a dozen male analysts. One snuck up behind him and got him in a hammerlock. While he's telling me these stories, I'm thinking, 'Well, either you've never fallen in love with a patient and have no idea of what it feels like, or you have but you've decided the experience is too dangerous to talk about. Either way, you're uncomfortable, and you're telling me condescending anecdotes about women who can't control themselves.' However, I had really scared myself with the coffee shop meeting, so I pushed on and admitted I was attracted to this patient and was having a hard time controlling the situation. He grew extremely serious then and gave me many reasons why I should stop immediately. He talked about ethics. Then he told me that if I wanted a partner, surely I wouldn't choose one who is mentally ill — think of the rigidity, the fragility, and so forth. Next he said it wasn't fair to the patient, and that part of the discussion upset me. My intention wasn't to hurt or betray him in any way. It was terrible to think I was taking advantage of him. Finally, he said that I was flirting with professional suicide."

After meeting with this man three times, Dr. Norman ended the consultation. At the time, she felt the doctor neither empathized with her feelings nor wanted to wade into dangerous waters. Later, she thought that a more important reason for their failure to start a useful dialogue was his disdain for the patient she loved.

"I got precisely the kind of response that I expected and feared. What else could an ethical doctor say? I couldn't imagine him saying, 'Isn't love grand?' But that was where I was — in love — and that's what I wanted to talk about. I wanted to tell someone about this secret attraction and have them take it seriously. I would have gotten further with the doctor if he had expressed admiration for my patient. After all, I'd spent an hour telling him what a fine person he was — his job, his accomplishments, his close relationship with his children. It's too bad the doctor couldn't have drawn me out on this. If he'd taken my feelings of love seriously, then I think we could have talked about how you treat a person you love. We could have discussed different plans of action and tried to see which would benefit my patient the most." And would that have made a difference in the long run? Dr. Norman sighed. "I don't know," she said a bit wearily. "Possibly not."

Dr. Norman finally confided in a friend, where she found a welcome but dangerous mixture of compassion and concern. Although still having bad dreams about being labeled an abusive, exploitive doctor, she began to calm down when reminded that it was not a sign of mental instability to love a person with bipolar illness. These people frequently marry and have notable careers, her friend reminded her. Also, she thought that the majority of human beings would see nothing wrong if a doctor and a patient became a committed couple after therapy was over. Dr. Norman was taking a chance with her patient's well-being and her own career, but her friend dismissed the idea that she was either abusive or crazy. Of course, what the friend couldn't describe because she wasn't a doctor were the difficulties that lay ahead.

Dr. Norman finally broached the topic of termination with her patient after a year of treatment. She told him she was no longer objective enough to be his therapist. If the relationship persisted afterward, it was against the rules and was dangerous. "I even gave him several articles on therapist-patient abuse," she remembered. And was he alarmed? Dr. Norman chuckled to herself. "No. No, he was not. Once he became angry and said it was nobody's business what we did after therapy was over, but more often he tried to make me laugh about it. He would pretend to be testifying against me in court, and he would use quotations from the articles I'd given him. They did sound pretty funny coming out of his mouth."

Having talked over the situation, Dr. Norman referred her patient to a doctor in a neighboring town. Several weeks later, they began to spend time together. "I admit now that it was nerve-racking. It was an awful way to begin or, rather, to conduct a relationship. At the same time, it was a relief to get out from under the doctor-patient framework. We found that the relationship gradually got more normal as time passed. We've known each other nearly five years now, and the therapy is a minor part of our history. I think the power got redistributed along the way and came into about the same sort of balance it would in any pair with our temperaments. Not exactly, but about the same.

"The relationship has gone through several phases — some close, some not very close. We had to undo some of the intimacy that therapy generated prematurely or rather one-sidedly. It's been difficult."

One of the few difficulties that Dr. Norman and her former patient have not yet had to face is rehospitalization. The two have decided that when it happens, she will not visit him. That would reveal too much. But why has this patient, who suffered an episode every year or two, been free of symptoms? Had her love cured him?

"Absolutely not. No. That's not the way the illness works," she said.

So how did she explain the five-year hiatus?

"Well, I think when people are in stable relationships they take better care of themselves. The incidence of all kinds of illnesses goes down. They live longer."

But wasn't that the same as saying that love was therapeutic? That it had helped her former patient more than medication or therapy?

Dr. Norman paused uncomfortably. "I see what you're driving at, and yes, of course, love is therapeutic, but I can't bring myself to say that when the relationship starts as doctor and patient that it's wise to . . ." She paused again. "You'd think after nearly five years I'd know the answer to that question," she finally said. "I've gone through so much to give this relationship a chance to develop that it's really hard for me to criticize it without feeling I'm betraying my friend and myself. Also, the friendship isn't over. The jury is still out. But I do know this: loving is difficult enough under the best of circumstances, and with a patient the circumstances are close to impossible. I would never do it again."

Like several of Freud's contemporaries discussed earlier and more specifically like Douglas, who fell in love with a resident at a halfway house, Dr. Norman stumbled against the largely unarticulated hazards that lie in wait for the lovestruck clinician. Not only did the attraction place her in a middle world, where she could not relate to either doctors or patients in a conventional way, but it also set her against the mental health care system. She became angry at the hospital and the doctor she consulted both for devaluing the person she loved and for failing to understand her own feelings. This is important for two reasons. First, it raises the question of which comes first — the forbidden love or the sense of being a critic and an outsider. Perhaps love in all its forms pushes therapists into the role of critics. Second, even if there were no rules at all regarding sex with former clients, the idealistic revolution that every lovestruck clinician wants to start represents an unwanted challenge to the mental health care system. No Medicaid clinic, for example, wants to reexamine every aspect of its treatment policy to see if its practices would adequately serve beloved friends and lovers instead of patients on welfare. Similarly, no doctor in private practice wants to embrace the long days and low pay that a physician like William Carlos Williams, who openly adored his patients, was willing to accept. For better and for worse, the way in which Western countries care for the majority of the mentally ill could not continue in its present, business-like form if clinicians let themselves fall in love with clients.

Dr. Norman's story also illustrates the point that clinicians who become entangled are usually lonely and somewhat naive. Like so many others we have observed, Dr. Norman ignored the attraction in its early stages, assuming that she had the power to turn off her feelings for a patient at any time. In addition to this dangerous underestimation of love's power, her story highlights the dilemma that lovestruck therapists face when they finally decide to put on the brakes. They have risked so much for the relationship that they find it almost impossible to stop without betraying themselves as well as their former patients. Finally, this story can't help but suggest that patients with sufficient confidence and power may be helped by a loving relationship — even with a therapist. Until doctor-patient couples can talk openly, however, we will not know.

~~~

A third, still larger category of practitioners who become entangled with patients and former patients is composed of naive, poorly trained, and insensitive clinicians. These are the men who can't believe they've done anything wrong in dating a former client, say, or in lavishly complimenting a patient's legs. Although such naiveté is technically possible, given the absence of training in this area until recently, the people I interviewed all found naiveté mixed with what they called "insensitivity," "a macho attitude," or "stupidity." For example, a man I'll call Dr. Betz, of a Pacific Northwest board of examiners, told several stories about "dumb and misguided therapists who don't see how their actions can possibly be perceived as hurtful." These are the men who come into his office screaming "foul play," he said, demanding to know why a complaint had been made. The false steps that brought them before the board ranged from complimenting a woman repeatedly, especially on her looks, criticizing a husband or boyfriend and telling the patient she needed a better man, giving hugs and squeezes, meeting outside the office, and *never* asking how these actions were viewed by the patient. When confronted by the charge of sexual harassment or seductiveness, such clinicians were astonished. According to Betz, this type of practitioner is far and away the most common offender. In his estimation, "there are four, well, fourish of them out there for every two psychologists who are lovestruck and for every one who is a sociopath — the truly egregious offender." It is interesting to note that when one of these insensitive therapists encounters a woman with considerable ego strength, the result is often immediate divorce. Patients have described stomping out of a doctor's office at the first off-color remark. "And I'm not paying!" more than one shouted over her shoulder.

The final type of therapist — and one that attracts so much publicity that there seem to be a lot of them — is the doctor who is obviously crazy. When sexual abuse at the hands of a lunatic needs to be illustrated, the story is usually told of a psychiatrist who worked on the adolescent unit of a state mental hospital. This man, who was probably schizophrenic, gradually came to believe that his semen conferred eternal salvation. God had told him this. Thus, following what he believed was divine advice, the doctor systematically set out to have intercourse with every patient on his unit. He had sex with several of the acutely disturbed teenagers before being discovered and hospitalized himself.

Another example is that of Suzanne King, a Boston psychiatrist who was sued by three patients. They claimed that she conducted therapy from her bed at home, wandered around the room in her underwear, went to sleep during sessions, moved two male patients into her home, and went to great lengths to get pregnant by these men. Luckily, there are few such loose cannons careering through the therapeutic community, and as a group they come in a distant fourth after the insensitive, the lovestruck, and the evil opportunist.

Official taxonomies of therapists who cross the line stop here. Although a fifth category clearly exists — doctors and patients who have developed what is touchingly called "a real relationship" — it has become so unfashionable to say so, and so dangerous to admit to being in such a relationship, that almost no one says a word. Even when a big national survey found that 13 percent of doctor-patient relationships ended in marriage or a committed relationship, this sizable minority was ignored. Fifteen years ago a clinician could write, "It is, of course, possible for a therapist to genuinely fall in love with his patient. After all, therapists are human beings and not immune to such feelings." But now stories that acknowledge this fifth category are passed among clinicians more quietly. For example, two women — a doctor and a patient who have been together for over five years — are so concerned with guarding their secret that they fly from Boston to New York whenever they need therapy. Carter Heyward, the Episcopal priest and professor at the Episcopal Divinity School in Cambridge, knows of "nearly a dozen couples [made up of professors who are clerics and their clients or students] who have gone underground for two years, five years." Dr.

Betz remembered that "where I used to work, it was common knowledge that two senior analysts had married former patients. It wasn't discussed, but it was commonly known. They stayed happily married as far as anyone knew." Elsewhere, a psychiatrist treated a woman who stated that her former doctor had terminated therapy and started an affair with her. She wanted the same treatment from the second therapist. "I want to have intercourse with you," she demanded, "*right now.*" "No," I said to her. "I'm tired. I've worked all day." The woman dropped out of therapy, returned to the original therapist, and, to her second therapist's consternation, "married the s.o.b. The guy was twenty-five years older than she was and had back pain. But I have to admit that as far as I know, they're doing O.K." He went on to explain that "I didn't feel there was a great power differential between them. Because they had terminated therapy before the affair began, she had a choice. Not that termination guarantees a choice," he added quickly, "but it sometimes makes a choice possible. I think it did here."

Such stories about what other therapists do circulate after hours, although now they are likely to be introduced tentatively. My sense is that roughly half of all senior clinicians know a therapist or professor of psychiatry who currently maintains a relationship with a former patient. Although it is fashionable to say that this fifth category is minuscule, no one really knows.

Dividing any collection of individuals into groups to help us understand their behavior is demanding, and never more so than when the individuals themselves won't talk openly about the behaviors that determine the categories. As long as this is the case, the groupings will be crude. Perhaps there are five kinds of clinicians who become involved with former clients, perhaps more. At the very least there are two — the insensitive, walled-off person, who has no understanding of the patient, and the overly empathic clinician, who has trouble controlling his or her actions. One climbs on a patient like a life raft. The other closes his eyes and starts down the primrose path.

When the explanation for erotic attraction is sought within the clinician himself — in his personality rather than his actions — then the softhearted talk about wounded healers and the hardheaded discuss genetics or disease. The idea that certain talented people pass through periods of "creative illness" and emerge as wounded healers has been around for at least two hundred years. In psychoanalytic circles the concept is usually associated with Henri Ellenberger, who long ago described the person in the throes of a creative illness as one who is so preoccupied with a problem that he is almost totally self-absorbed. Such a person feels lost, indecisive, and utterly alone, and onlookers may believe that he is physically sick or mentally unbalanced. When the crisis has run its course, however, a Darwin emerges from a bout of hypochondria or a Jung from waking nightmares with astounding new ideas. One way that such creativity has been explained is that the person "is more primitive and more cultured, more destructive and more constructive, crazier and saner than the average person." In other words, he or she lives among several extremes simultaneously and lacks the customary boundaries that usually keep these qualities separate. A man like Jung, for example, might experience an unnaturally wide range of impulses, feelings, and ideas — quite crazy, uninhibited thoughts — but a part of him would watch these kaleidoscopic dreams warily and try to capture useful insights. A mentally ill person lacks this cool observer, whereas the average person lacks the kaleidoscope. Obviously, the imaginative mixing of constructive and destructive thoughts can be dangerous in a clinician. When the best and the worst are so closely intertwined, patients get hurt by the same ambitious, appealing, and independent thinkers who add greatly to the field. "Why are the doctors with the most thought-provoking ideas so often the ones who have sex with their patients?" asked Mr. Anderson, who we will meet again in the next chapter. And why, asked Laura Brown in an article on the harmful effects of sexual relationships with former clients, does it seem that the "popular and sought-after . . . therapists" and those "in positions of leadership" are the ones who have affairs? One explanation is that big talents are often accompanied by big liabilities.

A different explanation comes from psychogeneticists — clinicians who attempt to explain our behavior on the basis of genetic inheritance. They point out that the genes we have today evolved hundreds of thousands of years ago, when *Homo erectus* was ranging through the savannas as a hunter-gatherer. Our environment has changed dramatically, especially with the development of agriculture in the past twelve thousand years, but our genes have not. We still have the genetic equipment that makes for good nomads. As Kalman Glantz and John Pearce pointed out in *Exiles from Eden,* "Most people are living in an environment they do not understand" — and have a hard time handling.

Applying the concepts of sociobiology to therapy, scientists theorize that male clinicians are likely to view their patients in about the same way that males have viewed other people from time immemorial. That is, they will see young female patients as potential lovers and older female patients as mothers or relatives. They will see male patients as rivals unless they are very old or young. Female practitioners, on the other hand, are likely to respond to older male patients as possible partners and to younger ones as children. At the same time, "the genes that hold culture on a leash" prompt patients as well as clinicians to act in old, old ways. Female patients, like females for half a million years, are likely to be attracted to the most powerful and established males in the community — older men who can protect them and their offspring and who presumably have genes that will ensure success for their children. Women are attracted to men who are competitive, assertive — if not downright aggressive — and physically robust. In other words, they are attracted to potent males or healers with relatively high levels of testosterone. They are primed to say yes to such a man.

As we will see later, psychotherapy is rapidly turning into a field that is much less welcoming to the potent, macho healer. Perversely, perhaps, I am saddened by this. And reminded of a story. One cold November night I took a man in his seventies who was complaining of chest pain to the emergency room of a hospital. I accompanied him to an examining room, where it was determined that he was suffering acute arrhythmia, and I was standing in the doorway when his heart stopped altogether. Before I understood what was happening, the emergency room exploded into activity, led by a maniac in scrubs who burst on the scene bellowing directions. In seconds the patient was wired up to a defibrillator.

"Clear! Clear!" shouted the doctor with an urgency that seemed to slap the nurses away from the body. The awful sounds of a jackhammer came from a machine as bursts of electricity were sent into the patient's body. One eye on a screen, one eye on the patient, the doctor crouched at the side of the table as if preparing to throw himself at his unseen adversary. "*Got 'im!*" he suddenly screamed, and there was in that triumphant, fiercely combative howl nothing less than a personal victory over death.

I have witnessed moments only slightly less dramatic with the mentally ill, and again, it was the passion of a driven, powerful, and quite possibly dangerous doctor that made the difference between life and death. They are liabilities, these wild clinicians, but from time to time nothing less will do, and I am sorry to see them leave the field.

Although no behavior is determined by genes the way eye color is — and, in addition, our many genes urge us in different and contradictory directions — it is interesting that the pattern of doctor-patient entanglements observed in surveys largely follows the pattern that sociobiologists would predict. Older, powerful male clinicians have sex with younger females of child-bearing age, whereas female clinicians tend to form liaisons with male clients of their same age or older. As E. O. Wilson maintained, the history of both the individual and the society "is guided to a more than negligible extent by the biological evolution that preceded it." If we demand different behavior from clinicians — behavior that biology is reluctant to support — then the effort required for such a change will be considerable.

Among those who believe that every clinician who crosses the line is sick rather than unusually creative or ordinarily masculine, the tendency is to distribute diagnoses. Jung was a borderline, the minister who left town with the high school girl was narcissistic, Douglas and Dr. Norman had poor impulse control, and the doctor with the magic sperm was psychotic. According to a British clinician, the typical American view is that "therapists will only offend if they are in some way dysfunctional." This system has its advantages. For one thing, it puts a comforting distance between "sick" and "well" practitioners, and for another, it explains deviant behavior in terms of poor socialization, childhood traumas, and unbalanced neurotransmitters — all causes familiar to clinicians. For example, some psychologists conjecture that therapists may cross ethical boundaries because they are so uncomfortable with anger and sadness that they insist on treatment's going well even if they have to hug and kiss their clients to make them happy. Another "sick" reason is that some clinicians are so angry at authority that they seduce clients to show their defiance. An increasingly popular possibility is that offending clinicians had seductive, adulterous, or abusive parents. Perhaps therapists who have been sexually abused themselves are more likely to seduce their clients. Jung confessed to Freud that "as a boy I was the victim of a sexual assault by a man I once worshiped." Otto Rank was introduced "to erotic experience in my seventh year through one of my friends, for which I still curse him today." However, many clinicians accused of sexual misconduct have not been abused, and the relationship remains unsubstantiated. The behavior of a large group of errant clinicians — say, a hundred thousand, or 10 percent of the million-plus doctors, therapists, and aides at work today — cannot be understood by cross-examining the few who are brought to court.

If we do not wish to classify therapists who act on erotic attraction by analyzing their personalities — calling them wounded healers or giving them diagnoses — we can look at their stated motivation. When a group of psychiatrists were asked why they had become sexually or romantically entangled, 73 percent answered for love or pleasure, nearly 20 percent said it was part of the therapy, and a small number admitted they simply lost control. Interestingly, when women were asked why they became involved with a client, a different picture emerged. Citing the fairy godmother complex as culprit, clinicians at the huge Learning from Women congress argued that "boundary violations among women clinicians begin as an attempt to rescue and nurture" and "women aren't out for *pure* power the way men are." "Women's mistakes are well intended." Sociobiologists would agree. For a woman, the urge to form a sexual liaison is more likely to mean a lengthy commitment than for a man. Not always, of course, but on average. The few studies available suggest that although female clinicians fall into all five categories of unethical sexual relationships, the majority are lovestruck.

Finally, we can look at the kind of therapy these clinicians practice. The usual way this question is posed — is a Freudian more or less likely to fall for a patient than a behaviorist or a humanist? — has not shed light on the matter, but another way of asking it does. The more profitable query is: What role does the doctor play vis-à-vis the client, that of protector, expert, teacher, or colleague? Do these different stances or, more accurately, these doctor-patient duets put clinicians at different risks for sexual involvement? And do they influence the nature of the entanglements that ensue?

Becoming a fully functioning human being, increasingly able to appreciate the wider world and one's place in it, is a long and difficult process that Alan Flashman views as a stairway with uncomfortably narrow steps at the bottom and ever wider treads toward the top. And, said Flashman, a child psychiatrist in private practice who also teaches at the Hebrew University in Jerusalem, because patients enter therapy on different steps, effective therapists need to adapt their work to the kinds of relationships or alliances that characterize each step on the stairway. Thus, when a distressed patient comes into therapy saying in effect, "I'm desperate! Don't change me!" the kind of relationship a therapist needs to establish with this person is very different from the rapport requested by a person who says, "I'm ready to do things differently. Can you teach me how?"

In simplest terms, there are four levels on which the somewhat similar businesses of living and doing therapy proceed, and as the stairs ascend, individuals become what Flashman and others call increasingly "differentiated." Not only does a person with a moderate degree of differentiation see himself as distinct from others, but he also sees others as existing apart from himself. His wife, for example, is not solely a person whose job it is to care for him. He sees that she has goals and desires unrelated to his own. He can even imagine his own mother in roles that have little to do with him — as his father's wife, as a business-woman, perhaps, and as someone's friend. "Mom" can now be a real person, and not only in connection to him, although this was precisely the case when he was a child and far less differentiated from her.

Therapy helps people ascend the stairway, and a good therapist takes the role the client is capable of giving him and works from there. Always tugging upward, toward greater differentiation, the practitioner simultaneously tries to broaden and delineate his client's social relationships. Conversely, he tries not to drag the patient down with statements or actions that tell her she exists solely as he, the therapist, sees her or as he needs her to be.

Starting at the bottom of the stairway, we encounter persons who see others as entities who only give or withhold. Conversely, these patients see themselves as receptacles for what others give or refuse to give them. When they think of their mothers, for example, they understand them solely as women who provide or refuse to provide what a son or daughter needs now. In such a world, life becomes the attempt to force these two-dimensional providers to give enough — a strategy that never satisfies. Patients at the bottom of the stairs have remained enmeshed in perpetual debates about getting what they need; their whole existence seems limited to engaging in these futile arguments. They are stuck. They are tired. And they are afraid. Such people can enter therapy only as an extension of these debates, however, and the only therapist they can perceive at first is a two-dimensional figure who gives or withholds. Such people are not ready for the talking cure. A therapist's interest in changing them will automatically be experienced as withholding, as telling them that they cannot have what they want. All that these patients can tolerate is a protector who won't ask them to change. With such a therapist, they can pour out their frustration and disappointment — their way of presenting themselves and their dilemma. They need not fear that the protective therapist will contradict them, for he or she understands that, like unhappy children, they first need a sympathetic ear and only later a guide who is skilled in using indirect approaches.

Next on the stairway, according to Flashman, are people who come into therapy saying, "O.K. You're the expert. Tell me what to do." Such individuals tend to have muddled relationships that they sense need fixing. Since the doctor is the expert, they expect him to prescribe behaviors that will make them and their families feel better. They are not interested in testing new ways of relating with the therapist, but they intend to follow his directions at home. In family therapy, the "homework" that the expert therapist might assign would be for a husband to take his wife out to a restaurant without the children once a week. Without explaining what he intended, the therapist would hope to underscore and strengthen the division between parents and children.

Higher still, and standing on treads that are wide enough to accommodate three-dimensional friends and relations, are individuals who wish to improve their techniques of dealing with the world and themselves. They want a teacher, and like a good student, they enter therapy prepared to interact with their mentor and expecting to take over more and more of the work themselves. With these patients, the therapist enters into the treatment rather than directing it from outside. He or she interacts with the patient and, in addition to showing by example how a more differentiated person speaks and acts, promotes an alliance that nudges the patient up the stairway.

At the highest level are patients who are actively exploring their lives. They go to a therapist either for validation of the progress they are making on their own or for collaboration.

"Many people enter therapeutic relationships because of a pressing desire to collaborate on some of life's central issues," wrote a humanistic psychologist. "A large number of my colleagues prefer the notion of assisting our clients. . . . Instead of medical recovery models [of treatment], humanistic psychology finds a friendlier climate in the idea of the wondrous uncertainties of journeying with our clients."

Whether protecting, directing, teaching, or journeying, a good therapist adopts the role required by the patient, but because all roles are not equally agreeable to all clinicians, many find themselves doing most of their work on just one or two steps. When a famous clinician like Hans Strupp asserts that the doctor-patient alliance is like a parent-child relationship, it suggests that he does much of his work toward the bottom of the stairway. When, however, Leston Havens maintains that a clinician must love his client or James Hillman describes the relationship as a kind of love that is tender and close, it suggests that these men work at the upper end of the staircase. Regardless of the level, however, the task is always to move the patient toward a more differentiated perspective, and at no level is this goal served by romantic fusion, which at least temporarily narrows and *un*differentiates the lover's outlook. To put it another way, romance is not the answer to any of the requests that patients make along the stairway.

If attraction is acted on nonetheless, the resulting relationship is likely to play itself out in different ways, do different kinds of damage, and need different treatments depending on the place along the stairway where it develops. These different scenarios go a long way toward explaining the debate that rages over what to call doctor-patient sex. "It's incest!" many women insist; indeed, if the erotic entanglement develops between a woman precariously balanced on a narrow step who first and foremost needs protection, then it is in some ways similar to incest. Both involve females who are so dependent on their protectors and so grateful for their attention that they cannot easily break free when sex enters the picture.* If, on the other hand, the liaison occurs between a truly cold clinician and a woman who has said, "Just tell me what to do," then

---

* Constance Dalenberg, a psychologist who does research on countertransference and abuse, has found that especially among women who have been abused as children, therapy starts with "a parental feeling." These women report feeling very young and very grateful for their therapists' attention. They are "sweetly loving of their therapists," Dr. Dalenberg says, "and this is where the therapists get trapped." Thinking the client is cute and the devotion she offers touchingly innocent, the therapist lets himself cross ethical boundaries. (Personal communication.)

terms like "rape" or "con job" seem more appropriate. With teachers and their students, people speak of "taking advantage" or "exploiting." And in cases where a doctor and patient collaborate as fellow explorers, sexual relationships that start after the therapy is over are comparable in some ways to adultery or even to ordinary love. As has become apparent before, when the variety of sexual relationships that occur between doctor and patient is acknowledged, it becomes possible to make sense of some of the conflicting claims and accounts that surround the issue.

Pulling together all these ways of categorizing therapists, it appears that the clinician most likely to get called up on minor ethical charges is the insensitive, self-centered, and poorly trained man who has a suburban private practice and can't believe that his hugs or his comments could be offensive to his patients. When the complaint is a sexual relationship with a patient or former patient, however, the most likely clinician is a middle-age, lovestruck man who, trapped in a poor marriage or recently divorced, reaches out for comfort. This man is also likely to have a suburban private practice, a lucrative, well-respected one at that. Although somewhat cynical about his profession's prospects, he is often an assertive and even charismatic leader in his field. Having the credentials and responsibility that go with such a position, he is greatly admired by most people who know him — the very model of success. This man feels he has found his soulmate, and at some point in the relationship he trades places and becomes the person in need of comfort. "Well, I am dying now," wrote Rank to Nin. "Come to my rescue." Or from Jung, "Return to me in this moment of my need, some of the love . . . which I was able to give to you at the time of your illness. Now it is I who am ill."

Behind the insensitive and the lovestruck come the hardened breakers of hearts, who repeatedly satisfy their longings with patients they care nothing for, and finally the psychotic. The media coverage this last group receives makes it appear larger than the others.

When it comes to typifying the female clinician most likely to cross ethical boundaries, little can be said except that she probably thinks she's in love, and she is at least as likely to enter a homosexual affair as a heterosexual one. Nor is there enough information to describe the clinician who is most likely to form a committed relationship with a patient, although he or she probably works near the top of the stairway. It is possible, however, to describe the clinician least likely to form a sexual liaison with a client: she is a happily married female social worker at a hospital or clinic. Although she does not have a powerful position, she is proud of her profession and the part she plays in it.* As we will see, her tribe is increasing.

Turning to clients, it comes as no surprise that the people who become involved with clinicians are as varied as the doctors themselves. After all, even exploitation is a relationship. It is a deal struck between greed and need. Leaving aside for the time being the lunatic doctor who rapes and the insensitive therapist who insults or misleads — neither establishes much of a relationship — we are left to wonder what patient is attracted to the hardened breaker of hearts, the less malicious Dr. Lovestruck, and the occasional doctor who sacrifices therapy to obtain a partner. In terms of diagnosis, the one label that is consistently linked to doctor-patient sex is "borderline." For example, when doctors at the Menninger Clinic reviewed every known case of sexual misconduct from their files in a ten-year period, they came up with a profile of the vulnerable patient, and she was a borderline.

Their report stated that "the typical patients are those with borderline personality disorders who have complained of 'emptiness' and have displaced object hunger [the desire to be connected to people] with a propensity to seek out affect-intensifying experiences [thrills]. They have a history of childhood sexual abuse or a history that suggests it."

Other hallmarks of a borderline personality include frantic efforts to avoid being abandoned, a pattern of intense, unstable personal relationships, impulsiveness, intense anger, and a wobbly self-image. So popular has the diagnosis become that it is applied freely to people living and dead, even when several of these core traits are missing. Jung, Spielrein, and Hillesum have all been called borderlines. Although the disorder

---

* I am reminded of the "portraits" of the man least likely to die of a heart attack that used to be drawn by insurance companies. As I remember these composites, they depicted a thin, unassertive, happily married man who didn't smoke or drink and who worked as a mortician's assistant — a low-stress job. No man wants a heart attack, but not all would trade places with the mortician's assistant. Similarly, no woman wants to be exploited in therapy, but how many are willing to avoid male therapists to reduce the risk, and how many feel it's essential to get a male therapist's point of view on their problems?

was hardly known twenty years ago, it is now said to afflict some five million Americans, most of them women. (This is equivalent to saying that roughly 4 percent of American women are borderline.) Called "the women's illness of the '90s," the malady is associated with sexual abuse and a frustrating emptiness that is always in need of being filled. It has become a metaphor for our current discontents.

What little research there is on the kind of clients who become erotically entangled in therapy strongly suggests that women who have been abused as children, either sexually or physically, are overrepresented in the ranks of the sexually involved. These women are more likely to be sexually attracted to their therapist — male or female — than women who have not been abused. Like women with a borderline personality disorder, those who have been abused seem to have greater difficulty differentiating deep concern or warmth from sexual attraction.

Turning to patients who establish long-term partnerships with their doctors, they seem to be "the reliable neurotics," women or men who are willing to take over the therapist's job of nurturing and caring. Mrs. Ferenczi probably fell into this category, as did the student lovers of Tausk, Reichman, and Horney. The patients of such analysts sense their loneliness and hurt and offer themselves as comforters.

Regardless of the historical period or the kind of therapist, the woman most likely to be swept into a doctor-patient imbroglio is physically attractive, under forty, white, and relatively successful. This generalization has been recognized for a long time, and to my knowledge no one disagrees. But what happens next is another matter. Does she fall in love with her therapist? Or does she get caught in a strange state called transference? The consequences of and the choice of treatment for doctor-patient entanglements depends on the answer, but there is no agreement.

5

Transference and
the Power Imbalance

> We misrepresent the character of an experience, in-
> cluding the experience of psychotherapy, if we think of
> the past as a reservoir of objects or events that are
> capable of enduring in the present like bricks mortared
> into a wall.
>
> — *Irving Singer*

Transference, and the power imbalance it helps to create, together form the foundation on which all politically correct accounts of doctor-patient sex are erected. Held up as one of Freud's greatest insights, transference originally referred to the unconscious transferring of feelings from the past — especially those needy, worshipful feelings that young children have for their strong, protecting parents — to the psychotherapist. Transference love (or transference hate), Freud said, represents a new edition of an old relationship that is superimposed on the therapist. This both helps and hinders the therapeutic process, for while the patient's feelings of dependency and desire fuel the therapy, the neurotic form of the transference relationship itself — the insistence on obtaining gratification from the perfect comforter (or punishing the perfectly awful "parent") — is the problem that is holding the patient back and must be overcome. Good therapy, then, manages to keep the transference going to provide impetus for the work that eventually convinces the patient that it is useless to continue looking for perfect providers and protectors. If the transference is not allowed to blossom — by restricting therapy to three sessions, for example, by holding a client at arm's length, or by the patient's frequently switching therapists — little work will be undertaken, but if the transference is acted on, and the therapist tries to be the perfect partner that the patient hungers for, the patient is likely to repeat all her old mistakes and learn nothing. In fact, Freud thought she might be worse off than before.

In a paper on transference love, Freud wrote: "If the patient's advances were returned it would be a great triumph for her, but a complete defeat for the treatment. . . . She would bring out all the inhibitions and pathological reactions of her erotic life, without there being any possibility of correcting them; and the distressing episode would end in remorse and a great strengthening of her propensity to repression. The love relationship in fact destroys the patient's susceptibility to influence from analytic treatment."

Freud also observed what he called countertransference in himself and his disciples. This term connoted the unconscious feelings and desires the analyst felt for the patient — his hope that she would fill those deep needs his parents had tried to meet. As early as 1908, Freud was collecting information on countertransference from one of his least favorite patients, a Frau C., who flopped disagreeably in and out of treatment with lots of analysts, always hoping to find the perfect protector and inadvertently generating volumes on countertransference.

"Frau C. has told me all sorts of things about you and Pfister," Freud wrote to Jung. "I gather that neither of you has yet acquired the necessary objectivity in your practice, that you still get involved, giving a good deal of yourselves and *expecting the patient to give something in return.* Permit me, as the venerable old master, to say that this technique is invariably ill-advised and that it is best to remain reserved and purely receptive. . . . I believe an article on 'counter-transference' is sorely needed; of course we could not publish it, we should have to circulate copies among ourselves."

Of course, not everyone agreed with Freud's interpretations of transference. Although Ferenczi believed that his patients transferred their old desires to him, he worried that Freud and his followers actively enticed patients into thinking of them as heroes. Analysts love feeling superior, admired, and adored, Ferenczi observed, and by interpreting everything patients did or dreamed about as reflecting their feelings for the doctor, a transference love was gradually fabricated. It was like a joint myth. To his diary he confided his belief that "a large share of what is described as transference is artificially provoked." Yet most analysts insisted that the transference was none of their doing. The admiration wasn't encouraged, they insisted; it was the patient's "distortion." In Ferenczi's opinion, this explanation helped them feel superior and remain relatively uninvolved. Although Ferenczi favored a closer relationship with patients than Freud, he did not want the role of hero. In the natural course of analysis, doctor and patient grow to know each other in a fairly realistic way, Ferenczi believed, and in so doing, the hope of the perfect love is gradually given up.

Jung also favored involvement with patients rather than reserve. In his article "The Psychology of Transference," written long after he had broken with Spielrein and Freud, he advocated a daring exchange. As he saw it, the doctor took on the patient's troubles and the patient borrowed the doctor's strengths. In this operation, "the doctor . . . exposes himself to the overpowering contents of the unconscious and hence also to their inductive action. The case begins to 'fascinate' him." In fact, as the two get under each other's skin, "the patient then means something to him personally, and this provides the most favorable basis for treatment." Jung believed that a doctor has to "catch" a patient the way he would catch a cold, and he spoke of "psychic contagions" and of feeling possessed. "The patient's destiny involves that of the analyst," and both of them battle their way through the illusions they have created together — illusions that lead to misunderstandings and perhaps more dangerously to "a most disconcerting impression of harmony."

Jung seemed to be saying that countertransference is as essential a driving force as transference. The doctor's fascination with the patient motivates him to attend to him or her just as the transference motivates the client. If the doctor is so self-sufficient or so sufficiently analyzed that he does not respond to patients with longing, nothing much happens in the analysis. (Although many clinicians disagree with this idea, those who work with severely disturbed, isolated patients are more likely to understand what Jung was saying than those who treat neurotic patients who are connected to husband, wife, friends, and others.)

Although Freud's ideas have been modified in dozens of ways, his intuition that doctors need to stay just out of reach of their patients has remained central to the vast majority of clinicians. Call it being objective, being reserved, or being professional, most practitioners find a way of holding their emotions at a distance.

"Long ago I settled on playing the role of the patriarch — the good daddy — as a way of controlling the countertransference," said Robert Blanchard, the former director of a small clinic in Massachusetts. During his forty years of work with all kinds of patients, he "became the benign father and my patients became, you see, the children. That kept us both safe." He paused. "I've often wondered if that didn't put them into the role of children too . . . too forcefully. I meet some of these people thirty years later and they still think I'm Daddy and they still act like children. Of course they're not children in their other relationships, but they are with me. That's the relation we agreed upon. It worked well for me and kept us both securely in our chairs. Still, I don't know if the father-child relation is always the best way to do it."

Today transference is used to mean not just the unconscious but the full range of feelings that a patient has toward her therapist. Realistic liking and disliking, conscious thoughts, and subterranean stirrings are all lumped together. What do patients think of transference? Not surprisingly, they are rarely asked, partly because they are supposed to be unaware of transferring old feelings into a new setting, and partly, I think, because clinicians like the concept of transference and don't want it challenged. Nevertheless, two observations are worth making. One is that for clients who are forced to attend therapy — prisoners, many children, hospital patients, and some chronically ill patients — the clinician often remains a mere annoyance to be tolerated. Another is that people can rarely point to more than two or three important, powerful therapists in their lives even though they have been in therapy with four, six, or even twenty-six different doctors. "Only a few were significant," said a man who has lived with bipolar illness for thirty years and can recall talking with more than a dozen therapists during this time. "One was like a kindly father to me, and I liked that. We just talked. Others were very busy. Some barely tried." It makes no sense to me to say that such a patient — and his numbers are legion — is clamped into a transference love with all fourteen of his former doctors.

Whenever transference does occur, however, the patient bestows on the doctor all the strength and wisdom she thinks he will need to protect her. At this point, any semblance of equality goes out the window — at least for the time being. The doctor has been given magical powers. Ethel Person, an analyst who has written on love, believes that transference is a natural outgrowth of our fears. Both in religion and therapy, she asserts, we try to tame the terror of the human condition by bestowing on God or a therapist enough power to give us a sense of security. Of course, this creates a new set of worries. What if the powerful protector gets angry and leaves? What can we do to keep him happy? "Haunted by our own helplessness," as Person puts it, the less power we have, the more strength we will imagine our therapist to have. Among patients who feel truly helpless, the transference is so strong that the therapist can seem to be a god.

But how can we be sure that any of this is true? According to the philosopher Irving Singer, who wrote a trilogy on the history of love, transference is a brilliant idea in need of severe pruning. There are two problems. First, although our impression of everyone we meet is influenced by people in the past, there is no way of telling *how much* the discovery of a new love is really the rediscovery of an old one. Second, the memories we have of our parents — what they did for us and what we desperately wanted them to do for us — no longer exist in their original form and cannot be used as a model for a therapist. We have memories, all right, but they are less like home movies in the head than they are like clouds that, shifting and rolling, allow us to see what our present emotional climate prepares us to see. In Singer's trimmed version of transference, parents and therapists are both authorities — both people whose love and appreciation matter to the patient. And the patient is likely to do and believe whatever he or she thinks will secure that love. In other words, patients' ongoing attempts to get their therapists to love them is the key element in transference, not the resemblance that may or may not exist between the patient's parent and the therapist. In this version, it is the profoundly lonely patient, rather than the helpless one, who will do almost anything to secure her therapist's love.

One final comment needs to be made on transference, namely that all love, in or out of therapy, involves transference. We urge on each of our new loves the attributes we would like them to have, and the best loved of these qualities come from deep in our past. We also present ourselves to our lovers in ways that will elicit the kinds of comfort and protection we want and remember. Thus every emotionally charged relationship unconsciously imposes these transferred dreams onto the less exciting observations we call reality. Whenever we transfer old hopes to another person, we give them power both to help and to harm. This brings us to the subject of power.

~~~

It has been said that "the history of madness is the history of power," and the same could be said of lunacy's little sister, neurosis. The current concern that psychotherapists are abusing their power over patients — and especially over their female patients — is the latest chapter in a long book on precisely these struggles. Separately and together, women and neurotics have threatened the Western ideal of passion securely controlled by reason. The major themes in this ongoing dialogue — how and how completely should the doctor overpower insanity — are beautifully illustrated by the controversy over Mesmerism. Mesmer's mysterious "power of the eye" and "authority of the voice" not only controlled certain forms of madness but also seemed suspiciously akin to the very passions it set out to conquer.

Franz Anton Mesmer (1734–1815) developed what is known today as hypnotism; he is also credited with being at least the godfather of psychoanalysis. Because he consistently questioned his own amazing cures and tried to test his results, his career is said to mark the entry of psychotherapy into the realm of science. Initially a student of theology under the Jesuits, the restless Mesmer turned to law and then to medicine. He received his degree to practice medicine at the late age of thirty-three and almost immediately sidestepped the necessity of working by marrying a wealthy widow. The two lived on a huge estate and entertained the musically sophisticated of Vienna. Mozart's first opera had its debut in the Mesmers' private theater.

At the age of forty, Mesmer discovered what he believed to be a form of magnetism in human bodies. An ethereal fluid flowed from the stars into almost everything, he thought, and it circulated as electromagnetic currents. He found these currents in paper, bread, wool, stones, glass, water, dogs, and people. If obstructed, they caused disease. This magnetism had most forcefully come to his attention in the person of a Mademoiselle Oesterline, who suffered an apparently incurable frenzy that gave her pains in the teeth and ears followed by delirium, rage, vomiting, and fits of fainting. Because conventional doctors could do nothing for her, Mesmer treated her with magnets. Concentrating intently on what he believed to be magnetic disturbances in her organs, he drew magnets over the young woman's body again and again in an attempt to redistribute her "mineral magnetism." The treatment precipitated what the French are fond of calling *une crise*, a crisis that marks a profound turning point. Apparently Oesterline writhed around a good deal during treatment, breathing heavily and crying out. She sounded to some like a woman having an orgasm. Afterward, she became languorous, then sleepy, and finally content. Her symptoms departed, never to return again. In fact, the young woman eventually married Mesmer's stepson.

Mesmer, meanwhile, went on to challenge his own theory and redefine it. He came to the conclusion that his magnets had no influence at all on his patients. But the doctor did. Renaming the central force "animal magnetism," Mesmer developed a technique that always began with the doctor's sitting knees to knees, or at the very least thumbs to thumbs, with the patient and staring into her eyes. The object was to use his own healthy distribution of animal force to pull her animal magnetism into line. It was hoped that she would become agitated, then excited, and finally experience a profound crisis — an internal revolution. Padded rooms were provided for recovering patients.

Mesmer's colleagues were as appalled by his technique as they were envious of his success. Trained in the classical method, eighteenth-century doctors did not touch their patients — ever. In fact, they didn't even speak to them in a language they could understand but used Latin, the better to influence their souls. Such men were deeply suspicious of Mesmer's intimate methods. Even when Mesmer used glass wands or metal bars rather than his hands to get the magnetism flowing, women responded with a volcanic outpouring of emotion. This wasn't medicine, the conventional doctors maintained, and they shunned the technique. Nevertheless, dozens of unmanageable women were sent to Mesmer by baffled fathers and frustrated husbands. For several years he enjoyed a dazzling success. He continued to produce truly marvelous cures (using what we would call suggestion) until an unusual patient, a young, blind pianist, was brought to him and the treatment let him down. Maria-Theresa Paradis was the eighteen-year-old daughter of an extremely wealthy civil servant. Blind since the age of three and a half, doctors could do nothing for her, but Mesmer was given a try. The first several sessions produced no change in Paradis but apparently stirred in Mesmer himself a kind of fascination — an agitation, a determination — as if the treatment were working in reverse. Finally, concentrating all his animal magnetism on the young girl, Mesmer simply willed her into an intense level of excitement — and for a few moments she could see. It seemed like the beginning of a miracle, and the hopes of the entire family were reawakened. The treatments continued. The lovely young woman claimed that she was gradually regaining her sight, but her original doctors were skeptical and urged that she be formally tested. The tests showed that Paradis could only see in the presence of Mesmer. Her family was furious. Their hopes were dashed, and so was Mesmer's reputation. When the girl seemed to lose her sight permanently, and could not see even during her sessions, Mesmer was profoundly shaken. Despondent at his failure and also at losing touch with the entrancing Paradis, he left Vienna, permanently left his wife, and temporarily left his career as well.

For three months Anton Mesmer walked in the woods and talked to trees. Gradually regaining his self-confidence, he decided to introduce Mesmerism to Paris. During this time he also experimented with adjusting his own magnetism — what we would call self-hypnosis. According to an account written by a contemporary, Mesmer mesmerized Mesmer to relieve a "blockage in the lower part of the body."*

In Paris, Mesmer was immediately caught up in a second cycle of success, scandal, and rejection. Initially there was an overwhelming demand for his treatment, and he was prompted to develop ways of magnetizing groups of women simultaneously. He also trained assistants. Predictably, ordinary doctors became alarmed, and as happens whenever a treatment transgresses a social taboo, they demanded an

---

* Some historians of medicine speculate that Mesmer was impotent in part because no gossip of a sexual nature ever circulated about him. It is possible that he developed self-hypnosis to treat a sexual problem, but we are not sure.

investigation. Louis XVI obliged by appointing a commission which included Benjamin Franklin and other members of the Société Royale. They produced a Secret Report, concluding that Mesmer was an impostor and his "cures" merely a trick of the imagination. Moreover, the report noted, the treatment was dangerous. Not only did the charms of the female patients affect the physician, but the women's weakened state made them susceptible to the powers of the doctor. "The danger is reciprocal," the report noted and went on to ask if the strange magnetic fluid that the doctor regulated and that produced undeniable changes in the patients was not the equivalent of love. But the question was intended to be rhetorical. Although the report expressed an obvious fascination with the intimate exchange of power and sensuality that passed between Mesmerists and the women they treated, its authors could not overcome their squeamishness. As continues to happen when sexuality appears in therapy, it seemed safer to regulate than to investigate. Doctors and patients alike stepped back from the heart of the matter.

Although Mesmer left Paris and wandered around Europe until his death, his ideas continued to circulate outside academic medicine. Among his followers, a new generation of Mesmerists induced a magnetic sleep (a hypnotic trance) and directed their patients' attention to concerns that might be disturbing them. The treatment became more conservative, and it became routine to include a chaperone in the sessions. Among the public, however, the concept of Mesmerism moved in the opposite direction, and the treatment was imbued with increasingly fantastical powers. Although the Marquis de Lafayette failed to find a receptive audience for Mesmerism in America in the eighteenth century, American practitioners trained in France established themselves as "American magnetizers" after 1815. In England, magnetism took more easily. In fact, the English were so impressed that statesmen became concerned that "magnetic spies" were coming over from France and using "the authority of the eyes and voice" to read minds and plant thoughts in diplomatic circles. It was believed that persons with great animal magnetism could work on others even at a distance with their lethargy-making, knee-nailing, eye-screwing, and dream-working techniques. In the popular mind, Mesmerism became synonymous with seductive manipulation — and remains so. Women still accuse their doctors of mesmerizing them.

Mesmer confronted many of the same questions concerning the ethical use of power that we do today. At least in the West, where most people are in favor of treating "unbalanced" individuals by restoring reason to its dominant position over passion, the question is not "Should a doctor try to outsmart the low cunning of insanity?" but "Should he use only reason to overpower the unreasonableness of the patient?" Is he still a good doctor if, like Mesmer, he uses something akin to the seductive power of madness to control madness itself? Here is the irony that made Louis XVI's panel and so many others nervous: people were going into therapy to have their reason restored to its dominant place by a treatment that depended on passion. This joining of combustible emotions seemed entirely too difficult to control. Regardless of what Mesmer said, his actions proclaimed that the therapist's passion or magnetism was essential in treating emotional problems. In other words, therapist and patient alike are caught in the crossfire between logic and emotion. Not only is the patient waging a civil war between reason and passion, old brain and neocortex, angel and animal, but the therapist is too, albeit in a calmer and more informed manner. Some clinicians in every age have acknowledged their own passions and concluded that living in a crossfire and treating a patient's crossfire at the same time is difficult but necessary. However, they have never convinced the majority that the power of both passion and reason are essential to therapy.

From the patient's point of view, the interesting questions to ask about power are different. Leaving legal questions aside for the moment, patients' two big questions concern safety and respect. Can I trust this doctor not to hurt me if I reveal my darkest secrets, my deepest feelings, and my wildest hopes? And where do I stand with him or her? Am I expected to play the role of a child? A student? Or is the therapist my adviser? Although many factors contribute to a person's sense of power vis-à-vis a doctor — not least the point on the stairway where they enter therapy — emotional components like transference and the magnetic attraction of the therapist usually outweigh socioeconomic differences such as age, income, education, and gender. In other words, the ingredients of the power imbalance are primarily the deep, half-conscious mingling of old needs and new hope in the patient and the animal magnetism of the therapist. Discrepancies in socioeconomic status between doctor and patient are present but generally less important. The "authority of the pocketbook" is easier to understand and counteract than the infamous "authority of the eye."

When power is misused, harm results, and of all the kinds of harm that therapists inflict on their clients, the damage done by sexual acting out is the most common basis for formal complaints. Although an Exploitation Index administered to psychiatrists suggests that many mistakes are more common — nearly 70 percent of the doctors said they had sometimes revealed sensational aspects of their cases, the same number accepted gifts, half said they were gratified by the power they had over the patient, and others failed to return calls, failed to stop therapy when it was doing no good, failed to limit addictive drugs, and so forth — the complaint that gets the most attention is sexual entanglement. Not only is this accusation more likely to appear in the media, it also accounts for half of the money spent on settlements. In addition, it occupies its own branch on the self-help tree and has become an almost surefire way to get published in the scientific literature. Some clinicians, in fact, maintain that sexual exploitation has generated its own illness — the Therapist-Patient Sex Syndrome. Like rape and incest, involvement with a therapist, these clinicians say, traumatizes the patient and inflicts "deep, diverse, lasting, and sometimes permanent harm." The broad, general symptoms include guilt, ambivalence, emptiness and isolation, suppressed rage, and an impaired ability to trust.

There is no doubt that patients bear the brunt of the damage when therapy turns into an erotic entanglement, although whether this constitutes a separate emotional illness is debatable. Until recently, evidence of harm came only from anecdotal evidence — a woman like Spielrein confiding in her diary or one like Katherine explaining her fears and confusion to a subsequent therapist. Now surveys of psychotherapists who have treated the aftermath of a doctor-patient entanglement are being run, and formal studies that compare women who have and have not been erotically involved with a therapist are being undertaken.

Some of the losses are so obvious that no studies are needed to clarify them. For example, the patient whose therapist begins acting like a lover immediately loses a valued ally. Not only does the patient lose an objective adviser and a confidant, but she also loses an expert witness (if needed for a custody settlement, for example) as well as the possibility of returning years later for additional therapy. The therapeutic relationship

that she may have spent several years and a great deal of money establishing is gone with the first kiss. "I needed those [therapy] hours to talk
about my problems to an objective person," said Barbara, a school-
teacher we will meet in Chapter 7. "But he wanted to talk about himself
— *his* work and *his* disappointments. He'd tell me how attractive I was
and why we'd make a good match, and I was flattered. But I needed
therapy, not compliments."

More personal forms of damage — a loss of trust in men, a loss of
confidence, and an erosion of self-regard — are more painful and more
difficult to assess. At present a controversy does *not* rage, although it
should, on who can best evaluate the harm and on what evidence such
evaluations should rest. Most of our information comes from surveys of
clinicians (not patients) and from adversarial accounts that are designed
to clobber the other side, not study the situation.

One small survey run in 1983 found that nearly half the practitioners
who returned the questionnaire had treated at least one patient who
reported having sex with a former therapist. No questions were asked
about the harm this may have caused, so in 1991 a much larger survey
was sent out to remedy this omission. Again, half the respondents
reported that in the course of their careers they had seen at least one
patient who had been intimately entangled with a prior therapist. Some
87 percent of these patients were women. When asked how many of
these patients had been "harmed" by the encounter, the clinicians estimated between 80 and 90 percent. Only 5 percent of the patients seemed
entirely positive about the experience, they reported, another 3 percent
had married their former therapist, and 17 percent seem to have recovered. Thus three quarters of the patients were judged by the subsequent
therapist to still be hurt by their earlier encounters. There is an obvious
bias here — women who were content with a doctor-patient intimacy
would not return to therapy as regularly as women who felt hurt — but
in this survey there was no way to balance the numbers. In addition, the
patients themselves weren't asked to evaluate the experience, and without their voice it is difficult to tell whether the harm resulted from the
former lover's being a therapist in particular or a cad in general. Although it is not fashionable to challenge any statement that draws
attention to the dangers of doctor-patient sex, it is important to realize
that the oft-quoted statement that 80 or 90 percent of patients are
harmed is the roughest of rough estimates.

What do we actually know about harm? Studies have yielded mixed results, although *none* has suggested that sexual involvement is helpful. One, noting that "patients vary in the degree of exploitation that they subjectively experience," quoted a woman as saying she would never report a therapist she made love to because "he was the most comforting therapist I ever had." This reaction was fairly common only among women who felt they had initiated the sex or that the idea was mutual. Even among these patients, however, if the relationship ended, they were likely to feel that the therapist had broken his promise to love them forever. After all, a therapist is supposed to know about love and not make promises he can't keep.

Another study, in which women who had been sexually involved with a therapist, doctor, or dentist were compared to similar women who had received therapy with no sexual involvement, found that a whopping 95 percent of the first group felt greater mistrust and anger toward men in general and suffered more physical symptoms, such as headaches and painful menstrual periods. The two groups had expressed the same amount of distrust and same number of aches and pains when therapy began. The distress these women felt was particularly acute when sexual abuse was already part of their history and when the therapist was married. What hurt them was the sense that they had been pulled into a liaison and then betrayed. Simultaneously, they lost the therapy that had been supporting them and were forced to confront the new problems that went along with having an extramarital affair. These findings have been supported by consumer groups such as the University of California's Post-Therapy Support Project, which identified anger and mistrust as key issues for women in erotic relationships with therapists.

In recruiting patients who had become sexually involved with their doctors, dentists, or therapists, the study inadvertently came in contact with eleven men who had had sex with their caregivers. Ten were heterosexual, and they "indicated that the sexual contact was a positive experience." The one homosexual said the experience was negative. Unlike the women in this study, the majority of the men failed to follow through and fill out the history and questionnaire. It is possible that those content with the experience are less interested in talking about it, but other explanations are possible. It also seems possible that sexual liaisons in therapy don't affect men and women in the same way.

If we turn from surveys and studies to gut feelings, every explanation imaginable can be found for why and how sexual relations in therapy harm patients. At one extreme is the conviction that every single person gets harmed even if he or she doesn't feel any hurt and even if such a person remains married to the former therapist. The author of a self-help book who takes this position said that it is critical "for women, especially those who do not easily identify themselves as victims, to recover an awareness of the underlying wounds that led them into an exploitive sexual relationship." He complimented a woman who "felt like the wounded, rejected little girl," for she understood how truly powerless she was in therapy. When another woman objected, saying she should have left her seductive therapist because "I knew it was wrong," the author-doctor replied, "No, you were helpless." Although she insisted that his attitude was patronizing, he insisted she was in denial.

At the other extreme are clinicians who believe that only about a third of persons involved with therapists will be adversely affected. Their natural passage through life will be set back, both by the experience and by how it is handled in their family and community. Another third "will be pulled forward painfully." The hurt and confusion will initiate a productive period of questioning, as can happen when any two people fall in love under difficult or impossible circumstances. If family and community support the patient, a different but equally important lesson can be learned. For the final third of patients, there will be little impact of any sort.

Certainly there are patients who insist on disregarding their sadness and disappointment, just as there are patients who turn their lives in a better direction as the result of what they call an impossible love affair. My guess is that almost all patients who feel pressured into having sex with a doctor or former doctor are harmed, as are those who have been sexually abused before. (It is estimated that the previously abused make up 40 to 60 percent of women who become entangled.) As for the rest, which may include a larger number of heterosexual men than anyone realizes, I don't feel there's enough information to estimate how many get hurt.

In discussing the harm that befalls women seduced by therapists, three similes are common, as noted earlier. Each casts therapists and their clients in significantly different roles. One is that doctor-patient sex is like incest and its victims like helpless children. Another is that such a relationship is like rape. Criminals force themselves on innocent women. A third comparison suggests that adultery provides the best model, with loneliness and yearning the major players in the drama. Knowing at what stage or place on the stairway a patient's therapy was helps to explain the different analogies, all of which seem to apply to certain situations. The case that Phyllis Chesler presented of Stephanie, whose doctor kissed her crudely, or Carolyn Bates's account in *Sex in the Therapy Hour* of a doctor who insisted on five-minute quickies during the hour have elements in common with acquaintance rape. On the other hand, the psychotic doctor who thought God wanted him to impregnate an entire ward sounds more like criminal rape. There is an altogether different feel to the story that will be told in Chapter 7 by Barbara, a woman of forty who fell in love and "nearly committed adultery" with her married therapist.

Yet neither rape nor adultery provides a model for forty-four-year-old Marilyn, who married the leader of her sobriety group and lived to compare the relationship to incest. When she was twenty-nine, with a history of sexual abuse and one illegitimate child, possibly from a cousin, Marilyn was forced by the Department of Social Services to sign herself into a detoxification center or lose her daughter. While she was in this program, she fell in love with the social worker, a man sixteen years her senior, who led group counseling sessions. The two moved in together shortly after she was discharged and were married within the year. They reclaimed her daughter and had a child of their own. Later the family moved to an island, where the social worker ran an outpatient clinic.

After the couple had been married a dozen years, Marilyn was badly injured in a car accident. Flown off the island, she required months of hospitalization and rehabilitation. During this time she became extremely anxious and felt she could not tolerate being separated from her husband. Ashamed of her fears, she described herself as feeling like a helpless child. In talking with therapists at the hospital, her husband's earlier role as her counselor was revealed, and Marilyn began to believe that many of her fears stemmed from an unhealthy reliance on her husband. He had remained a father figure for her, she said, and she was the child. She recalled that whenever they disagreed, he always had the right answer and the last word. When it came to running the household, he managed the money and the education of the children while she did what she was told.

Marilyn came to believe that her husband had chosen her because he knew how vulnerable she was and how easily she could be manipulated. He had installed himself in her life as both "father" and lover with the result that she now felt the same hurt and confusion she had suffered earlier in life with her cousin and others. What she had assumed was love now looked more like exploitation to her, yet even to think such a thing about the man she depended on completely was frightening.

Although many people would not see Marilyn's married life as an example of sexual abuse, almost everyone can understand the difficulty she has had in separating herself emotionally from a man who protected her, apparently loved her, and also bullied her into doing things his way. Marilyn admitted that she did not enter the relationship with many strengths of her own. She stood at the bottom of the stairway, in need of a benevolent protector. A vulnerable, previously abused patient, she not surprisingly felt robbed of a chance to grow up by a therapist-client entanglement, even a committed and in some ways well-intentioned one.

~~~

Turning from the harm that doctor-patient relationships inflict on the patient to the harm they inflict on the community and the therapist, the story is much shorter. In a closely knit community, the knowledge of doctor–former patient relationships spreads quickly and causes trouble. For example, once the therapist's colleagues or students learn that he or she is dating a former client, they are likely to split into factions. One may condone the action — it may appear to be a committed relationship or they like the clinician — but another will see it as a betrayal of the profession or a personal affront. Divisions occur as well among patients or parishioners who may discover that their leader is dating a former follower. "So why not me?" or "Am I next?" they ask. "Can I tell this person how attracted I feel without starting something?" "Has he been telling me the truth?"

"That's one of the biggest problems with misconduct," said Mr. Anderson, the young pastor who treated the rector who ran off with a high school girl. "When a person you personally admire breaks the rules, you have to go back over everything he's taught you and check it for authenticity."

Not long after Anderson was given the impossible job of counseling his own rector, he left the ministry and enrolled in the John D. Finch School of Psychology, on the West Coast, a spiritually oriented program within a seminary. "Finch was strong," Anderson remembered. "He was totally devoted to the integration of religion and psychology, and he had written several books on the subject. I enjoyed them. I enjoyed him. He struck me as a very committed person. A lot of conviction. I remember taking notes when he lectured and thinking, 'Wow, this is good stuff. He really sees the science and spiritual parts as inseparable.' I embraced much of his philosophy as I made my own integration of the two. You see, I thought I'd dropped out of the ministry, but Finch made me see that I was doing a minister's job. I was still attending to the needs of others."

With increasing energy and enthusiasm, Anderson threw himself into his new career. Several of his fellow students went on long, silent retreats — they called them "intensives" — held far to the north on Finch's private property. Students lived in individual cabins there for a week or more at a time. They thought and prayed and received intensive psychotherapy from Dr. Finch, a licensed psychologist.

"Then," recalled Anderson, "rumors began to fly that several women were having sex with Finch during the retreats. They were under the impression that it was part of the treatment. We'd get these notices in the mail about the school's position and what was happening. One day they took Finch's name down from the front of the building. One day — just gone. Another day they announced he'd lost his license to practice.

"Do we have to go back and reevaluate the whole process?" he and the other students asked. "Can we trust what professors teach us?"

Years later, Anderson has concluded that Finch's unethical behavior gave both him and the academic community a bad shaking, but it did not destroy either. "I think most important experiences in life are a mixture," he said, "and if you have the resources — *if* you do — then you can sort the bad from the good." As with patients, so with students — the strong survive a mixture of good and bad treatment; the vulnerable get hurt.

Of course, therapists get hurt too. Although many slip out from under their mistakes, those who lose their license or liability insurance cannot be reimbursed from third-party payers, and this drastically curtails most careers. For some, the cost of earning their license back — paying for supervision while restricting their practice — is too steep, and they are forced to change careers. If they are successfully sued, it can mean financial ruin. Some escape censure but feel great remorse.

However the harm caused by doctor-patient sex is explained and whatever the number of sufferers, it is clear that, like psychotherapy itself, unethical liaisons have grown tremendously in the past fifty years. Professional associations have not been able to stop their members from flirting, abusing, seducing, and occasionally marrying their clients and former clients. When lists of clients' rights and codes of ethics fail, the law steps in.

6

There Oughta Be a Law

If only it were all so simple! If only there were evil
people somewhere insidiously committing evil deeds,
and it were necessary only to separate them from the
rest of us and destroy them. But the line dividing good
and evil cuts through the heart of every human being.
And who is willing to destroy a piece of his own heart?

— *Aleksandr Solzhenitsyn*

"We have developed a very sophisti-
cated technique for helping people," said a wise analyst in his later years.
"Trial and error." On hearing this, clinicians used to chuckle. Now
someone is almost sure to say "Yes, and for every error we make, a new
rule is created." Let me give an example.

At a correctional institution for convicted sexual offenders, a young
female therapist made a mistake that added a new rule and three pages
of paperwork to the busywork already in effect, not only at her institution but at all the other facilities managed by the same vendor or
company. She kissed a con. A fellow therapist reported:

Whenever something bad happens like this — like her kissing that
con and getting caught — it makes trouble for all of us. She was up
in one of the classrooms on the top floor, and she was seen by a
correctional officer in an embrace with an inmate. The officer
reported the incident, and by the end of the day the therapist was
"escorted" off the grounds — fired. So she applies for unemployment and is denied by the facility here until she hires a lawyer and
forces payment on the grounds that she had never formally agreed

to the no-embracing rule. Now [the vendor who provides the institution with therapists] is feeling threatened. They have to show the state that these incidents will never happen again, so they write up a three-page list of rules that everyone has to sign. I mean, we have to sign every single rule so we can be denied unemployment if we break any of the regs. And that's not the end of the paperwork.

The other bad thing is that there are never good feelings between the correction officers who believe in punishment and the therapists who believe in . . . well, in trying to fix these guys, and after this kiss thing we are really on opposite sides of the fence. We're angry at her too. Our job is harder because of the message she sent to the cons and the reaction of the vendor. The bottom line is always the same. The room we have to work in gets smaller and smaller.

Psychotherapists throughout the country in all kinds of settings agree with this man's evaluation. As the rules intended to protect the emotional well-being of clients and the financial well-being of managed care companies multiply, the room that therapists have to work in — the areas where they can use their own judgment and make their trials and errors — gets smaller and smaller. Is this protection necessary for the emotionally distraught client? Or are we trying so hard to eliminate risk from an inherently risky business that we are in danger of throwing the baby out with the bathwater? Convincing arguments can be made for both positions.

It is not surprising that psychotherapy is being regulated. As recently as thirty years ago, the talking cure was a cottage industry practiced by a small number of analysts and therapists on a tiny fraction of the population, but today it is big business. In 1990, for example, it is estimated that Americans spent some $10 to $12 billion for office visits to their therapists. As in any industry that affects millions of people, regulations are imposed to protect consumers.

At the same time that therapy has become an industry, its practitioners have become increasingly secular and nontraditional. Fewer therapists say they believe in God, for example, than almost any other professional group, including chemists. Likewise, more describe themselves as independent thinkers than those in other professions. Therapists are therefore less likely to feel bound by traditional values than almost anyone else. This is not to imply that most are anarchists, but it does underscore the observation that in a multicultural society, there is no one accepted code of conduct for everyone. As we have already seen, when traditions no longer guide our actions, legislation steps in to prevent chaos. Thus in the late 1970s and 1980s, as therapy grew into an industry and as both doctors and patients held increasingly diverse expectations, regulations came marching in. But why has sexual abuse been singled out, over all the other bad things a therapist can do, as the most important mistake to regulate? Why not go after sins of laziness and neglect, arrogance, anger, and avarice?

There are several reasons. First, sex is often a metaphor for power and control, and the traditional male claim to power may be the real sin that the new regulations are addressing. Discussing power in terms of sex rather than economics, for example, has advantages. It is simpler and more dramatic than tackling broader topics and often more profitable — literally. Writing about it, regulating it, and correcting the consequences make a lot of money for a lot of people.

Whether we see the present concern for doctor-patient sex as developing from an earlier concern for child abuse or from the consumer movement, the underlying issue is the redistribution of power. As women have demanded more power in all aspects of their lives and have flexed their new muscles by insisting on being free of unwanted sexual attention — no pats on the fanny, no catcalls, no grabbing, no rape — regulations have been enacted to support their requests. In simplest terms, as women gain control over what happens to them, men lose control over what they can do, and rules are the means we use to enforce this redistribution of rights and responsibilities. Each new rule creates a new group of people who are legally protected and a new group of villains as well. For example, when New Jersey passed a controversial rape law in 1992, stating that signs and threats of force were not necessary to prove rape, cases that hadn't even been considered rape under the earlier legislation were brought into court. As the definition of rape expanded, the number of men who were now considered rapists expanded, just as the number of women who now felt they had recourse to legal action expanded. Can a woman in New Jersey brand a man a rapist simply by saying that he persuaded her to have sex when she didn't want it? The rest of the country waited attentively for the answer. The combination of power politics and sex makes such questions irresistibly interesting.

Quick to realize that sexual abuse is currently one of the most acceptable explanations of emotional unhappiness, authors of self-help books have made millions by telling women how to identify the signs of abuse and then how to progress from victimhood to survivor. Trial lawyers, therapists who specialize in sexually abused women, self-help leaders, and a new kind of administrator, called a risk management or human rights representative, all earn a living off sexual abuse, including doctor-patient entanglements. Some therapists claim that "a sex-abuse industry" now exists, made up of people who see sexual misconduct everywhere and profit handsomely from it.

Finally, regulations are imposed on any industry that fails to regulate itself. Although in the 1970s professional organizations of psychotherapists finally drew up codes of ethics that explicitly banned sex with clients, these rules were more like a "salute to the flag for therapists than a bill of rights for clients." Malpractice was neither actively uncovered nor punished under these codes. Consequently, the judiciary stepped in.

In 1973 the American Psychiatric Association adopted a code of ethics that formally banned sexual contact between doctor and patient. Citing the Hippocratic Oath, which speaks of abstaining "from all intentional wrongdoing and harm, especially from abusing the bodies of man or woman, bond or free," the APA was the first group involved in psychotherapy to explicitly ban sex during the time a patient was under the care of a doctor. Other professional associations followed suit — the American Psychological Association in 1977, the American Association of Sex Educators, Counselors, and Therapists in 1979, the National Association of Social Workers in 1980, the American Association for Marriage and Family Therapy in 1982, and the American Psychoanalytic Association in 1983. These organizations had had ethical codes before, but they did not single out sexual relationships with patients from general abuse.

It is worth tracing the development of one of these codes, briefly, to observe both the reasoning behind the prohibition and the compromises that had to be made when the code ran up against existing traditions and legislation. In the mid-1970s, when the feminist group within the American Psychological Association (another APA) demanded that a specific prohibition against sex be added to the code of ethics, complaints of sexual misconduct were coming into the association at the rate of one or two a year. Three quarters of this trickle of complaints were being dismissed. Nevertheless, women insisted that abuse was occurring in therapy and that many more patients would come forward if the APA made it clear that sex in therapy was unethical. Thus an ethics committee sat down and drafted an apparently simple statement: "Sexual intimacies with clients are unethical." They gave three reasons. First, they believed that sexual contact with a client could only represent exploitation. After all, if the therapist fell in love, then he or she would terminate the client, refer this person to another therapist, and go about the business of starting a different type of relationship. (This currently unfashionable belief was fairly common in the 1970s.) Thus when a doctor initiated sex in the therapy hour itself, it indicated that his motives were dishonorable and his behavior exploitive. Second, the committee believed that good therapy could not proceed between persons who were sexually intimate, for objectivity went out the window. Third, they wished to prevent fraud. Therapists, they reasoned, shouldn't trick patients into thinking that they are receiving therapy when in fact they are receiving sex. When this new statement was added to the professional code of ethics, any psychologist who was a member of the APA (and many were not) could be brought before the association and reprimanded or expelled for having sex with a client. To plug an obvious loophole, state licensing boards agreed to adopt the APA's prohibitions so that all licensed psychologists would be covered by the same rules.

Legal disputes arose as soon as the new code of ethics was released. Was a woman who was given an I.Q. test one afternoon by a psychologist his patient? Was a student supervised by a psychologist his patient? (Supervision can include teaching, therapy, and/or collegial interactions.) Was a man who dropped out of therapy in January without notifying his therapist still a patient in March? The following January? The ethics committee reconvened to straighten out the confusion and especially to address the criticism that the ban didn't protect women whose therapists stopped therapy so that sex could begin. Although at the time only a single article in the scientific literature claimed that doctor–former patient relationships were harmful — and this finding was based neither on research nor surveys — the APA's Revisions Task Force felt these women needed protection.

After a great deal of deliberation, the ethics committee drew up a more inclusive statement. Once a person was a client for any reason, he or she was always a client. However, when the committee sent the revised statement to their own lawyers in the APA, it came back marked "unworkable." For one thing, therapists — like other Americans — are guaranteed the right of free association. The APA couldn't tell them who they could and couldn't befriend — forever. For another, the definition of client as "anyone who saw a psychologist for any reason" was too broad. Courts of law would throw out cases of sexual misconduct based on a phone conversation with a psychologist, an intake interview, or an hour of testing, which would weaken the APA's overall position. Eventually a compromise was reached. In December 1992, the prohibition of sexual intimacies was extended to cover former clients, meaning individuals who had been in therapy — as opposed to testing or training — and who had been out of treatment less than two years. (Although this prohibition contradicts a therapist's right to free association, the APA takes the position that ethical therapists should voluntarily forgo this right.) By covering this group of former patients, the ethics committee elevated one of the three reasons for banning sex — exploitation — to the sole reason. Preventing fraud or keeping therapists objective no longer seemed as important as preventing exploitation. In other words, the therapist was seen as so powerful that even a client who had left therapy wouldn't be able to say no. As one of the members of the ethics committee said, this argument "assumes that the basis of sexual contact is due to the exploitive tendencies of the therapist . . . as opposed to sexual attraction pure and simple, mutual infatuation, or even 'falling in love.'"

The two-year rule has been adopted by many professional organizations and most states, although a few insist that the vulnerability of the client lasts forever. However worded, these rules banning sexual intimacies with former clients net the greatest number of errant clinicians. It is much more common for a therapist to terminate therapy and start a sexual relationship than to try to combine the two.

Although the two-year rule has proved to be the most useful in sanctioning clinicians, its implications are at odds with several other beliefs that both clinicians and the public hold dear. For example, if we truly believe that a therapist is always and forever more powerful than a client, then the doctor is in a "superior" position and the client in an "inferior" position. But practitioners, especially counselors and therapists, are not comfortable with this situation. They insist on "the autonomy" of the client. This is especially true among feminists practicing relational therapy. Clients are free agents. They are able to enter into legal contracts. They can make their own decisions, including whether to take medications and when to start and stop therapy. They are held responsible for their actions, like other adults, and can be sued or arrested if they hurt their doctor or the doctor's property. It is difficult for therapists and the rulemakers to reconcile this autonomy with pockets of vulnerability, and as we will see, the wording of many state regulations concerning sex with clients and former clients reflects both the complexity of the topic and the ambivalence of the public.*

There is another way in which the two-year or forever rule is at odds with what psychologists say they believe. Although clinicians insist that scientific evidence forms the basis of their policies, no rigorous studies have been undertaken to show that a therapist has the same powerful influence over a person two days, two years, or two decades after therapy has ended. That members of the APA "act as if posttermination sex with

---

* Because it is the therapist who works under a professional code of ethics that limits sexual behavior, the therapist alone is blameworthy if a sexual relationship is begun. Patients cannot be blamed for trying to initiate sex — short of physical force — but neither can they claim that they are completely under the power of the therapist. Documentaries on sexual exploitation commonly have a woman saying, "If he had told me to rob a bank, I would have done it," or words to that effect. (See for example the clergy training film *Not in My Church.*) If her words were literally true and she would do *anything* the therapist asked, a strong argument could be made that the woman was legally incompetent and needed a guardian to protect her. My point is that a patient can't have it both ways. He or she can't demand the rights and protections of a competent adult and simultaneously claim to have lost *all* power and thus *all* responsibility. Nor can therapists continue to play fast and loose with competency, now defining it strictly, now loosely. In 1995, the New Mexican legislature was so annoyed with clinicians' handling of competency that they passed the Wizard Amendment. This would have required therapists to wear a dunce cap and wave a wand whenever they testified on competency. The amendment was vetoed by the governor.

clients is harmful does not directly prove it is." Thus a group of self-declared scientists find themselves building a code of ethics on what they think "might" happen — not a scientific approach. The unsupported belief that a former client forever thinks, feels, and behaves like a client is particularly troublesome in states like Florida, where sexual intimacies are banned in perpetuity, or in cases where a person in public office has had one or even several therapists. Do these therapists really have power over a senator or a judge *forever*? The rules say yes.

Finally, the APA's insistence that psychologists have enormous power over clients, former clients, and even potential clients has been successfully challenged in several arenas. Several years ago, the Federal Trade Commission forced the APA to abolish its restrictions on advertising. The association had argued that if clinicians were free to advertise, they might mislead vulnerable people by promising too much or by scaring them. The FTC said in effect that consumers can take care of themselves, so psychologists are no longer told how to word their advertisements. Another instance of paternalistic concern involved the APA's lobbying efforts to prevent the development of home kits for testing for HIV infection. The APA insisted that counseling is necessary, although no research has shown that talking over the results with a psychologist is any better than talking with friends or family — or even screaming all alone. Yet the APA feels people are too vulnerable to handle HIV testing without professional help. Clearly, no static line can be drawn between a doctor's and a patient's responsibilities, and the power on which responsibility rests will move back and forth between them as the culture evolves. Right now, power is moving toward the consumer.

The prohibition of sexual intimacies between professionals of all kinds and the people they treat, train, and serve has spread widely in the last decade. Several universities have put their professors on notice that students are off limits; other schools have nonbinding guidelines. In 1992 the American Bar Association's ethics committee passed a nonbinding prohibition against sexual involvement with clients. By contrast, in the United Kingdom, the code of ethics formulated in 1990 by the British Association for Counselling stated that "counsellors must not exploit their clients financially, sexually, emotionally, or any other way," but it imposed only a twelve-week "cooling off period" after termination. Longer periods may be necessary for some clients, it said. The formulators of the code acknowledged that ethical guidelines are increasingly necessary in a society where not everyone agrees on what is moral. At the same time, the weakness of regulating morality with laws rather than guidelines is that legislation imposes a single standard on a population recognized as having multiple standards.

But laws have been passed nonetheless. When it appeared that sanctions imposed by professional organizations, the loss of license, and lawsuits were not enough to control clinicians from becoming sexually involved with former clients, some states chose to criminalize the deed. The advantage, they said, is that the threat of a criminal record and time in prison cool all but the most ardent therapists. As well as a deterrent, a prison sentence is retribution as well. The disadvantages are that it is more difficult to convict a clinician of a criminal act than of an ethical violation — the standards of proof are more rigorous in criminal cases — and guilty clinicians no longer have reason to admit their mistakes and seek rehabilitation. In addition, criminal justice rarely provides victims with as much financial remuneration as lawsuits, and women who are willing to initiate a civil suit may be less willing to enter into criminal proceedings. Summing up the pros and cons, the authors of an article on criminalization stated that

> The arguments in favor of criminalization are that it serves as a deterrent, offers retribution, provides redress when other avenues are blocked, deals with unlicensed psychotherapists, makes victims' assistance funds available, and provides due process protection against false accusations. In opposition to criminalization are the arguments that civil and administrative measures already exist to deal with the problem, it may have a chilling effect on the reporting of misconduct, it may void malpractice insurance, it makes guilty psychotherapists place themselves in jeopardy if they acknowledge their wrongdoing in attempting to make amends, it removes control of the legal process from the victim, it fails to offer rehabilitation, and it singles out psychotherapists from other fiduciaries for more stringent treatment.

Wisconsin was the first state to decide that the advantages outweighed the disadvantages, and in 1983 it made sex between therapist and client a first-class misdemeanor. Three years later it raised the stakes and made the act a felony. In 1988 it required that therapists report any incident of therapist-client sex even if the client did not wish to press charges. Minnesota made therapist-client sex a felony in 1985 and legislated that the crime can be punished by up to ten years in prison and a $20,000 fine. At the same time, the state required mandatory reporting of therapist-client erotic involvement. Just as therapists in many states are mandated to report child abuse, elder abuse, and the abuse of the disabled whenever they hear of a case, they must also protect women from their therapists in a growing number of states — but only from sex. If a woman gets beaten up by a man, even a former therapist, the current clinician is not required to report the incident. He or she can ask the client what she would like to do and proceed accordingly. But if the same client says her former therapist kissed her on the lips during the last session or became her lover a year later, then in goes a report. Criminal proceedings are begun regardless of what the client wants. Colorado, Maine, and North Dakota have also made therapist-client sex a felony as have California, Florida, and Michigan. Fourteen states have criminalized doctor-patient contact, and at least five others are trying.

It may appear that criminalization has caught on in this country, that it is simply a matter of time before every seductive act both during therapy and for at least two years afterward will be brought to trial if discovered. However, that is not the case. Each of the present laws is a convoluted affair that reflects the uneasy political compromises that had to be made to ensure its passage. For example, in California, having sex with a current client is a felony, but having sex with this same woman five minutes after termination is *not* a felony unless the therapist has failed to refer her to another therapist and the client can prove that the termination was made solely to obtain sexual favors. Likewise, in Minnesota, a sexual relationship with a former client is a felony only if the client can prove she was emotionally dependent on the therapist or if he said the sex was part of her treatment. Michigan's statute reveals even more clearly both the bargaining and the double standard that underlie many laws: "Sexual intercourse under pretext of medical treatment" is punishable, *but only if the therapist is a male and the client is a female.* The statute does not apply to female clinicians who seduce male clients or to same-sex pairings. This certainly implies that males in Michigan think they have more power vis-à-vis their therapists than women do and don't need this protection. How can this be true? Is the law based on the power that is automatically bestowed on a therapist by a vulnerable client — Freud's "transference love" — or are we really talking muscle power? There is more thinking to be done.

States that have not criminalized doctor-patient sex have found other ways to make clinicians think long and hard before making a move on a client or former client. Massachusetts, for example, was the first state to prevent therapists from staying in practice without a license. Before 1995, a psychiatrist, psychologist, or social worker who lost his or her license could continue to see patients even though insurance money could not pay for these visits. If the unlicensed practitioner could find clients willing to pay out of their own pocket, then he or she could continue to practice. Now, however, if such a therapist appears to pose a risk to clients, he or she can be barred from all forms of practice. Again, it is interesting to note that in the United Kingdom, the only legislation concerning doctor-patient sex makes it illegal for a male on a hospital staff to have sexual relations with female patients — women considered truly unable to protect themselves.

Wherever doctor-patient sex has not been criminalized, civil suits represent a client's most effective weapon against a therapist. The client, typically a woman who has left therapy and taken a year or more to try to make sense of the confusion that sex with the doctor has engendered, talks with a lawyer and presents her case. The fact that she may have been willing or at least seemed willing to enter into a sexual relationship does not excuse the therapist's behavior. Consent is never a defense. What the client must prove to win an award of damages, however, is what is called "the four Ds" of malpractice liability — dereliction of duty that directly causes damage. That is, the client must convince the judge and/or jury that she has suffered injuries that result directly from her therapist's breach of ethics. Generally, this takes years to do — three years is the average time for a settlement to be made in several New England states — and the awards vary dramatically. When the *Boston Globe* looked into civil suits, its reporters "estimated" that the average settlement against psychiatrists was $417,000. In the same article, one of the founders of TELL, the Therapist Exploitation Link Line, was quoted as saying, "In the victim community, we say why go to the Board [of Registration in Medicine] — why bother? We say, go pursue the civil malpractice case and win some money to pay for therapy and maybe take a trip with the family."

In examining civil suits from all over the country, one clinician found that "damages vary tremendously — from trivial amounts to awards in the millions. No particular logic or reason seems to apply to the assessment of damages." The great range of awards reflects in part the cap that most insurance companies have put on malpractice claims arising from sexual misconduct. For psychologists, insurance companies will pay no more than $25,000. What any discussion of legislation and civil action cannot begin to present, however, is the depth of confusion and unhappiness that surrounds all these cases.

One person who routinely saw the heartbreak that attends the investigation of doctor-patient relationships is the person I am calling Dr. Betz, a member of the board of examiners in the Pacific Northwest. For eight years his job was to understand men and women who claimed to have been wronged by psychologists and to reconcile their version of the story with their therapists' account. How difficult was it to get the two sides to agree?

"Very difficult," said Dr. Betz emphatically. "In most of the cases we handle, there is nothing approaching complete agreement. Someone feels wronged by us."

This is not to say that the board does a poor job, only that it has a very difficult one. In the time that Dr. Betz has sat on the board, he has seen the number of complaints triple. The board members have a standing joke: "We say that if we stay in the business [of psychology] long enough, we'll each have a complaint brought against us." The complaints vary tremendously, Dr. Betz said, but about a quarter are about boundary violations — "everything from breaches of confidentiality to sex."

The first steps the board takes when a serious complaint is lodged — and "very few complaints are trivial" — is to launch an investigation and try to work out a "consent agreement." Such a voluntary accord is achieved when a complaint has been studied, a finding handed down, a plan for correction put into effect, and everyone signs off. In theory, this inexpensive and only moderately punishing process leads to reconciliation. Agreements can be reached quickly if the psychologist admits that he or she did what the complainant described. "Yes, I began dating the half-sister of a client," he might say, or "Yes, I sat on a disciplinary board when my client's child's case was being reviewed." When the infractions are minor and not considered major ethical violations, the doctor is reprimanded and sometimes directed to seek supervision, education, or therapy. Dr. Betz found that for the persons making the complaints, "it feels a little better when the board identifies a problem and asks the psychologist to get help.

"We should always offer the opportunity of sitting down together and talking the problem over," he continued. When complaints are caught early, the difference between the doctor's and patient's stories can be small and reconciliation more likely.

If the breach of conduct is more serious, however, and an egregious violation is substantiated, the consent agreement may stipulate that the psychologist pay a fine, up to $1,500. The acknowledged violation will make it difficult for him or her to renew liability insurance, get on managed care panels, and find new clients. The person who has brought the charge gets the satisfaction of seeing justice done and the public warned. The finding may also inspire the accuser to undertake a civil suit. "A small number of people use the board to get a free legal opinion before trying civil action," Betz said. Many consent agreements are not reconciliations in the sense of restoring harmony or goodwill, but they do express accord. Both sides agree on what took place, and their stories are reconciled.

The more frustrating cases are those in which agreement cannot be reached, and, said Betz, "this is becoming much more common." In such instances, the conflicting stories may be given a disciplinary hearing — a tense and costly affair with lawyers and cross-examinations. Each side uses whatever information it can find — substance abuse, diagnosis, divorces, traffic violations — to shame and discredit the other. Both doctor and patient are cross-examined in an effort to discover which one is telling the truth.

Betz implied that an important ingredient leaves the examination process when a case is handed over from the board's psychologists to law enforcement people. The latter decide that one of the stories is right and the other wrong. After all, their job is to form a judgment as quickly as possible. The board, on the other hand, seeks to find what is believable in both stories and thus to arrive at an understanding. "We hold the ambiguity for as long as we possibly can," maintained Betz. "It's difficult, but psychologists deal with ambiguity. We know its value. We can live with it."

Literally meaning "to wander around," ambiguity is one of those undervalued, underused resources that most people prefer to forget or actively avoid. For Betz, holding on to ambiguity means wandering through the contradictory stories that doctor and patient tell him and listening for what each story is trying to say, separately and together. One example he gave involved a male psychologist who fell in love with his patient and she with him. Deciding that it was more important to pursue the love than the therapy, doctor and patient agreed to terminate the treatment and start dating. Eventually they became engaged. Later still, the relationship ran into trouble, and the couple broke up. Not until years afterward did the woman file a complaint. The therapist was shocked by her betrayal and felt "extremely violated." As in many cases, there was no hard evidence for Betz to pursue. The literal truth of what had happened in the therapy sessions years before — who had said precisely what to whom — was unknowable. The words were gone, changed into memories. There was no videotape waiting to be found, and the only truth now available to anyone, including the doctor and patient themselves, lay in the two accounts that had been filtered and refiltered through the jumbled contents of two very different minds. So Betz wandered through the conflict trying *not* to make up his mind, a process, he said, that "takes an overwhelming amount of energy." The therapist told him that he had loved his former patient in an honorable way. He had not broken any rules, for at the time they met there was no ethical prescription to wait two years after termination to pursue a different relationship. On the other hand, the woman told a story of abuse, of being misled by the powerful wishes of her doctor. "I don't think either person is lying," said Betz. "I believe them both. They have two different interpretations of the experience." It is the nature of people, he said, to mold events into stories that fit their understanding of what life is about. The love affair really was wonderful for the psychologist, and what may have been wonderful for his former patient became a betrayal. "The victims' rights people don't like this attitude," Betz continued. "They want right and wrong separated — one in each account."

Nevertheless, what Betz heard from doctor and patient were two thoughtful stories that made sense separately but did not make sense together. What was he to think about this common occurrence? Betz implied that such disagreements point toward but do not engage larger questions; for example, how do two people who are not the same — not in size, power, temperament, background, or many other ways — how do they *know* if they are loving each other in a mutually satisfying and respectful way? It is a relatively new question for us to ask.

But these are not the points raised in a disciplinary hearing. In this case, the doctor was found to have used poor judgment by becoming involved with his patient a bit too quickly. Yet neither party was satisfied by the board's ruling. The doctor felt his love had been betrayed; the woman felt that he had been scolded for faulty timing, not punished for abuse.

Betz encounters many different kinds of disappointment, but most stem from divergent interpretations of a shared experience. Sometimes the person interpreting the experience is neither the doctor nor the patient. Not long ago, for example, a complaint was made against a psychologist by a nurse at a general hospital. She had found the therapist lying on a hospital bed with a woman who was awaiting surgery. The psychologist was fully clothed, but there he was, lying on the bed with his arms around his patient. For the nurse, there was no ambiguity in this scene: doctors do not climb into bed with patients. Nor was there ambiguity for the psychologist. He believes in the therapeutic value of touching, and he has persisted in holding clients to soothe them in spite of several complaints, all of which have been dismissed. Confronted with this latest complaint, the psychologist explained to Betz that his patient had asked him to visit her in the hospital and hold her to allay her anxiety and panic. The patient herself told Betz that she "felt very positive about the experience." She was grateful. The complaint was dismissed, leaving the nurse utterly mystified.

The case that gave Betz his worst moments, however, involved another liberal, nontraditional therapist who treated a woman for the better part of ten years. Holding was part of this man's treatment, and he used it with this client to soothe her. Whenever treatment stopped for a year or so, therapist and client remained in touch on an occasional basis. When she built a log cabin high in the mountains, she gave him a tour.

When she and her husband had twins, the therapist was invited to see them. Several times doctor and patient had coffee together, and once he gave her a ride into town when the roads were impassable to all but four-wheel-drive vehicles. At the end of ten years they parted amicably.

Some time later, the woman went back into therapy, this time with a female therapist. The two discussed the sexual abuse that the client had endured as a child but had not talked about before. The client began to feel that her earlier therapy paralleled the abuse in certain ways, and she recalled that there had been episodes of kissing and petting as well as holding. She also had the feeling that her first therapist was breaking the rules with other clients; in fact, she thought he was having sex with them. What should she do? After long deliberation she filed a complaint. "I do not think she had a vendetta against this man," said Betz. "She saw it as part of her recovery work — the healing process that she was going through with her other therapist."

When Betz began his investigation, the psychologist was adamant that "holding was it." He claimed that his patient had kissed him once but that he "set the limit right away." "I can't hold you if you kiss me," he remembered saying to her, and his notes supported his claim. Betz was impressed by the man's sensitivity to the fine line between soothing and seducing and by his deep concern for his patient. He had gotten supervision from several different people on this case, and when Betz checked with them, "none recalled any discussion of sex." Yet Betz persevered. He pressed the psychologist, challenged him. "When a psychologist is investigating another psychologist," he said, "it's so easy to identify with him. I put myself in his place. I feel how nerve-racking it is for him — a terrible experience. But I need to be unbiased. My job is to protect the general public. I'm working for the citizens of my state." Nevertheless, no additional facts surfaced. The therapist continued to say that nothing beyond holding had taken place. His client of ten years continued to say there had been sexual abuse. And Betz "couldn't figure it out. I'll never know."

Since no agreement could be reached, the case had to be either dismissed or sent to a hearing. "I had to be very explicit with her about what would probably happen in a hearing," Betz remembered. "In many ways she would become the accused. Her case could be made public, and the defense lawyer would seek to discredit her and her story in any way he could." And how did the new therapist react? "She didn't push the idea of a hearing. She was very supportive and let her client decide." Eventually the case was settled without a hearing, and the doctor was asked only to read articles on early childhood abuse and boundary violations. Again Betz was left feeling that here were two good people, each with a decidedly different interpretation of a shared experience. Both were believable. Both, in his opinion, were telling the truth.

Betz now thinks that whenever therapists and patients are deeply interested in each other — he quotes Leston Havens as saying, "You have to fall in love with your patients" — the words, looks, and touches that pass between them are continually being reinterpreted as treatment changes. Up and down and back and forth, the hug that is truly just a hug is seen for what it is when therapy is going well but reappears as abuse when treatment goes poorly. Conversely, the harmfully seductive clinch can be misinterpreted as affection and only after therapy be seen as exploitation. Given this level of complexity, what does Betz recommend? Caution — on both sides. He believes that the number of complaints will continue to rise, as clients feel more comfortable about speaking out, and that more and more complaints will be found in favor of the victims, as we become more knowledgeable about how individuals who have been abused as children respond to the unspoken neediness of their therapists. This trend toward investigating mistakes and misunderstandings rather than hiding them is a good one, Betz believes, part of a cultural change that is prompting professionals to clean up their acts. But, yes, it has a disadvantage. The new readiness to lodge formal complaints or launch lawsuits discourages almost all kinds of experimentation in therapy. "There is less room for creativity. That's for sure," he said.

It is the exception, not the rule, to encounter as able an interpreter as Dr. Betz in cases of sexual abuse. His appreciation of how meaning changes over time and his willingness to work with the ambiguity of evolving testimonies are rarely enjoyed by either doctor or patient. Far more often, the two sides face each other with no intermediary at all and, as a man I will call Attorney Blake learned when he accepted a case of alleged sexual abuse, the inability of old and young, male and female, accused and accuser to communicate can leave an entire community in confusion.

The case that brought these disjunctures to light for Attorney Blake involved two women, both parishioners of an Episcopal church, and a minister who was filling in for a year while the congregation selected a new leader. Trouble began in the middle of the high holy days when a seven-page, single-spaced letter arrived on the bishop's desk. "It contained allegations against the minister," said Blake. "Let's call him the Reverend Mr. Moorehouse. Something had happened.

"Now you understand," the attorney continued, "from the standpoint of criminal law, the only inhibitions on this priest are those on everyone — aggravated assault, rape, sex with a minor. Other behaviors between priest and parishioner are handled in civil actions in most states. The Episcopal Church has recently written down the steps to follow — a flow chart or decision tree, if you will — to see if the trouble can be handled internally or if civil action [a lawsuit] is on the way. This meets the requirements of its insurers," he added. "With the Reverend Mr. Moorehouse, the process of evaluation got very abbreviated, and that angered the parishioners, or I should say it angered the ones my age and older."

To his surprise, Blake discovered that in this case, "the natural division of sympathy" lay between those of different ages rather than genders. The men and women of the parish under the age of forty seemed to understand intuitively how a person could feel victimized by those who are supposed to be caretakers. The parishioners over forty seemed skeptical of abuse unless it was accompanied by an act of violence or a serious threat. These people are certainly familiar with the concept of mental cruelty — it was the basis for many a divorce before no-fault proceedings were possible — but they did not equate insensitive remarks or a hug with actions that led to lawsuits or jail. Thus, when phrases like "He broke my spirit" or "He raped my mind" are considered criminal offenses, they are puzzled. In fact, it now seems to Attorney Blake that the two age groups not only start from different assumptions and look for different kinds of evidence but may actually process the information differently as well.

The letter sent to the bishop charged Mr. Moorehouse with the sexual abuse of a parishioner during several church services. At the point in the Sunday service when the minister directs the congregation to exchange the peace of Christ — that is, to greet those around them with a handshake or a hug while saying "Peace of Christ" — the woman alleged that the rector came down from the altar, embraced several parishioners, and kissed her on the mouth. These allegations prompted the bishop to ask Mr. Moorehouse to suspend his clerical activities. Within the week, the bishop met with the Committee to Respond, reinstated Mr. Moorehouse with a single restriction — no one-to-one counseling — and offered pastoral support to the accuser. The woman began private therapy at the church's expense and received guidance from an advocate. Although Mr. Moorehouse was reinstated so fast that he did not have time to fully register his surprise at being asked to suspend his duties, the restriction made it sound as if indeed something had happened. Mr. Moorehouse disagreed. He called Attorney Blake and, realizing that an investigation would take months because it had been expanded to include a second woman who complained about a second priest, he waited for the bishop to hold a healing meeting with the entire parish. Accusers and accused were not to attend.

The parish meeting was a shambles. After the bishop assured his flock that Mr. Moorehouse and the women were getting the help they needed and after supporters of Moorehouse objected because the bishop's statement implied that he had done something wrong, one of the women made a surprise appearance to explain her unhappiness.

"Is it all right for a priest to embrace a client?" she asked, resting her charge on the shocking juxtaposition of the words "embrace" and "client." The other woman, who was charging that a priest abused her but without either physical contact or direct verbal references to sex, had admitted that "it is more difficult to explain [my case]. He was subtler. There was sort of an intravenous drip of innuendo and seduction. I couldn't tell I was being abused," she continued, "but now I know. Talking with my advocate helped."

A confused discussion broke out among the parishioners. "How can we heal the parish in this atmosphere of half truths and insinuations?" asked one woman. "We need facts. We know almost nothing." There was a discussion then of "subjectivity" and an entity called "strong denial." The idea was advanced that certain things could be done either by or to a person that could not be brought to light by ordinary questioning. Facts were not everything. "You people don't understand," said the woman. "You aren't in touch with the feeling." "If you thought the rector was trying to kiss you on the lips in church," said someone else, "why didn't you turn your head?" "Because of the terrible power imbalance," she answered.

Blake thinks the confusion that results from this mixture of fact and feeling, logic and intuition, is characteristic of many cases of sexual abuse. He has observed that older conservatives start from the assumption that a person's public life — his or her deeds and reputation — is more important to the rest of the community than that person's private feelings. Conversely, the young women who alleged abuse and the majority of parishioners under forty argue that the personal feelings that give meaning to experience form the center or keystone of a life. Given these different assumptions, the older generation wants to collect facts that will document deeds, while the younger, more liberal parishioners are more interested in empathizing with each other's feelings, a kind of communication that depends more on intuition than logic. When one side says, "We create our own reality" and "It's how you deal with the facts that counts," and the other says, "We need facts" and "You're contradicting yourself," the two groups are speaking different languages, and the ensuing confusion is not likely to clear up.

Although the charges against both priests were dismissed, the larger issue of miscommunication remained. For Attorney Blake the central question is, How can a person defend himself if private feelings are elevated to the status of fact? It seems to him that he grew up in a more homogeneous society, one where "everyone knew what was what." Now new voices make new demands and seek to expand, not just job opportunities and legal protection, but the very definition of the truth. Are there moments when Blake can imagine being left behind by these changes? Well, no. Not yet. But if women, blacks, Hispanics, gays, and other groups are successful in adding new standards of truth to the conventional one, he wonders how so many truths — so many different languages — can be combined. Fact, feeling, logic, intuition — if all these are mixed together with no common rules, how incomprehensible the public discourse might sound to his generation.

A year or so after this case, an elaborate system of background checks was initiated within this diocese, and Attorney Blake was again approached by concerned priests who wondered how they could protect themselves against the "hearsay and unsubstantiated information" that reference questionnaires could collect and against the use of this information, which was to be liberally shared among the church community. Especially worrisome was the impossibility of correcting erroneous material once it was filed — a system that took away one of the clergy's civil rights. If a parishioner misinterpreted an innocent statement or, as Dr.

Betz noted, *re*interpreted an innocent statement at a later time, the charge of "conversation for the purpose of sexual arousal" would go down as a permanent black mark on a minister's record.

"We feel that the Church is grossly overreacting to a problem and pursuing oppressive and regressive policies which have never worked in the past and are no more likely to succeed now," wrote a group of concerned clergy. "There is absolutely no evidence that these questionnaires will solve any problem; there is great cause to believe that this so-called effort to make parishes 'safe places' for parishioners will create such an atmosphere of fear and distrust as to render any effective pastoral ministry untenable." (The objections did not convince the Episcopalians to drop background checks as part of their campaign against abuse, but the issue was tabled for further study.) Psychiatrists, psychologists, and social workers — especially those who work with state-supported patients — are increasingly required to cooperate with background checks. The same problems concerning privacy, confidentiality, and fairness are at issue.

~~~

The new willingness to report abuse and to institute new regulations affects everyone in the field. From psychiatrists to unlicensed mental health counselors, everyone is seriously considering the advice to be more cautious and less demonstrative with patients, and some are considering as well the costs to themselves and their patients of the new policies of detachment. Kourtney Lyon, the director of a halfway house for the mentally ill, knows the tradeoff well, but unlike Betz, she believes that the new rules are not doing a good job of protecting the well-being of her clients. Instead, she thinks they are better at protecting the financial interests of agencies and institutions. Her clients get less warmth and enthusiasm from the now self-conscious staff while her employer, a state department of mental health, compulsively seeks to prohibit any contact that could possibly be construed as inappropriate.

"I'm practical," Lyon said, meaning that she devotes her energies to the art of the possible and has little patience for a mental health system that sets its sights on impossibilities. "In a halfway house we deal every day with what happens, not just with what is supposed to happen. And believe me," she added, "everything happens."

She should know. Lyon has headed one or more halfway houses for nearly twenty years and has earned the reputation of being the best. "If I had a kid who was schizophrenic," more than one psychiatrist has said, "I'd send him to Kourtney." And why is that? "Because the residents know I'm on their side," she thought, "and because I work harder to preserve them than to preserve the system." In other words, Lyon has learned to play a little to the left of the middle. She tries simultaneously to protect her clients from their own distressing symptoms of mental illness, from worried relatives, from each other, and from the anxieties of the system that shelters them. The more nervous any of these people becomes, the more difficult her job becomes.

Currently Lyon's biggest headache is the system. State agencies and the private vendors of health care that run many halfway houses have become so fearful of litigation that departments of mental health in many states have created Risk Management Teams to spot potential trouble. Departments also repeatedly revise and expand their policy and procedure manuals to cover troubles that just might snap back and sting the system. Anything connected with physical abuse or sex tops the list of dangers. Blows and angry threats of violence are seen as only slightly more dangerous than hugs, gifts, and sex itself. Especially where staff is concerned, the rules mandate no hugging, no touching, no gifts given or received, no expressions of affection in either direction.

"We say to our residents, 'You're not allowed to get a crush on us,'" said Lyon with a laugh. "These words come out of our mouth. Have you ever heard anything so silly? It makes you laugh because *we* are the ones who are supposed to be normal so we can help them be normal. That means we're supposed to teach them how the world actually works and what happens out there with love and jobs." She shook her head ruefully. "'I'm sorry, Dan or Bob,' I tell them, 'the rules say you can't fall in love here.' But it happens," she said with a shrug. "It will always happen." And when it does? "Then the rules get in the way. If I use my best judgment, I have to bend them to make room for common sense."

Fifteen years ago Lyon was assigned to a twenty-eight-year-old woman she calls Rebecca. Emergency Services brought the young woman to a small hospital in bad shape. Confused and paranoid, unwilling to cooperate in any way, Rebecca was apparently suffering her first schizophrenic break. She remained in the hospital for nearly a month and while there befriended Dwight, a thirty-five-year-old aide. The two would sit in the heavy wooden chairs in the dayroom and smoke and talk. Rebecca told Dwight that her marriage was a wreck. She and her husband slept in separate bedrooms in the beautiful house he had built for her. They had two babies, or rather she did, because her husband was a perfectionist and a workaholic who never came home except to criticize.

Dwight was sympathetic, as Lyon recalled. He had a shaky marriage himself and had been struggling to stay sober for the past four years. He listened to Rebecca five days a week without surprise or disapproval, and the staff watched them talk together with similar tolerance. "It's common," Lyon said. "Patients are scared, especially young ones or first-timers. Many become very attached to a staff member. It gets them through."

"In the old days," she continued, "I would follow many of the people when they went home, so I began calling on Rebecca every week. She was still badly shaken and quite paranoid. I could see the illness just under the surface. So I was surprised to notice this glow of happiness. She was a pretty woman, a nice person too, and she looked wonderful. I'd mention it — 'You look so happy,' I'd say to her — and she'd smile some more, then shut it right off. *Then,* completely by accident, I learned what was going on. I was in the park pushing my granddaughter in a stroller when I saw Rebecca and Dwight embracing. I pretended not to see them."

The next time Lyon visited Rebecca she told her what she had seen. The young woman burst into tears. "I'm so glad you know," she said to Lyon. "I felt like I was being false to you."

"The issue was trust," Lyon explained. "She wasn't close to any of her family, so I'd become her best friend in this new phase of life. She was convinced that meeting Dwight was the best thing that had ever happened to her. She could talk to him without hiding anything. He wasn't frightened of her illness like everyone else. 'Please don't tell,' she said to me. 'Don't turn him in.' 'Did anything happen on inpatient?' I asked her. 'That's all I need to know.' It hadn't, and in those days the rules covered patients only when they were patients, not when they went back to their normal lives. 'I can see this is a person you really care about,' I said to her, and we talked for three hours."

For six months a romance bloomed between Rebecca and Dwight.

As far as Lyon could see, the two were doing a lot of walking and talking, "lapping in and fitting together." When someone else saw them and turned Dwight in, however, the relationship came to an abrupt end. The hospital decided to make a point and fired Dwight. "He was an easy one to go for," said Lyon with a sigh. "He wouldn't fight back." So Dwight lost not only his job but soon his wife, family, home, and sobriety. "He started drinking *bad.*" Rebecca also went through a divorce but did not become acutely ill again. Fifteen years later she looked up Kourtney Lyon to tell her that she was about to graduate from nursing school. And did she remember Dwight? "Of course," she told Lyon. "He will always have a special place in my heart."

Nor has the Department of Mental Health forgotten Dwight. Although Rebecca's husband failed in an attempt to sue the department, new rules appeared shortly. Once a patient, always a patient, the policy now maintains, and there is no socializing with patients. Has the new rule solved the problem? "Of course not," said Lyon. "There's a man on a suspended leave of absence right now, *with pay.* He moved a patient into his house a couple of weeks after she got out of the hospital. I don't believe he loved her. It was sexual. The hospital tried to get this guy out fast, but he hired a high-tech lawyer."

Lyon thinks the new policies have protected some women — she's never heard of a case in which a man gets hustled by a female aide or doctor — but she doesn't think that the minimal protection has been worth the cost in self-consciousness. "We've become so very cautious now," she said. "We have to be careful of our reputation. Cautious and careful. We say, 'Don't give them anything to talk about. They talk enough already.' One of our workers got into an accident driving the van. Twenty miles an hour, not serious. When I heard, I rushed to the emergency room, and there she was strapped to a stretcher. As soon as she saw me she burst into tears. 'Oh, Kourt,' she cried, 'What will they make of this?' *The first thing out of her mouth.* What will they make of this. Can you imagine? 'I don't give a damn,' I told her, 'as long as you're all right.'"

"Cautious and careful" is the watchword during the holidays especially. "We're not allowed to take gifts," Lyon explained. "That's another sick thing. We go all out for the holidays here to teach them to *give.* Personally, I love gifts. I love giving them and I love getting them. I've bent that rule plenty of times, but in compassionate ways. One Christmas a resident presented each of the staff with a fifty-dollar money order. We were stunned. The women just looked at me like, what do I say? 'Thank you.' You say 'thank you' for a gift like that. Then right away I called the resident's mother and told her the rule. 'Oh, please accept his gifts,' she begged me. Her son had worked all year. He'd gotten his mother to ask us about sweaters and perfume, but he'd decided on money. So," Lyon continued, hands on hips, "we accepted, and we cashed those three money orders and took the whole house out for Chinese food. It worked out just fine. But isn't it too bad," she added, "that we couldn't sit down and talk about it with DMH people? It would be better if no one got punished automatically for falling in love or accepting a gift. Everyone should have a say in what happens."

Lyon believes that the system gets so caught up in preserving itself that it forgets that trust and affection are essential to the people it serves. "The department needs to trust us instead of all the time asking, 'What will it cost us?'" she commented. "Of course a house needs structure, but you can't structure love. Zoom, it hits you. It's going to happen. *All* of it's going to happen — crushes, lust, dead-end affairs, love. Like Rebecca and Dwight. He meant something to her that she'll never forget. That's my opinion."

~~~

So we return to our original question. Has the formal regulation of psychotherapy been good for clients? In several respects, the answer is a resounding yes. The new rules have educated the public. Everyone who reads a newspaper or watches television knows that sex is never a part of therapy. The public now talks knowledgeably about dual relationships, and most people have at least heard of a woman who successfully sued her therapist for damages resulting from sexual misconduct. In addition, the rules have promoted a more uniform level of professionalism in what has become a multi-billion-dollar business. Several surveys suggest that this includes a greater reluctance to risk sex with clients and former clients, but other explanations are possible. There may be a greater reluctance to admit to unethical behavior or, as we will see, the influx of women into the field may be responsible for the apparent decline.

A second advantage — but to managed care companies, hospitals, and clinics, not to patients — is that the new regulations offer protection from costly civil suits. If a clinic or parish, for example, can show that it has performed background checks on its staff, trained them regarding sexual abuse, and made them sign each of the rules and regulations, it has a good chance of avoiding suits. In the past, the institutions that therapists worked for were the "deep pockets" that plaintiffs went after when they tried to recover damages. Regulations can sew those pockets shut. It seems ironic, but the same rules that protect the client from the exploitive therapist also protect the parish or clinic from the angry patient.

The disadvantages of increased regulation fall into two areas. The very nature of the therapeutic alliance changes. Regulations move therapy away from an intimate and intensely private exchange between two people toward a contract among largely invisible yet active business partners, each of whom has a say in how the treatment should proceed. Although it still looks as if therapist and patient were alone together in an office, the invisible presence of risk management personnel, licensing board members, insurers, and accountants all press on the clinician and demand part of his or her attention. In a very real way, all therapy except that paid for out-of-pocket is a meeting of business partners. Especially when the therapist is filling out forms in the client's presence or making decisions that go against both of their wishes, the client becomes aware of sharing the hour with others. Regulations encourage the cool side of therapy.

In addition, the clinician's own style changes. When the realm in which clinicians are free to use their own judgment is reduced, they are forced into a partnership with rulemakers — a situation they either accept or fight. There is no third option. Neither accepting nor fighting the regulations improves the clinical skills of *ethical* doctors, although it is hoped that compliance corrects the negligent. Clinicians who agree to report cases of abuse whether or not the abused want this, who fill out background checks, who send treatment plans in triplicate to insurers, managed care companies, and state agencies, and who perform a dozen similar, time-consuming tasks are in fact becoming more cautious clinicians and, as both Dr. Betz and Kourtney Lyon pointed out, less personally responsible and less creative. Home visits have all but disappeared in the clinic I work for and, I have heard, at most others. So has communal gardening and landscaping — even hiking, unless done in a group. These activities "might" be interpreted the wrong way. Someone "might" sue. Yet seeing where a person lives and working alongside him provide information that is not available in any other way. When it comes to hugging and touching, the level of alarm rises precipitously. As Dr. Betz said, "Any therapist who holds his clients routinely is going to be brought up on an ethics charge sooner or later."

One route open to the cautious counselor — and one taken by an increasing number of clinicians — is to avoid treating borderline patients or anyone who acknowledges prior abuse. These are the patients most likely to sue, so one way to avoid trouble is to avoid them. No case did more to drive this point home than Dr. Margaret Bean-Bayog's unconventional treatment of Paul Lozano, the Harvard Medical School student who subsequently killed himself. "This case had a terrorizing effect on the psychiatric community," wrote Dr. Bean-Bayog, "so that lots and lots of people are practicing defensive psychiatry, avoiding the really difficult patients, transferring all their assets into their spouse's name, burning their journals, because my private fantasies were stolen and used as an example of malpractice in the most horrifying public crucifixion that you could ever imagine."

Dr. Bean-Bayog went on to proclaim that her case set serious talking therapy back "because the seriously ill, like the sexually abused, will no longer have a place to go because therapists will be afraid of treating them, fearing this will happen to them." In fact, she continued, "the people who work with the sick patients . . . are now considered crazy. . . . They are now considered to have 'poor judgment.'"

"Sad, but true," commented Dr. Johnson, a psychiatrist from Georgia. "Many of my colleagues have adopted precisely the conservative attitude she described." "This is mainly a problem in private practice, not clinical practice," countered Pat Markert, the director of a small suburban clinic. "Our clinicians are not biased against borderlines or any other kind of client." However, she acknowledged that practicing defensively — guarding the clinic's interests first — is a fact of life for private practitioners as well.

Among doctors unwilling to practice defensively, some react to the new constraints with fury. "I think the reason managed care is horrendous to people is because it takes control away from physician and patient," said Alexander Vuckovic, a psychiatrist at the prestigious McLean Hospital in Belmont, Massachusetts. "There is the question

'What the hell are these people doing being my partners? Have they gone through residency? Why are they participating in the care of this patient? Leave me alone!'"

Dr. Vuckovic's "Leave me alone!" is echoed by thousands upon thousands of clinicians. Among the most vociferous are those working with the desperately ill — with suicidal patients who will kill themselves if they aren't hospitalized, for example. In Massachusetts, the death rate among the chronically mentally ill has risen 79 percent in less than five years — the same period in which money-saving plans for privatization have gone into effect. It is not surprising that in a 1995 poll designed to measure the satisfaction of psychiatrists, only 51 percent indicated that they would choose psychiatry as a profession if they were making the choice today.

Also frustrated are the new relational therapists, as we will see at some length in Chapter 8. Mostly women with specific ideas for improving therapy, relational therapists believe that the relationship that gradually forms between therapist and client is the sine qua non of good therapy. Yet with managed care companies discouraging long-term care and regulations making hugs and walks suspect, how much room is left for the "authentic" relationships that these therapists insist must develop?

Clergy and pastoral counselors, who, like therapists, rarely have a hand in formulating the rules meant for their moral improvement, are also furious at regulations that seem to drop from the sky. "There was virtually no input from this diocese, and the questionnaires were simply dropped upon us in a paternalistic way," stated the clergy opposed to background checks. "We were simply directed to comply and submit. . . . The overwhelming feeling about these questionnaires is that they are offensive, invasive and designed to demean clergy and lay employees of the Church. The questionnaire is illegal and unenforceable, excepting that with the new National Canon clergy will no longer have civil rights."

Hand in hand with fury and frustration goes the sadistic treatment that some clinicians feel their colleagues are passing on to patients and to one another. The line between defensive and sadistic can be difficult to draw, and some relatively minor acts of sadism, like the premature termination of clients the moment they mention sexual attraction, can be construed either way. Although it may sound barbaric to break off a mutual relationship that has developed in the course of a year or more as soon as a client says she has sexual feelings for the therapist, it is not difficult to appreciate the therapist's fear. For example, when a California psychologist who both teaches and treats sexually abused women was sued for allowing sexual thoughts to persist in therapy (she didn't terminate the case), for fostering dependency (she answered all the client's phone calls, even at midnight), and for not being sufficiently informed (she asked for supervision on the case), her colleagues were so horrified that they became anxious about cases of their own and more willing to terminate problematic patients.

"Even when an ethical complaint is dismissed, as this one was," said the psychologist, "it is so awful that no one wants to go through this. I went through a period of withdrawal after the case. Do I want to continue treating these women? Shall I try to change my style?" If the answer to the second question had been yes, a certain amount of businesslike sadism would have entered this woman's practice. She would not have answered phone calls after six P.M., and she would have terminated cases as soon as sexual attraction was mentioned.

A peculiar form of sadism was reported on a survey of patients who became sexually attracted to their therapists. Some of these women said they had been badgered into developing a sexual transference, then humiliated for having sexual feelings. They reported that their male therapists appeared flirtatious, egged them on, interpreted their dreams and gestures as expressions of attraction, and finally urged them to admit how much they desired the therapist. When most of these women tentatively agreed — "O.K. I guess you could say I think you're attractive. I've had a daydream or two" — the therapist struck them down. "Well, I'm *not* attracted," one of them is supposed to have said. "May I remind you of the ethical restrictions," said another. In each case, the woman felt tricked, angry, and humiliated. (I have noticed that the psychologists I supervise react to increased rules and restrictions in one of two ways. Either they work much harder to make up for the loss of closeness that rules bring with them or they ignore the rules. "The system doesn't respect me or my clients, so why should I trust their rules?" is their attitude.)

Of course, either side can be sadistic, and a minor disadvantage of any regulation is that a few bad apples will turn any rule to personal gain. One client said openly, "I decided to make money on this fellow." She played her therapist skillfully, and he did not have the self-control or moral standards to resist. Then she successfully sued him. "I'd like to do it again," she said.

There is nothing astonishing about the mixture of welcome protection and disagreeable cost that accompany the new regulations. Rules work this way. Especially when political power is being taken away from some men and given to some women, it is to be expected that all sorts of bargains and compromises will attach themselves to the original intentions of the new rules. In spite of inevitable imperfections, recent changes in the therapy business have given us three new players: a better educated and more assertive client, a more regulated and more mercenary health care system, and a less autonomous clinician, who has become either more conservative or more frustrated. Together, these three will lead therapy down bumpy new paths toward shorter, less intimate, and more uniform treatment, the outcome of which is difficult to predict.

When it comes to enforcing the new mandates, the picture becomes still more complex. Not only is it difficult to reconcile the stories told by doctor and patient — accounts that evolve over time — but it is equally difficult to reconcile the needs and desires of the diverse populations in our society. Every regulation that protects one group from the actions of another takes power away from someone else. Nevertheless, some rules go into effect with relative ease — they seem to fit the society — whereas others require a great deal of energy to hold them in place. Regulations that constrain doctor-patient entanglements seem to be the kind that "cost" a lot to enforce. Not only are patients inconsistent in reporting cases of sexual involvement and boards of registration inconsistent in applying sanctions, but clinicians themselves aren't sure the rules are a good idea. They "vote" against them in two ways. First, although 98 percent *say* they are opposed to unethical sexual practices, more than 2 percent become embroiled, and second, almost none is willing to turn in an offending practitioner. "What is amazing to me," said Dr. Betz, "are the numbers of psychologists who know a colleague who is practicing on the fringe but don't do anything about it." Why does telling a male clinician not to seduce a female client seem so difficult?

A sociobiologist would probably say that whenever society passes a rule that biology is reluctant to follow, a great deal of effort is required to enforce that regulation. An example is any rule that asks men not to act on their desire for willing (or apparently willing) women. As noted earlier, men have actively been on the lookout for available women for hundreds of thousands of years. For millennia this was the best strategy, and men who were sexually forward had more offspring than those who were not. We see the results today, even though this strategy may no longer be useful. Among clinicians, it is the males who do some 85 percent of the seducing, and in the few studies of patients who physically initiate sexual behavior, it appears to be the males who touch their female doctors more often than the other way around.

Basically, a society has two options in a situation like doctor-patient sex: it can take the easy route, letting gender continue to determine who has power and who remains vulnerable, or it can train its citizens to redistribute power without regard to gender (or race, religion, and so on). In the first instance men will continue to dominate, and although this route is easy in that it is "natural" or deeply habitual, it produces pervasive social injustice. As a woman, I'm not in favor of it. The second option has its own problems, however. To control the ingrained sexual strategies of *both* men and women, an elaborate system of regulations must be put in place to constrain what bodies quite naturally want to do — and not just wanton bodies, all bodies, all people. Thus, with the second option, the problem becomes the loss of personal freedom that accompanies regulation. As a psychologist, I resent this plan. I do not want a managed care company or a board of registration whittling away at my freedom to treat as I see fit. Yet if I vote for an old style society, I will not have a profession at all.

One final irony. Nearly twenty-five hundred years ago, in a socially unjust society based on gender, Hippocrates asked doctors to take an oath. They swore that they would treat their patients well and take responsibility for their actions. Now, in a more socially just society, in which regulations take over the job of preventing exploitation and, like a net, hold us in positions where we will do the least harm, the Hippocratic Oath becomes vestigial. Whether or not the words are spoken, its job is being taken over by policy statements and the law.

~

7

Repairing the Damage

Treatment of patients who have been sexually abused by a prior therapist tends to be exceptionally difficult and complex.

— *Janet Sonne and Kenneth Pope*

Doctors talk a lot, but no one tells you how to get over these things.

— *"Barbara"*

A happy life is the best revenge.

— *Samuel Butler*

Ｏne of the few things that everyone involved in doctor-patient sex agrees on is that the story a woman tells herself about her involvement with a therapist changes over time. People are natural storytellers, and especially when they seek to make sense out of an experience that is unexpected, confusing, and incomplete, they are likely to describe the event over and over again from slightly different points of view until they find an account that makes sense. "Perhaps we were in love," they say to themselves as they try to fit the details of the experience into a love story. "Perhaps it was my imagination." "Perhaps it was a misunderstanding." "Perhaps I've been taken for a ride." If the event can be discussed openly, each possible explanation is typically worked out with friends, who support or challenge each version of the story with experience of their own. "Yes," a friend may say, "that's how I'd feel too," or "No, if he *really* loved you he wouldn't have broken it off." Eventually these commentaries are worked into the story, and the woman who has had an upsetting relationship with a therapist settles on the account that best explains what has happened to her. But in searching for what a doctor-patient entanglement means, open discussion and support are almost never available, and the process of making sense of the experience limps along in solitude. Because the relationships are unethical (and in some states illegal), the therapist insists on secrecy. If either party is married and the relationship is — or was — adulterous, doctor and patient feel doubly constrained to keep silent. The same is true if the patient's moral code does not allow for sex outside marriage, if she knows other people who go to her therapist, and so on. With the first extra-long hug or the first confession of desire, a very lonely process begins for both patient and doctor.

"I still don't know whether I've been sexually exploited or deeply loved," Barbara began, jumping straight into the confusion that caught her off-guard three years earlier and still disturbed her. "I think about what happened a lot, but I still don't know the whole story."

At forty, Barbara was living in a historic suburb of Philadelphia, her husband had a good job, and their two daughters were in school. She wasn't sure what to do with her excellent education, and she didn't know why she was upset so much of the time. Not only was she having panic attacks, but she and her husband were not getting along. She turned to a psychiatrist for an explanation — a man whose ivy-covered home and office stood, she noticed, at a crossroads.

"I was in therapy with Dr. — with this man for eighteen months. I quit a couple of times because I felt it was inappropriate. But some was helpful. One thing he did that really helped was encourage me to work. He was a cheerleader for me. He pumped me up. I got a half-time job in the reference department of a university library and then a full-time job. He believed I could do it. I don't think my husband was so sure." The doctor also prescribed medication that blunted the panic attacks and helped Barbara sleep. She was grateful, and initially she did not notice when the conversations in his gracious office turned from her private concerns to their shared interests. They discovered that each had a German Jewish grandparent, that each was married to a gentile, were the same age, and liked the same books. The doctor treated his patients with a mixture of encouragement and affection, and when Barbara got her first job, she tried to treat the students that came to her for help in the same way.

Barbara certainly did notice when the doctor started telling her about his sexual problems. When he spoke of his wife's lack of warmth and receptivity and of his own growing need to find an outlet for love, she became acutely uncomfortable. "'We need to stop,' I'd say, and he'd get really angry and tell me that I would never get better if I ran away from . . . ah . . . this topic. Maybe I should have been able to talk more about sex. It was hard to know. But especially after the weepy stuff, when he got so upset, I tried to leave."

Barbara was particularly disturbed about a book that the doctor kept telling her to read: "It was a murder mystery about a therapist and a patient. He mentioned it three or four times, so I finally looked it up in the public library. It's a disgusting book, and it was right out there where children could read it. 'Why did you want me to read that awful book?' I asked him. 'I couldn't even finish it.' 'Because it's a caricature,' he told me. 'Not all therapists who make love to their patients are like that.' It was an opener, I'm sure, but when I told him I didn't appreciate his remarks, he flipflopped and said, 'Oh, you misunderstood me. Nothing will ever happen between us.' He'd get scared, I think, and retreat. Also, and this is really disgusting, he kept rubbing the inside of his thighs as if he was on the verge of doing something."

On several occasions Barbara and her doctor almost discussed what was going on between them. Annoyed at his frequent references to transference, Barbara wrote a skit about trying to buy a peppermint ice cream cone from a clerk who was also a psychiatrist. (Peppermint is her favorite flavor, and the ice cream was so obviously a symbol for her doctor that she later referred to him as Dr. Peppermint.) Initially, the psychiatrist-clerk claims that the peppermint ice cream is frozen solid and thus not available. He tries to give her a substitute, but when she holds out for what she really wants, he insists that her desire is a case of transference. "You don't want peppermint, that's a transference from strawberry," he says. No, she tells him, even as a child, I cut the strawberry off the Neapolitan and traded it for vanilla. "You like the peppermint for its healing properties," says the clerk. "It's a transference from Pepto-Bismol." No, no, says Barbara, that's not it either. "You want to be young again," counters the clerk, reminding her that she ate peppermint ice cream with hot fudge sauce at college. No, she insists, she doesn't want to be twenty years old. Finally Barbara asks a crucial question. "Why do you have the peppermint here if you can't sell it?" To this question — which asks the doctor why he seems to be offering love when clearly he cannot deliver — the clerk says weakly, "To study your reactions." "Unfair," snaps Barbara, "You're driving me nuts. . . . I'm getting out of here." "Wait!" cries the clerk. "Maybe the peppermint will thaw. Wait . . . wait."

Barbara took the story to Dr. Peppermint and read it aloud. Obviously impressed, he roared with laughter and asked to keep it. When they met the following week, he was wearing a peppermint pink shirt and had a sad expression on his face. He had gotten the point of the skit. This patient whom he found so congenial wanted to find love — somewhere — but all he could offer was titillation. Therapy was much more valuable to her than that, but in spite of her needs and her preference, he had covertly chosen to flirt.

Again they almost talked, Barbara recalled. "He said that in the real world we were both equally responsible for what happened, but in this setting, he was more responsible and would be held more responsible." To Barbara, this sounded like an admission of mutual attraction, a way of saying that something was happening to both of them. She managed to say that "what was growing" was like an orchid in a hothouse. In her opinion, it would not survive outside the office. "He said that it could never be taken outside, and what did I want to do? I think I said I didn't know, and we changed the subject."

Unfortunately, the subject did not change at all. Dr. Peppermint continued to straddle some indefinable line — sometimes listening attentively and sensitively to her, sometimes rubbing his thigh and teasing. If she drew his attention to these provocations, he would say she was the one who was being seductive. "Me!" she responded in surprise, "I wear L. L. Bean turtlenecks." Intermittently, Barbara would leave the hothouse, but she couldn't stay away. "It was already too late," she said. "Weeks would pass and I'd miss him. I'd be reading a book and say to myself, 'He'd love this book. It's just the kind. . . .' And back I'd go." And leave again. And return.

After Barbara started therapy, she had two nightmares that repeated themselves from time to time but in different settings. One was always about a gift: someone was giving her a present, and she was excited because she knew it was going to be wonderful. Yet no matter how it was wrapped or presented, the box was always empty. She would awake feeling great disappointment. The second dream was more frightening. She was being beaten up in a public place and no one would help her. No one noticed. She might be sitting at a football game or wandering through a bookstore. People would approach her, and she knew she was going to be beaten, but no one looked at her, and the game went on.

Barbara thought that both dreams described her life *before* as well as after going into therapy. But how could she escape? How could she face the disappointment that the first dream portrayed and get on with the business of getting her own gifts for herself while feeling as vulnerable as the second dream depicted? She sensed that what she needed was safe and reliable support before the real work of therapy could begin. However, at the end of eighteen months, she felt less supported than ever. Her marriage was suffering, she had lost all sexual desire for her husband, she was having bad dreams, and she felt frightened. She left Dr. Peppermint and did not return.

To help make sense of her confusion, Barbara subsequently saw five different therapists — four men and a woman — but all of them were reluctant to talk about her well-known doctor. "One therapist told me I was delusional," she said, "because a man like my doctor would never do a thing like that. He said I needed an antipsychotic medication. I told him my doctor stopped billing me halfway through the year. I think that's when he wanted the relationship to change, but he still didn't believe me." Another psychiatrist, after meeting Barbara once, wrote to her family physician (without her permission) and said, "It is clear that this patient is reenacting her unhappy marital situation with therapists." The female doctor was more sympathetic, at least in theory. She kept repeating, "I feel such concern for the women who do not get out in time," and "You're so lucky to have gotten out." Barbara felt that this woman dismissed her unhappiness as trivial because she left therapy without being raped. "She wasn't looking at me," said Barbara. "I was back in the dream, and no one was willing to help me."

The insensitivity, moral laxness, and cavalier paternalism that Barbara encountered in all of these doctors predictably set her search for understanding back many months. "Am I making a big deal over nothing?" she asked. "Am I really psychotic?" Luckily, she bounced back from these destructive encounters with a new willingness to fight. She complained to the therapist who dispatched a hasty opinion of her without written permission. She looked up the diagnoses each gave her and wrote down the symptoms. "I can't be all five of these awful types at the same time," she told herself sensibly. Barbara concluded that her story was like a projective test — an inkblot — for therapists. Each came up with a different diagnosis and a different interpretation of her experience depending on their own fears. This might make a fine dissertation for someone, she thought, but did not help her in the least. It was the same with the books she read on the topic. Everyone knew what was wrong, but no one wanted to listen to anyone whose story was not cut and dried. For a time, the indecision she felt was almost paralyzing.

After three years, Barbara is still unable to settle completely on a single version of the story, and she thinks this is why the experience still lingers in her mind. It often feels as if the reckoning has a life of its own and is taking its time settling into a credible account. But there has been progress. When Barbara first left Dr. Peppermint, her recollections of therapy changed shape and direction so fast and so often that they were like a flock of sparrows wheeling across the sky. One instant they flew in formation and made perfect sense. The next moment they scattered, and her understanding was gone. At that time memories of affection and misery alternated so quickly that the explanations each seemed to support barely had time to form.

However, as Barbara tinkered with her story — now pushing it toward a classic account of abuse, now reading more honorable motives into Dr. Peppermint's behavior — two contradictory stories began to emerge. In one, doctor and patient loved each other; seductive remarks were just what they seemed to be, compliments were genuine, and teasing was really irresolution — caution. "He alternated. I alternated. Both of us were smart enough not to let it go further. We protected each other." Barbara called this version her "impossible love story," and it made her sad. "Impossible love *is* sad," she stated simply. "When I reread Shakespeare's late sonnets, I said to myself, 'He's out of control.' Shakespeare's like me — in love with someone he can't get to and who doesn't treat him well. Of course, *he* turns the torment into art. I felt a little bit better after reading him," she continued. "I thought to myself, 'I may be unhappy, but I'm in the best company in the world.'"

In the other version, "Dr. Peppermint is all wrong, and I'm an innocent victim. This is what I believe when I'm angry." And she had many reasons to be angry. Her doctor stopped being her therapist and tried to be something else. Because he was lonely and wanted to flirt, she lost an understanding ear and a confidant. She was also angry that he didn't play fair, alternating seduction with denial, then blaming the confusion on her. This sequence of events was not seen as caution or irresolution when she was angry. But most of all, she was angry because he promised her something that she very much wanted — love — but that was not in his power to give. He shouldn't have started what he knew he couldn't finish, she thought. Did this degree of selfishness make him a bastard? Well . . . not quite. As Barbara saw it, Dr. Peppermint probably fell in love with her — "I think he'd say it was love" — and that was not his fault. How he handled his feelings was the problem. He should have transferred her care *before*. But before what? "Before he stole my heart," she said. "That's the irony of this whole thing. He took my heart."

Like Spielrein and other women whose stories Barbara was familiar with, she felt hurt and betrayed no matter which version of the story she told herself. If she believed that she and her therapist loved each other, then she paid good money for a broken heart. Even professional relationships, she might conclude, are treacherously insecure, and love that has nowhere to go is indeed bitter as well as sweet. If, instead, she was a helpless victim taken advantage of by a bad person, then she didn't experience love at all. All that affection she felt toward, as well as from, Dr. Peppermint was an illusion, all that new confidence she gained from his compliments, a scam. These radical subtractions left her distrustful and insecure as well as just angry. "I still go back and forth," she said. "Neither story explains the experience to my complete satisfaction."

In spite of her ambivalence, something happened to Barbara. Before she began looking into her predicament — into the history of love, into herself, into doctor-patient relationships — she felt helpless. "He's spoiled me for other loves, for my husband, and my marriage," she said then. "He's become an obstacle, and I am the one who is stuck." As in her dream, no one helped. Later, after fashioning alternate versions of her experience, she felt that while the accounts of impossible love and abuse still contradicted each other, they were hers. She was the author. Starting at the time she wrote the skit about peppermint ice cream, progressing through her readings of Shakespeare, Spielrein, and others, and leading to recent revisions she made in her stories, Barbara gradually took her past and her future into her own hands. Predictably, dreams of empty promises and vulnerability troubled her less, although they did not disappear altogether. Barbara understood that she couldn't change the events of her therapy or erase the betrayal, but she could decide for herself, gradually and carefully, what the experience meant. "No one tells you how to get over these things," she had said with annoyance many times before. Since then she found, unexpectedly, that healing is a lot like art. Both of these long and laborious undertakings take painful contradictions as their raw materials. Both put opposites together in surprising ways. "I hold on to that idea," she said, a touch of pride creeping into her voice. Today, Barbara is moving ahead with both her stories. She has been accepted into a Ph.D. program in history and may write her dissertation on doctor-patient intimacy. At the same time, she is seriously considering making a formal complaint to the Pennsylvania Board of Registration. "I would like an apology," she said. "It's about time."

~~~

Some therapists — and I'm one of them — see considerable progress in this movement from helpless confusion to tentative pride and independence. Barbara has lived with contradictory feelings for a long time, which is neither easy nor comfortable. Now they are coming together under the heading "a good man handles desire badly." She seems increasingly free to express both the affection she felt for her doctor and the anger that his mishandling of the situation merits. That, I would argue, is one of the larger signs of maturity. Nor does she insist on explaining every last detail of her experience. If she has a last word to say on the subject as she turns her attention elsewhere, it is that "life contains pockets of things we never figure out."

As with Spielrein, Hillesum, and others, we can draw two conclusions. One is that Barbara struggled a few steps up the stairway — got better — in spite of Dr. Peppermint. This judgment implies that it would have been better if she had never met the man and instead had received therapy from someone else. Much of the time, Barbara herself thinks this is true. Or we can conclude that Barbara made progress because she received treatment, albeit poor, from a man who loved her, and that although this hurt and confused her, it also lit a fire under her as nothing had before. This in no way excuses Dr. Peppermint's self-centered desire to flirt with her, but it does suggest that love, *when handled responsibly,* may play an essential role in therapy. We will return to this dangerous idea in Chapter 9.

Other therapists would not see progress in Barbara's story. For them, she is yet another example of an abused woman who, unsupported, has sunk into compromise and submission. This attitude is common among leaders of abuse groups, for most of them believe that the only true story is one that describes exploitation, not affection. "We typically get women coming to us in acute crisis," said Nancy Avery, the codirector of BASTA, the Boston Association to Stop Therapist Abuse. "They are seeing that what they thought was going on [with their therapists] isn't." In her groups for clients who have been abused by therapists or clergy, Avery hears women ruefully admit that they thought their therapist loved them and was trying to help them by becoming intimate. Feeling singled out as particularly wonderful, such clients initially believed that their fondest dreams were coming true. They had been chosen, not just by any man, but by a therapist, who really knew how relationships work. As the liaisons progressed, however, doubts crept in. Sworn to secrecy, these women began to wonder why they felt so bad — why they cried more and, like Barbara, had nightmares. Sensible decisions became impossible to make, and they were obsessed by fantasies. Again like Barbara, when the erotic relationship or the memory of it felt like an overwhelming betrayal, these women were prompted to seek help. Barbara chose psychiatrists with no special expertise in therapist abuse; others joined groups like Nancy Avery's.

"We have learned that victims of therapist abuse pass through five stages," said Avery. "At first, their self-blame is enormous." New members of the group are certain that they brought the sexual intimacy down on themselves. They think that the way they dressed or the fantasies they entertained caused the misconduct. Avery and her colleagues explain to such women that they are never to blame because only the therapist operates under a code of ethics. Furthermore, the blame they feel is a defense. "They want to believe they have some control over what happens to them," said Avery. Their argument is that if sexy dressing caused the abuse, then conservative dressing can prevent it. But this is not the case. The second stage is similar. Still holding on to the idea that the client should have controlled the situation, members of the group now blame themselves for not spotting the danger in time. "How could I have been so stupid?" they ask. "Where was my common sense?" Avery said clients in this stage are tormented by feelings of shame and despair.

Most dangerous of all the stages is the third, when a great rage is unleashed at themselves and their abusers. "A high percentage become suicidal," claimed Avery. Most get through this period with "black humor." The real work of recovery begins in the fourth stage, when women ask the critical question: "Why did this happen to me?" Avery said that at this point they look into their pasts to see why they developed into such vulnerable women — women who would naturally misinterpret an exploitive "invitation" as a genuine offer of affection.* As they begin to see patterns of abuse in their history, they enter the fifth stage, which involves learning to spot abusive situations, and protect themselves — a valuable lesson. "People do want to take responsibility," she maintained.

As Avery's clients "get the story straight" and move from the idea that they may have fallen in love to the possibly truer one that they have been exploited, their guides and counselors respond in an equally emblematic or archetypal way. As Katie Roiphe noted in her book on the women's movement on college campuses, students who listen to their peers speak out against abuse characteristically respond with three messages. First, "It is not your fault." Second, "We believe you." And third, "We love you." These are the same messages that BASTA's clients receive and that Katherine was grateful to find waiting for her when she started talking about her relationship with the Reverend Mr. Blanford. "There are wonderful, fantastic people out there who accept me," she said. "It was a huge relief." Support and exoneration were not the messages that Barbara received — not from her subsequent therapists, not from Shakespeare, and not from Spielrein or other Jungians. Her story

---

* Although support groups say they help women distinguish exploitive offers from genuine offers of affection, only one kind of offer — the bad kind — is acknowledged in therapy. Even if a woman's therapist tells her he's in love, acts in love, and is not connected to another woman, the groups I have spoken with will not consider that the love could be real. It can't be real, they say, because the therapist knows his love will hurt the client. This is like saying that no interracial couple in the 1950s was in love because both were certain to get hurt. To say love makes a mess of therapy is not the same as saying it doesn't exist.

was shaped by other responses, and it is not surprising that it is quite different from those that emerge from Avery's group.

Research on hundreds of men and women strongly suggest that when the experience to be explained is unclear, the influence of advisers and confidants is surprisingly great. Therapy has been described by James Hillman as a contest of singers, which is to say that therapists, often unconsciously, seek to impose their understanding of the world on their clients. They seek to influence their clients' stories. Especially when people are upset and uncertain, this is easy to do. In a study that has become a classic, students were divided into two groups and given a dose of adrenaline. Unbeknownst to them, each group had a "mole" in its midst who agreed to react to the drug in a certain way. Thus in one room, as the subjects waited for it to take effect, one student started saying, "Hey, I'm revving up. What a rush." As these students felt their heart rate accelerate, most tended to go along with the positive story and experienced the adrenaline as a high. Meanwhile, in the other room, the mole was sowing alarm: "Oh, I don't feel good. I think I'm getting sick." Again, the majority of students took their cue from this subject and told a negative story of the "trip."

These accounts help to point out the malleability of stories formulated in times of uncertainty. If Barbara read Shakespeare's late sonnets and heard a man whom she admired calling his misery the pain of love, then she was likely to tell a similar story unless other options were more forcefully supplied. Likewise, if a woman went to a therapist who believed that anthropology and evolutionary theory offered important insights into sexual misconduct, she would emerge with a somewhat different story. Under the influence of a therapist who sees professional abuse as yet another instance of men and women acting like Neanderthals — the men ever on the lookout for extra women, the women drawn to powerful, successful males — she might emerge with the understanding that flirtation in therapy is not acceptable even though predictable from a genetic point of view. She might also be encouraged to work on her own old habits as well, at least noting how natural it feels to look for love and protection from a male who has all the signs of success.

The stories that women tell themselves about their erotic involvement with therapists are varied, but not equal. The version that is truest to the facts, is most comprehensive, holds together best, and is acceptable to other people is likely to be a better guide than the others. It is rare, however, that any one story gets high marks in every category. Barbara's story of loving a man who handled desire badly is more comprehensive, for it includes their profitable exchanges as well as the hurtful ones, but less straightforward than an account of a "snake" who simply set out to exploit a client. As a result, Barbara's account may teach her more about the common contradictions of life, whereas the second story may be better at bringing short-term relief. Martin Seligman, a psychologist well known for his work on depression and "learned helplessness," said much the same thing when he warned people to pick their explanations with care. He was especially worried by the widespread popularity of blaming others, for although it was an appealing consolation, he felt the disadvantages outweighed the initial lift provided by victimhood.

"These kinds of explanations make us feel better," he said at a convention in 1994. "They shift the blame to others, thereby raising self-esteem." By itself, however, this agreeable feeling accomplishes almost nothing at all, he maintained, and comes at a considerable price. Labeling oneself a victim goes along with feeling hopeless and being passive. Nancy Avery agreed. Being a victim was not where a woman wanted to reside for the rest of her life. It was merely a step on the way to becoming a survivor, but, she felt, a necessary one.

So how do women like Barbara or Katherine find a therapist who will encourage a useful story? For the most part, by trial and error. Because "most [psychotherapeutic] technologies are developed to sustain and promote the interests of the dominant social groups," clients who can afford it shop around until they find a like-minded therapist. The two then settle down to reedit the client's story in a way that will seem natural and right to both. When the story to be untangled involves doctor-patient abuse, however, only therapists with extreme points of view are easy to find. As Barbara discovered, an alarming number of therapists still brush off stories like hers as pathetic fantasies. At the other extreme are therapists who know *in advance* that all doctor-patient intimacy is exploitation and work to get clients to agree.

"There is no place in the treatment of abused women for moral neutrality," thundered Judith Herman when asked if a doctor-patient liaison could mean different things to different people. "I've heard the argument that it can have different meanings," said Nancy Avery. "That's a wishy-washy unwillingness to take a stand."

Because doctor-patient intimacy is so wrapped up in gender politics, and because in this country it is erroneously assumed to take only a single form — exploitation — everything about the topic is polarized. Women seeking to make sense out of erotic involvement with a counselor will find this polarization in treatment too. Unfortunately, they will not have an easy time finding a therapist who does not know beforehand *either* that doctor-patient involvement does not happen (or is not damaging) *or* that it must represent exploitation.

Regardless of the therapist a woman chooses, one of the things she is likely to say is that she wants something returned to her. "I want the control back in my life," said one young woman. "He stole my heart," said Barbara. Or, as Katherine put it, "He ran off with my peace of mind." The feeling is that men like Dr. Peppermint have stolen something precious, and their patients want it back.

The well-known Jungian psychologist James Hillman believes that what they want back is their innocence; they want the betrayal that has occurred in therapy undone and trust restored. This, he said, sounds reasonable but is not realistic. He maintained that forming a relationship of perfect trust, in which one is protected from all the desires of the therapist and from all the disastrous mistakes of one's own that could also wreck the therapeutic relationship, "means really to be out of harm's way and so to be out of real life."

Katherine's story illustrates this point. When she was toyed with by her minister, she slid precipitously from a state of innocence and naiveté to one of disturbing worldliness. Not only did she lose her illusions about the purity of the clergy in general and Mr. Blanford in particular, but, of equal or perhaps greater importance, she awoke to her own capacity to crave physical love, burn with desire, and even lie to her son. This may sound harsh, but in fact Katherine found herself capable of thinking in ways that felt evil and disgusting. Although the entanglement was in no way her fault, it suddenly introduced her to her own dark side. There is no way to forget or undo that. And for many people there is a special place in hell for the person who has held that dark mirror up to their face.

Hillman maintains that as painful as betrayal is in therapy, marriage, or anywhere else, once it has occurred, the objective is not to undo it and retreat to Eden but to learn from it. Among sterile ways of dealing with betrayal — ways that produce no learning — are revenge, denial (nothing happened), cynicism (love is a cheat and therapists are prostitutes), self-betrayal (the real me wasn't involved and didn't get hurt), and a paranoid insistence that life should be free of risk. "The paranoid demand for a relationship without the possibility of betrayal cannot really be based on trust," Hillman stated, making the point that relationships involve love, and love always carries with it the possibility of betrayal. The desire to eliminate risk, he continued, is an attempt to strike a deal and manage power, not an attempt to start a relationship. "It is a retreat to a logos relationship [a contract], enforced by word, not held by love."

So what are the Barbaras and Katherines to do once they have been betrayed? Hillman's prescription is not comforting: "It may well be that betrayal has no other positive outcome but forgiveness, and that the experience of forgiveness is possible only if one has been betrayed. Such a forgiveness is not a forgetting, but *the remembrance of wrong transformed within a wider context,* or as Jung has put it, the salt of bitterness transformed to the salt of wisdom."

"Easy for a man to say!" roared one of my colleagues. "Nice deal. The therapist messes around with a client, then the client is supposed to thank him for giving her the opportunity of *forgiving* him!" But this woman missed Hillman's interlocking points. First, he was not saying that betrayal is what any client wants or needs from therapy. Once it has occurred, however, Hillman argued that forgiveness needs to be part of the response. Second, he was speaking of the betrayal in relationships of deep affection. He believes that doctor and patient share a unique bond, "a kind of loving . . . not reducible to other more familiar forms." Sometimes, however, this love jumps its boundaries, and both doctor and patient are swept away. Finally, he understood that hatred and bitterness are neither the opposite of love nor the absence of connection. The vengeance that seems popular today represents a different but often equally intense bond. If the client is truly to be free of the unworkable love she shared with her doctor, she must deal with the experience of being wronged, *and* she must also forgive.

"There is no cure for impossible love," wrote another Jungian, Jan

Bauer, the author of *Impossible Love*. "Anger, disillusionment, bitterness, hurt, and humiliation are all part of the return trip." It draws us deeper into ourselves and "also into longing, and this will not, should not, ever cease. . . . This longing keeps us in proximity to our souls."

No matter whether a therapist regards doctor-patient entanglement as exploitation, a terrible initiation, or an unfortunate learning experience, none denies that recovering is difficult and painful.* Coming to terms with the experience is complicated and time-consuming because the whole person needs help, not just a piece of an individual, and the accumulated feelings of a lifetime need airing, not just a selected group of them. Added to this is the difficulty of finding a therapist who doesn't think he or she already knows what the real story is, a clinician who will listen.

~~~

In turning to the training and retraining of therapists — for rehabilitation is largely the retraining of errant therapists — and in asking what forms of dissuasion have been tried and which work, we have an improbable story as a guide. It is the legend of the mad poet Majnun and Layla, the woman he loved. Based on Arabic folk legends dating from the seventh century C.E., it is, on one level, a love story — the Islamic culture's equivalent of Tristan and Isolde or Romeo and Juliet. But on another level it is the story of Majnun's father and his attempts first to stop and then to understand the impossible relationship that his son had chosen. The wise sayyid tried every tactic that has been used to dissuade lovers. Each one has its counterpart in our current efforts to train and, if necessary, reform therapists. Understandably, the focus of such training is the handling of love and attraction, not sociopathic behavior.

---

* Clinicians also agree that prevention is preferable to treatment, and consumer groups have published a number of pamphlets to educate consumers about the dangers of sex in therapy. The Department of Consumer Affairs in California has put out "Professional Therapy *Never* Includes Sex," which was modeled on "It's Never OK: A Handbook for Victims and Victim Advocates on Sexual Exploitation by Counselors and Therapists," published by the Minnesota Public Education Work Group. Research suggests that clients who have read a brochure on sexual misconduct are significantly less naive and more assertive than those who have not. (B. E. Thorn, R. C. Shealy, and S. D. Briggs, "Sexual Misconduct in Psychotherapy: Reactions to a Consumer-Oriented Brochure," *Professional Psychology: Research and Practice*, 24 (1993): 75–82.)

The story of Layla and Majnun began in the desert of Arabia, where the chief of a nomadic tribe prayed for a son. This powerful man had great herds of goats and camels, fine rugs, and glittering jewels, but no son to carry his memory forward into time's trackless dunes. At last his wish was granted when quite late in life his wife bore a son, who was named Qays. A beautiful and well-tempered infant, he soon grew into a child known for his many talents. Given a book, he learned to read. Given a pen, he learned to write. Given classmates, he learned to converse in a kind and charming manner.

One day the precocious daughter of another chieftain arrived at the school Qays attended. She too was both beautiful and gifted, and because her hair was lustrously black, she was called Layla, which means "night." Qays and Layla stared at each other in the classroom for many days and became entranced. Soon Qays neglected his studies and started whispering "Layla, Layla, Layla" under his breath. It was said that both Qays and Layla became intoxicated with the scent of the flower that has no name.

Finally Qays could stand it no longer, and he burst from the classroom, shouting "LAYLA! LAYLA!" As he ran through the markets and bazaars, the people who heard him shook their heads sadly. He is "majnun," they said to one another, which in Arabic means "crazy."

When Layla's father heard that his daughter's name had been broadcast through the streets by a madman, he immediately confined her to a tent in the desert. But when Majnun's father learned that his only son was smitten with love, he was less alarmed. With a promise of great riches, he went to Layla's father and tried to arrange a marriage. Layla's father would have none of it. His daughter was not going to marry an unbalanced lunatic. The union was impossible. He would never agree.

Majnun's father returned home and faced his son. "Love's fool," he said to the young man. "It is time to forget Layla and choose another."

Thus began the sayyid's long battle to convince Majnun to give up his obsession for a woman he could never possess, for a union that was tainted by the very force of his desire. Surely there are other girls as beautiful as Layla, the sayyid told his son, girls as slender as the cypress whose skin smells like flowers.

Less poetically, errant therapists are routinely told that if they don't date patients, there are still several billion women left to choose from.

But Majnun was not interested in other women any more than the lovestruck therapist is interested in someone other than his client. In his delirious state, Majnun couldn't even see other women. Afraid that he could not make his father understand that he had no control over his choice, he ran away into the desert. There he sang of Layla and tore his clothes. When he eventually collapsed on the sand, a group of shepherds took him back to his father's tents.

Clearly needing a stronger method of persuasion, the sayyid next tried to cure his son by taking him to Mecca. Majnun was carried there on a litter and brought to the holiest of holy places. "My son," said the chieftain, "ask Allah to save you from your passion. Pray to him to end your madness and to cure you of your obsession."

The secular parallel is a trip to the therapist — a special therapist who has been trained to unravel the complexities of therapist-client abuse. There the offending therapist asks that his neuroses be uncovered and resolved. Not surprisingly, this form of rehabilitation has been neither well received nor effective.

Nor did the trip to Mecca cure Majnun. "Oh God, let me not be cured of love, but let my passion grow!" he shouted as he touched the stone. "Make my love a hundred times greater than it is today! And let me love for love's sake!"

When Layla's father heard of this blasphemy, he demanded that Majnun be punished for refusing to give up his perverse love. Dutifully, Layla's kinfolk rode off into the desert to find Majnun, who had again taken up life as a hermit. At the same time, Majnun's people set out to force the young man to come home. They too were angry that he was bringing shame down upon them. If the persuasion of family and the counsel of priests could not convince this stubborn young man to give up Layla, they would force him to forget her. The parallels with the criminalization of therapist-client sex are obvious.

But again reasonable tactics were no match for Majnun's unreasonable state of mind. Ripping open the side of a tent, Majnun escaped from his own people and, by slipping through the desert like an animal, avoided the tribesmen from Layla's camp as well. He hid in the great spaces of the desert, living on grasses and composing songs to Layla that he sent to her on the wind. Even when his father was near death and wanted only to provide for his son, Majnun would not return to the village.

"You could not rescue me," said Majnun when he heard that his father had died, "but you shared my suffering. You were my companion, my protector, my pillar. Now that you are gone, I have no home in your heart."

This was a turning point for Majnun. Aware that his father had been steadfastly on his side once he accepted his son's obsession, the boy began to realize that his only consolation, like that of his father before him, lay in sharing the suffering of others. Only a community of shared loss gave him comfort, and conversely, only men and animals who had lost their mates could bear to be near him. Gradually lions, gazelles, ants, and serpents took up residence in his cave. By day they hunted for food, and by night they lay peaceably together.

Modern analogies for shared suffering are hard to find in the literature of rehabilitation. As I will argue later in this chapter, it is only when a person is helped to commit to a greater love — not when he or she is told to stamp out an attraction — that an obsession can be transformed into constructive sadness. Such transformations start in suffering, however, and often progress when that suffering is shared with a "father." Although experts on sexual misconduct routinely assert that such wise parental figures are available — that supervisors are waiting in their offices to help the wavering, lovestruck clinician — both surveys and informal stories suggest the opposite. For one thing, when clinicians in training are polled, a third or fewer say they can talk freely with their supervisors. The rest say either that they don't feel comfortable discussing desire with their supervisor or that the supervisor avoids the topic. "That's for you to discuss with your personal therapist," trainees are told. For another, stories from clinicians who did discuss attraction in supervision are not invariably marked by empathy and understanding. "You don't have a crush on *her*," Douglas was told. "You wouldn't pick a partner who was bipolar," Dr. Norman heard. Supervisors aren't always eager to understand what lies behind the attraction, which is not surprising. Unless the supervisor him- or herself can talk comfortably about crossing ethical boundaries — at least in fantasy and imagination — how can he or she extend genuine empathy to the clinician? From all reports, it is not easy to find a steadfast father — or mother — among supervisors, one who dares to speak openly about the love that flares up between doctor and patient and that hurts so much to forgo. It is a forbidden topic but one that interns and residents need to hear about, not in an abstract way, but from their mentors' own experience.

Time passed, and Majnun persevered in loving Layla. In one part of the desert Layla ate dry grass to stifle her sobs, and in another Majnun grew crazier. People were afraid to go near him. They were afraid his animals would attack them. Finally Majnun felt a change come over him, and he prayed to Allah. "Do not let me perish now," he prayed. "Do not let me lose my way."

The next morning a great peace descended on him, and with it came news from Layla. She had heard of his father's death and wished to share his grief. She also told him that she had been given in marriage but had never submitted to her husband. Majnun wrote her a letter, telling her of his continued love, and when she received it, she asked the messenger to bring Majnun to her so that they might look at each other one last time.

The two finally met in the moonlight outside a tent, but they could not approach closer than ten steps for fear of being consumed by their passion. Majnun sang his loveliest song for Layla and disappeared. Shortly afterward she died with her lover's name on her lips and was buried in the desert. When Majnun learned of her death, he and his animals went to her grave. Majnun lay on the sand above her body for a month while his animals kept everyone away. When Majnun the mad poet finally died, his animals kept watch, and only when the sun had reduced his body to dry bones did they depart. Then Majnun's kinsmen gathered his dust and buried it at Layla's side. The Arabs say that no one has ever loved as truly as Layla and Majnun.

Obviously I am not implying that therapists who fall for clients even begin to feel the desire that Majnun experienced or are capable of his control and loyalty. I suggest only that the tale illustrates the futility of stopping love by force or reason alone. We have seen that the second largest number of therapists brought before boards on charges of sexual misconduct have been moved by an attraction they call love. It also appears from the majority of reports on rehabilitation that telling them to stop does not lead them along a new path.

Gary Schoener and John Gonsiorek, who together have handled more than a thousand "impaired practitioners" at the Walk-In Counseling Center in Minneapolis, share the common pessimism. Although they feel that remorseful therapists can be rehabilitated, as can therapists who become erotically involved because of inadequate training or personal distress, they have seen rehabilitation plans fail too often to be hopeful. Personal psychotherapy and supervision, they know, can turn into bull sessions. Errant clinicians can drop out of the rehabilitation plan and practice without a license. Even the carefully selected supervisors who serve as role models of ethical behavior can inexplicably undo the work they have accomplished by becoming involved with a patient themselves.*

In an effort to plug some of these loopholes, limits may be placed on the impaired clinician's practice. For example, he may not be allowed to work with single women during a period of probation, and he may be urged to change his style: no more hugging. (Because women often make up three quarters or more of the patients in a private practice, such a prohibition, for two years, say, often forces a therapist out of the field.) Finally, for intractable offenders, vocational training is offered to help them embark on a different career. This policy — requiring therapy and/or supervision for the remorseful and limiting their practice while they receive it — is increasingly common for both psychotherapists and clergy. Nonetheless, few believe that present methods are sufficient.

At least three major changes need to be made. One is in the initial training of psychotherapists. To address the two largest categories of unethical behavior, insensitive erotic remarks and acting on attraction, two kinds of instruction are required. The simplest appears to be sensitivity training, and many graduate programs have incorporated material from women's studies to teach young therapists what are and are not provocative remarks and gestures. Far more difficult is the discussion of

---

* At a seminar on countertransference, Andrea Celenza related that as directors of the country's largest program to rehabilitate therapists, Schoener and Gonsiorek took great pains to find several supervisors to evaluate the progress of errant clinicians. One of these men was senior to all the rest, and soon he had treated so many of these cases that he had more experience rehabilitating therapists than anyone else. Schoener and Gonsoriek were thus understandably shocked when this doctor was brought up on charges of sexual abuse. "How could you do it?" Schoener was said to have asked. The doctor replied that he had put the experience in a box in his mind, where it seemed isolated from everything else he knew. "And it was exciting." Schoener admitted that for some men, whatever, or rather whoever, is forbidden has incomparable appeal. (Cambridge Hospital, Countertransference, Engagement, and Boundaries, April 9, 1994.)

sexual attraction; students as well as professors are uncomfortable with the topic, and neither can tell of their own experiences unless the attraction was reined in without a single slip.

Dr. Constance Dalenberg, a psychologist who treats abused women at a trauma research institute in San Diego and conducts research on sexual abuse in therapy, is one of a small number of clinicians who are using videotapes to get discussions started about sex. "We must focus on the initial attraction," she maintained. "Students are naturally afraid, but they need to be taught to accept it and use it." Dalenberg uses tapes made by professional actors that depict therapy sessions in which seduction is covertly or overtly the agenda. The tapes are stopped at critical points and the trainees asked to state what they would say to the seductive client. "Out!" is the most common rejoinder, as if the goal were to get sexual attraction out of therapy and keep it out. But this is not the goal. Dalenberg's research has shown that when attraction enters therapy, as it often does, the best strategy is to talk about it and to "own it." The best outcomes involved therapists who treated sexual attraction as an expected part of therapy and proceeded carefully but without pulling back. Bad outcomes occurred when attraction was not discussed at all or when the therapist pinned the sexual tension on the patient.

At the same time, young clinicians need to respect the power of these attractions. As Dr. Norman discovered, thinking that surely a doctor can control love is the pride that cometh before the fall. She went on to make a point similar to Dalenberg's, namely, that running away was not the answer. After saying that "just by falling for this man, I felt kicked out of the club," she added, "The reverse is more like it. Only when you have truly fallen for a patient and looked at your work and the mental health system from the point of view of a lover have you become a fully experienced therapist. Love should be viewed as a dangerous rite of passage."

A second change that needs to be made in retraining is to acknowledge that different therapists need different rehabilitation plans — ones tailored to their place on the stairway, as Alan Flashman might put it. The married practitioner who falls for a woman who is expecting him to act like her father needs far more directive treatment than one who becomes engaged to a former client who was journeying with him, much as Pálos was with Ferenczi. Like clients, clinicians too come into rehabilitation with different questions.

The third change involves our attitude toward love in therapy. As long as we continue to deny that therapists fall in love with clients, we will not be able to train students adequately or rehabilitate lovestruck clinicians. The story of Majnun contains a lesson: love listens only to love. Counselors like Douglas and doctors like Dr. Norman agree and, as we have seen, a similar belief inspired the training program at the Jung Institute in Zurich, where lovestruck trainees were urged to talk openly about the wonderful qualities of their loves. This same idea is familiar to Catholic priests, only in their case, they are urged to develop consistent control over their natural desires by focusing on their greater love of God. Can clinicians learn anything from celibate clergy about reliable control?

~~~

Father Walsh, a Catholic priest and the rector of a small, isolated parish, is not, alas, a simple soul. His early hopes of living an uncomplicated life dedicated to the service of God eluded him more quickly and completely than they did most other aspirants. By the age of nineteen he was beginning to discover — and by fifty-four had fully acknowledged — that wit, rather than purity, and cunning, rather than simplicity, were the gifts he had brought with him into the world. There was also sadness. This great hulk of a man, who is welcomed by everyone as he moves through the churchyard in his loose white alb or walks down village streets, has a deep, rich laugh that comes straight from a reservoir of sadness. No one knows exactly why Father Walsh is sad — he is Irish, and it could be bred in the bone — but it is clear to all that he has earned the right a hundred times over to comfort his flock. A character, they call him, a passionate eccentric. Neither naturally outgoing nor easily familiar, he holds himself at a distance, as if his passion needs an empty space around it for safety's sake.

"Perhaps," began Father Walsh slowly, "perhaps to be intimate a person must be radical — a radical and courageous character." He paused, his great freckled face frowning with deep concern. "Jesus is a courageous character, you know. And Saint Francis. Neither man avoided the struggle." Abruptly Father Walsh began telling a story, several stories it turns out, that circle around the struggle that he believes lies at the heart of intimacy, what it is like for him and why it is dangerous.

"Do you know Mr. Edmund?" he asked. "His wife is dying of cancer. I visited yesterday, and I saw in her eyes those looks that say, 'I wish I had more time' and 'I'm scared.'" She did not express these deepest of misgivings, however, and Father Walsh sensed that like many people close to death, she had been given a last task to perform for her family: not to scare them with her own fears. "'Are you afraid?' I asked her, knowing that no one close to her had the strength to bear her answer. 'Yes,' she said. So I recited a Jewish prayer, 'The Messiah will come. Even though we die, the Messiah will come. The Messiah is here.' She wept, and I think she felt relieved. They love me in the hospital," he added with a smile. "Even in my most despairing moments, I am good there. I relate to the dying." But was it difficult to baptize a dying baby? To give the sacrament of anointing to the unprepared? And be the one willing to ask the hard question? "One does not count the cost in this calling. We are privileged to witness the most important moments in many lives. These are the times when people are playing for keeps and the stakes are high. You have to be willing to have your heart broken."

Apparently veering away from the concept of intimacy as the willingness to enter the common struggle, Father Walsh began another story: "I gave first communion to a young boy last week. My, he was spiffy in his blue blazer. Blond hair, all scrubbed and clean. After the service he came walking solemnly up to me, and I felt a great urge to hug him. I'd just fed this boy his first real meal — the body of the Lord. But I hesitated. We're inclined to be careful today, and then I asked myself, 'Where am I going with this? If I am *like* Jesus, what would I do?' So I gave him a headlock. I could be criticized, but if we are to be intimate, we must be willing to be embarrassed, rejected, criticized — in a word, sentenced. We are not meant to tiptoe through our days."

Father Walsh's enormous tiger cat trotted onto the porch and hoisted herself onto his lap. Rolling over on her back, she lay like a pig in the sun, shamelessly waiting for her stomach to be scratched. She batted his hand coyly as automatically he started to stroke her. The priest's thoughts moved to a different kind of struggle with intimacy. "A woman once came to my parish," Father Walsh recalled. "I was in the kitchen making coffee. 'I need to tell you something,' she said. 'Can we go in your office? Would you close the door?' On my part, I am thinking she wants a mass card. When I am in the church I am safe. I have signs of the Lord all around me, no thoughts of danger. Suddenly she blurts out, 'I am madly in love with you. I can think of nothing else.' I was taken completely by surprise. The Holy Spirit truly gave me the words, and I said to her, 'As a male, I am immensely flattered, but I love your husband, your children, and yourself — all together. Nothing will ever come of this.' The woman left immediately. She seemed embarrassed. Not too long afterward her husband died, but she could not confide in me. She accepted some books on grieving and asked me to bury the man, but it was awkward. I rarely see her, and I wonder sometimes if I could have said anything different." Does Father Walsh still run from encounters that involve physical attraction? "Oh, Lord in heaven!" he blurted out, "I struggle. My whole life has been a struggle to be authentic, and it's been very hard." It has taken him many years to learn about love.

Father Walsh said that he has lived among powerful expectations. From the beginning, the Church expected him to be one kind of a person, "the guys" expected something else of a man, his mother, brother, and sister something else again. "There is a special set of expectations when you're young and trying to fall in love," he said. "I couldn't do that dance. I was afraid." So, like many another Irish Catholic adolescent, his first answer to love's invitation was a flat no. He dove into seminary, eager to avoid intimacy. For a time it worked well, and his calling protected him. The clothes he wore indicated that he was not like other men, and the only time he listened to people talk of love was in the confessional. "I was very protected. Initially it's a relief."

By the time Father Walsh had finished seminary and was ordained, however, three of his classmates had committed suicide. What still haunts him about the deaths of these "wonderful, bright, nervous" young men — one friendly, one ambitious, one "a maniac with his hair parted in the middle" — is that he suspects each of them was afraid of all kinds of intimacy. They didn't really know each other, he said. Their deepest thoughts were not revealed to anyone, and "this creates a dreadful mess." He believes that young students need to let someone into their lives and hearts in spite of the danger involved.

"Do you see?" he asked. "We are caught. The more unmarried we are, the more vulnerable we are to love, affection, flattery — all those things. The heart is ready to run wild. Yet if we shut the door on love and intimacy once and for all," he continued, "we're in a coffin cut off from life." So what should priests do? "Oh, it's not something you *do*. It's not accomplished by your own ingenuity."

After years of struggling to remain open to love yet celibate, Father Walsh has learned, or been given, as he would say, an important lesson: "The heart can only be harnessed in the service of love. We manage love with greater love.

"There is no woman I have ever, ever met that I would sacrifice my vocation for," he said. You mean your job? Your calling? "The diamond," he answered. "The pearl of precious price given to a few. I have been entrusted with the sacred ministry of God, and I don't want to trade my status as a man chosen by Jesus Christ for that of a man chosen by a woman. I'm already taken. 'You are mine,' Jesus said to me, 'and I will be yours.' There are times when this feeling is very strong. Once, driving along the lake at night in the snow and rain, an understanding was given to me in grace. Another time it came before dawn as I was entering the church. I suddenly realized that I would never love Jesus as Christ himself has loved me — never. I burst into tears. I cried a towel, as the Irish say. But for those minutes I was enveloped by a cloud, by the voice of God. I was overwhelmed by the mysticism. These moments are the most intimate of my life. You see there has to be this intimacy with Jesus Christ in order to carry out the vow, in order to love and be intimate *in* the world without giving myself away *to* the world. Love listens only to love."

There were times, however, when the love of his life wouldn't speak to him, and whenever this essential counterweight was absent, Father Walsh's yearning threatened to sweep him away. He never became in-ured to beauty. He started to fall in love over and over and over again. As a teenager he had first yearned silently for an Italian girl with eyes the shape and color of almonds. In middle age he went to Rome. It nearly killed him. "WHY DON'T YOU TALK TO ME?" he shouted to Jesus. "Even my cat talks to me!"

Father Walsh's brand of intimacy — active, unafraid of disapproval, but precariously balanced — has been sustained "so far" by a still greater love to which he has pledged his heart. That vow holds him like hands, at times lifting him up, at times holding him down against a grinding wheel to sharpen him like an ax.

"A vow is not taken once," he explained. "It is lived out every day. It is grown into, like a marriage or a title. It is not an answer, but a tension among forces that pull me in different directions. It suspends me between desires, and leaves me vulnerable. Every day there's the possibility that your heart — my heart — will be stolen or broken. With this job," he concluded, looking me straight in the eye, "comes a characteristic ache of the heart."

Father Walsh has discovered several fundamental truths about all who seek to serve others. First, he has understood that they must remain open to love *and* vigilant against acting on sexual attraction. His vow of celibacy is no more a solution to this problem than a clinician's code of ethics. Both vow and code merely announce to candidates the particular kinds of tension that come with the job and must somehow be tolerated. Like good priests, good clinicians do their work suspended between conflicting desires.* Second, Father Walsh has understood that to manage the tension between love and desire, only a greater love can be an effective counterweight. Rules, fines, threats, common sense, and supervision as commonly practiced are flimsy defenses against passionate attraction. Force and reason have been tried for centuries without a great deal of success. So has fearing and hating the attraction itself — calling women evil, calling romantic love "sadistic" and "childish," calling men pigs, or calling patients ridiculous partners. Buddhists used a meditation that consisted of imagining the body of a woman as a bag of excrement. Christian monks used a similar exercise. But the remedy did not work, noted the poet and philosopher Octavio Paz, "and brought on the vengeance of the body and exasperated imagination." Yet more than a few supervisors use essentially the same tactic — "not *her*."

"It takes God a long time to fashion a mature and holy priest," David Rice commented in his study of priests who broke their vows of celibacy and left the priesthood. There were no quick tricks or tech-

---

* When Gillian Rose fell in love with a Catholic priest, she discovered that her presence at his side — as they walked to the post office or sat chatting in public — released and revealed the sexual tension that existed between the priest and all his parishioners. Young girls blushed. Older women engaged in a pleasant form of rivalry. Had they been lovers, however, Rose believed the reaction would have been anger: "Not for the vow betrayed, but for the withdrawing of his gift of sex — which was integral to the social efficacy of his priesthood — from all to one" (*Love's Work: A Reckoning with Life* [New York: Schocken, 1995], pp. 68–69).

niques to deflect the urge to plunge into physical love. Celibacy, he continued, must be grown into. In comparing priests who stayed in the church and were content with their calling to those who left, Rice discovered that happy, effective priests often possess four qualities. First, they like their work. Next, they have a private life that includes activities not associated with their profession. In addition, they distance themselves from the agenda of the church bureaucracy, and last, they have an intimate relationship with someone — a friend and confidant, a therapist, a prayer group, a sponsor in AA. All of these qualities seem to be ones that would help clinicians as well, and all seem self-evident except the curious observation that effective priests step back from officialdom. Rice explained that priests needed to dissociate themselves to some degree from the business or bureaucratic side of the church in order to maintain their sense of autonomy. Although obedient to their bishop, priests had to also feel free to make many decisions on their own and to take personal responsibility for them. If they became company men, Rice said, burnout was sure to follow. There have been many periods in the history of the church — and at least one in the history of organized therapy — when the institution's agenda went against what Rice called "honest, loving service." The priests who survived, he maintained, are the ones who dissociated themselves to some extent from the church in an effort to best serve their people.

Thus, like Father Walsh, Rice's productive priests manage their unruly urge to love with steadfast devotion to both Jesus and their parishioners, with an abiding belief in themselves, and with acceptable forms of intimacy outside the church. Love of something greater than a romantic union with an attractive patient and a steadfast desire to grow into this greater calling seem to be more effective ways of managing attraction than viewing it as the enemy.

"That's it," murmured Father Walsh as he shifted in his wicker chair without disturbing the cat. "Dedication, not control."

"Take Monsignor McFlaherty at eighty, God bless him," he continued. "I can still see the man, tall and thin — well over six feet — with white hair parted in the middle. He made quite a picture in his black cassock and biretta, standing on the church steps or striding up the hill to the rectory. The man truly lived for his people, and most of them knew it. His whole life was for them. But the things he did — Holy Mother of God — he would never get away with today. One day he started a summer camp for kids in the parish. There was a flu epidemic, so he simply loaded as many boys and girls as he could fit into his car and took off to the countryside with a bunch of tents. No background checks. No rules about touching. He just swept them out of the city and camped out. He was a tornado. He believed he could find water with a divining rod too, and the bishop finally had to ask him to stop wandering through people's backyards with a stick in his hand. A rumor was starting that he was practicing magic. And opinions. Father McFlaherty had strong opinions, and he expressed every one of them. For instance, he called every woman he met 'Mary,' and if they said, 'But Father, that's not my name,' he'd tell them, 'Well, it ought to be.' The man was bombastic. No holds barred. No tact. Yet he always gave something to the men who wandered up to the rectory and asked for a handout. They came up from a state hospital, you see, and they wanted cigarette money. They'd tell you anything to get it, but Father McFlaherty would say, 'I'd rather be conned than ungenerous.'

"But the monsignor's hallmark, you might say, was tap-dancing on the steps of the Church of the Most Precious Blood. He'd appear after the mass in his cassock, with red buttons swaying down the front of him, collar to hem, and his crimson sash jumping as he jumped. He knew a couple of routines, and he'd shuffle step to the right, then back to the left — kicking this way and that way until everyone was laughing and clapping. Six-foot-three, he was, and I can still see him at the front of the church at eighty, dancing around his people.

"Frank knew what he was supposed to do in this life," Father Walsh said, suddenly frowning, "and he did it so fearlessly that . . . how can I put it, that he was doubly valuable to the people he served. They knew he was on their side, and they also knew he would do anything to help them — not just anything within his jurisdiction, but anything at all. It was the freedom that went along with Frank's dedication that was so appealing. I think that's the winning combination — a man who is utterly dedicated and utterly free. Now I ask you, why is that so difficult to come by?"

~~~

From McFlaherty, Rice, and Walsh the messages are clear. If therapists are to remain reliably chaste with their clients, excellent training must be provided both on the natural perils and attractions of the doctor-patient relationship and on the somewhat eccentric nature of clinicians themselves. Specifically, each aspiring therapist needs to know what his or her particular gift is and what weakness or wound shadows that talent. Supervisors who are willing to talk of love, seriously and personally, need to be available, and not just in the training period but throughout a clinician's career. Also important are the pride and confidence that come from retaining a large degree of autonomy or independence in a profession that is generally respected. A harried and demoralized clinician is not likely to be good or reliable. Yet the autonomy of licensed clinicians is being cut back. Finally, as Rice's study of contented and discontented priests suggests, the consistently ethical helper takes personal responsibility for his actions. In other words, he retains the freedom to make his own decisions and thereby sees his work as a reflection of his character and not merely of someone else's policy. It is this combination of independence and utter devotion, as Monsignor McFlaherty lived it and as Father Walsh practices it now, that marks the great priests and the best of the wounded healers.

However, as we will see in the next chapter, it is not clear whether independence and devotion will also mark the next generation of managed care providers.

III

WHY CAN'T
WE TALK
ABOUT LOVE?

The appearance of sexuality continues to be an obstacle, a stumbling block, preventing researchers and practitioners from pursuing their investigations beyond these appearances into what I will suggest are the deep affective ties at the heart of the doctor-patient attachment.

— *Léon Chertok*

No therapy works unless I love my client. But publicly I cannot acknowledge this love. In fact, I must pretend *not* to have this essential ingredient.

— *Alan Flashman*

At a seminar on the feelings that clinicians have for their patients — a week-long affair dramatically called "Surviving the Storm" — I made marks in the left-hand margin of my notes every time the word "hate" was said and marks in the right-hand margin every time "love" was spoken. I also noted how often each concept was followed by comments and questions. At the end of five days, "hate" had been discussed nine times more frequently than "love," and if we hadn't spent an entire morning on the Bean-Bayog–Lozano case, the ratio would have been closer to forty to one. Similarly, when "hateful," "loathsome," and "detestable" came up, they triggered a comment or question roughly three quarters of the time. When love for a client was mentioned — not love *from* a client, but a question such as "How did you handle your love for this woman?" — there was silence. In these next two chapters, I will try to discover what clinicians believe are the active ingredients of therapy and why they would prefer *not* to investigate the possibility that one of them is a deep, emotional tie — not sex, but a kind of love.

Today, the clinicians to answer these questions are women, not only because they presently make up two thirds of all psychotherapists and are increasing in number, but also because they are particularly receptive to the idea that it is the therapist-client relationship that makes therapy work. Women are quite literally taking over the practice of psychotherapy. In psychiatry, psychology, pastoral counseling, and master's level counseling their numbers are rising, and in the field of social work their numbers are already high. At the same time, fewer men are going into these fields, and their absolute numbers are dropping. Not surprisingly, female clinicians have a different way of doing things, and although many forces impinge on the business of psychotherapy, women are also making their influence felt. One of the ways is by encouraging a relatively new school of thought called relational therapy. As we will see in the next chapter, relational therapy attempts to place therapist and client on a far more equal footing than conventional therapies, and it emphasizes the curative power of the relationship that develops between them. Not only is relational therapy welcomed by therapists and patients, who find it a natural way to relate to other people and an effective way to restore themselves, but it is also prompting a new look at doctor-patient ties. Ferenczi's ideas on mutual analysis and on the real relationship that develops in spite of a clinician's professional stance are more in vogue now than in his lifetime.

Ironically, the feminization of psychotherapy threatens to curtail some of the same inquiries it hopes to inspire. For one thing, many of the women who support relational therapy are emphatically unwilling to consider that attraction may be part of the picture. For another, with women streaming into the field, the problem of doctor–former patient sex is likely to diminish, and with it the pressure to investigate its occurrence. Networks that serve victims of sexual abuse as well as seminars and workshops often advise clients that sexual feelings and actions have no place in therapy at all. The only permissible relationship, these forums emphasize, is a nurturing bond between therapist and client. There is such fear that any form of sexual attraction will lead to exploitation that Eros is not allowed into any serious discussion of therapy. In other words, it appears that although the new generation of female clinicians is taking a new look at the therapist-client relationship, many insist on doing so from the safety of a parental framework. They are bravely willing to discard the buffers that have traditionally held doctor and patient apart — Mesmer's glass wand and Freud's transference, for example — but only insofar as they can replace them with the conviction that therapy is basically a parent-child duet. As we have heard clinicians of both genders say, if a practitioner really feels like a parent, he or she is protected from acting on attraction by a powerful taboo. However, we have also seen that all therapy does not occur at the parent-child end of the stairway and that male therapists tend to form different kinds of bonds with their clients than female practitioners do. These forms of the doctor-patient relationship need to be included in our discussion. Relational therapists are taking a new look at a big piece of the doctor-patient relationship, but not at all of it.

To approach two interlocking questions — "How essential is the doctor-patient bond to effective therapy?" and "Is love a fundamental part of that bond?" — I will adopt a historical perspective. The last chapter looks at what clinicians have claimed makes therapy work. Everything from the doctor's learning to his caring, his personality, his experience, his hands, and even his bare body have been assumed to hold the key to helping a patient to change. Currently, a three-way match or fit among doctor, patient, and the goals of therapy is assumed to be necessary for effective treatment. However, in the course of thirty or more years of discussions, two aspects of this well-fitting relationship have been repeatedly stated but resolutely unstudied. One is the mutuality of the doctor-patient relationship, including the changes — sudden and profound or gradual and subtle — that therapy promotes in clinicians. The other is the characteristic fervor of a good doctor-patient relationship. The illogical and deeply emotional forces that underlie the relationship have seemed too close to romantic love to investigate safely. Sometimes called suggestion (Chertok) or magic (E. Fuller Torry), animal magnetism (Mesmer), intimacy (Nouwen), and very occasionally love (Havens, Hillman), these pre- or nonverbal communications run silently between doctor and patient.

As we have seen, the idea that doctor and patient resonate to each other's vibrations so immediately and unintentionally alarms clinicians as well as patients. Thus Mesmer backed away from the idea that it was *his* presence and *his* animal magnetism that affected the women he treated. The glass wands and metal bars literally put some distance between him and his patients. When a young woman Freud was treating threw her arms around his neck in amorous gratitude — a shocking gesture in his day — he wondered, but only briefly, if it was *his* presence and *his* attributes to which she responded. His glass wand was called transference. Today, as those two glass wands lose their credibility, we invent another — professionalism — to hold at bay our fear of finding an elemental form of attraction between doctor and patient. All such explanations that "prove" that the nonrational portion of the doctor-patient bond isn't real, even before undertaking research, have hampered serious investigations into the way therapy works and are now threatening to limit relational therapy's explorations as well. Of course, there are other reasons for keeping a discussion of love out of therapy, and we will look at many of them.

In spite of a dearth of studies in this area, I will argue that some form of love is necessary to long-term therapy. Although many observations could be made to support this position, I will cite only two. One is that the doctor-patient relationship has many elements in common with the Western tradition of romantic or courtly love as formulated in medieval France. Both represent an ideal — and in the history of the world, an unusual — way of treating another person. The other is that the "work" that both the doctor-patient relationship and love itself do in the world is the creation of individuals. Although only some clinicians — such as developmental psychologists, psychoanalysts, and pastoral counselors — speak openly of love's role in the development of a self, I will argue that in all long-term therapy, love is the shaping and molding force that creates and then maintains what we call individuals. Just as climate determines the shape and structure of leaves on a tree and as wind determines whether little ripples or enormous waves will form on the water, so the love that we give and receive establishes our stance and character. Psychodynamic therapies in particular are devoted to nothing less than enhancing or even building individuals, and the fortunes of serious, long-term therapy will rise and fall with the value we place on the autonomous self. This is not a choice for clinicians to make but one that society as a whole will determine. Given all the discussion of the regulation of individual freedoms both in and out of psychotherapy — as a substitute for tradition, as a necessary accompaniment of growth, and as a tool of social justice — we must wonder whether a large, technologically advanced, and culturally diverse nation can also manage to accommodate the luxury of individuality. If the answer is no, then therapy will serve that answer by becoming a business contract between adviser and advisee, whose main purpose is to prevent people from straying too far into left field or staying there too long. However, if the answer is yes, and the advantages of having a willful, independent, and even eccentric citizenry outweigh the disadvantages, then doctors and patients will persist in creating relationships of attentive wonderment — loving, valuable, and risky. The last chapter closes with a double example of relational therapy, which illustrates the benefits and dangers of affection.

~~~

I once had a patient who could not talk about certain aspects of love. I can still see her. She had straight black hair that fell just past her ears, and her brown eyes looked at me as if from a great distance. Sitting across from me, she would square her broad shoulders in order to meet head-on whatever unsettling ideas were bound to come across the room. It was not immediately apparent what her difficulty was or, rather, what invisible obstacle sat between us and deflected our well-intentioned attempts to communicate. Back and forth we would range over her childhood and adulthood, picking up clues, but nothing that led anywhere. Her stories and my responses curved around something, and curving, we always ended up where we began.

One evening shortly before Christmas she returned to the treasured memories of her grandmother. She saw again the paper chains she had taped on the door of her grandmother's apartment and remembered again how willingly she left her own apartment with its Christmas tree and presents to visit her grandmother, who had nothing for her.

"When she died, I was twelve," my patient said.

"And?"

"And nobody cried. Not one person."

"How about you?"

"Oh," she said matter-of-factly, "that's when I picked up the habit of crying in my sleep. I don't cry when I'm awake, but every so often I wake up and my face is wet. My mother told me it started after Grandma died."

Too many clinicians are where my patient used to be. If we cannot acknowledge, examine, enjoy, and lament the love we feel for our patients, then that love becomes an obstacle that distorts more of our communication than we realize. We cannot talk to our patients honestly in the intimate hour if we pretend that the tensions and wonderment we sometimes feel in the room form a one-sided, not-quite-real bond. Nor can we talk to each other — male to female practitioner, traditional to feminist therapist, clinician to administrator, clinician to lawmaker. A great deal is at stake here. To ask if love has a legitimate role to play in psychotherapy is to put a vital question to our entire society. What is the best way of doing business with another person? Whatever our answer, we should not respond in our sleep.

8

*Women Refashion
Psychotherapy*

Where one's gift is, there will one's faith be also.
— *George Santayana*

In a poem about Orpheus, the poet Edward Hirsch wondered how the grieving husband of Eurydice knew where he was going in the underworld. He concluded that it was not by reasoning or even by seeing clearly but by attending to his feelings — "by the ache in his left side." It could be said that Orpheus navigated using his yearning heart as a compass.

Like him, many women believe that they are guided as truly by their hearts as by their heads. In some fields and in some times, this dual navigation system has been said to make women less reliably logical than men, but in the caring professions in the late twentieth century, it is generally recognized that heart and head work very nicely together. This is certainly the belief of women in psychotherapy, which makes it powerful indeed, for as psychiatrists, psychologists, social workers, professors, and administrators, these women are literally refashioning the field. Not only are they promoting a more supportive and egalitarian approach to therapy, but they are also paying closer attention to their feelings for their clients. Theories that explain emotional change only in terms of logic or chemicals are not enough, they say. The result has been the development of relational therapy. Clinicians who use this approach consider the relationship that evolves between doctor and patient of primary concern. In some ways, it is like paying attention to transference and countertransference, except that relational therapists see this connection as a real one in all respects. It is the distortions of this real relationship that alert the therapist to the kinds of trouble that the patient characteristically suffers or that the therapist herself may have, and it is the improvement or healing of this relationship that constitutes the core of the treatment. More radically still, relational therapists insist, at least in theory, that the work accomplished by the therapeutic relationship is mutual. Therapist and client are healed together or they go nowhere — together.

A change in philosophy, no matter how profound, is not enough by itself to refashion a field. What makes the impact of women's thinking on psychotherapy so great is their growing numbers. This unexpected shift — what some call the feminization of psychotherapy and others refer to as the resegregation of compassion — is both a cause and an effect of the economic changes that are transforming the talking cure from an expensive specialty provided by a few highly trained physicians to a less expensive and more routine service provided by great numbers of less formally trained counselors. While psychotherapy is now available to a far greater number of people, recent rounds of public and private belt-tightening are restricting both the number of sessions and the kinds of problem that agencies and insurance companies will cover. The so-called normal problems of living, such as marital discord or sibling rivalry, are no longer paid for unless they can be described as more serious emotional problems. The three changes together — a new philosophy, more women, and fewer dollars — are pushing and pulling psychotherapy into new forms and will significantly affect doctor-patient sexual entanglements.

Psychotherapy has already undergone several dramatic reorganizations in the past hundred years, and a thumbnail sketch of its history suggests that the nature of the patient population goes a long way toward determining who the therapists will be. For wealthy, hysterical women seeking treatment in the early years of the century, an attractive but fatherly doctor seemed the right choice. Socially, these women felt more comfortable confiding in a respected professional, and emotionally, they seemed better able to recognize their repressed sexual feelings with a male doctor. However, when psychiatry expanded to embrace the study and guidance of children, female clinicians seemed a natural choice. With the advent of World War II, soldiers and sailors became the largest single group of clients, primarily for psychological testing but also for treatment. To serve the recruits as well as the shell-shocked, male clinicians were quickly trained. Although there were only thirty-five psychiatrists in the Army Medical Corps at the end of 1941, more than four thousand physicians and psychologists were testing or treating veterans by the end of the war. Women were largely excluded as therapists by the armed services during the war years, but they began entering the field in the late 1940s as psychotherapy took on the man- or, rather, the woman-in-the-street in addition to the casualties of war. When the National Institute of Mental Health was created in 1949 and the Veterans' Administration began training programs for clinicians at about the same time, opportunities opened up for both men and women. Because most of the money spent on the mentally ill and emotionally disturbed still went for the care of hospitalized males — mainly schizophrenics — male doctors were still seen as the mainstay of clinical practice. But not for long.

In the 1950s and '60s both patients and treatments began to change. Therapies that differed markedly from psychoanalysis were introduced — for example, nonmedical forms of the talking cure such as Carl Rogers's client-centered or humanistic therapy at one end of the spectrum and medical techniques that relied solely on medication at the other. At the same time, mental hospitals were being closed down and chronic mental patients moved to halfway houses and treated at community mental health centers. Soon the bulk of funds earmarked for mental health went for the treatment of outpatients. Everyone, it seemed, wanted therapy, but women most of all: mothers wanted help raising their children, women wanted solace when relationships ended, divorcees wondered what had gone wrong, and widows puzzled over how to live without a husband. By the thousands women asked for therapy, and many wanted to talk with another woman, not a man.

The United States couldn't produce enough social workers, Ph.D.'s, or M.D.'s to keep up with the demand. Training centers in universities and hospitals opened and then expanded. Professional schools designed expressly to train clinicians were started. Especially in the 1970s, women as well as men flocked to the growing field. By the 1980s a veritable tide of these new clinicians was sweeping across the country to fill positions in clinics and mental health centers. Suddenly, however, the money that had supported this expansion of services began drying up. Under President Ronald Reagan, both the discretionary funds that individuals used to buy private therapy and the public funds that supported treatment for the disabled shrank by about 25 percent. At the same time, states cut their mental health budgets, and insurance companies redistributed benefits so that hospitalized patients and those on medication received more but outpatients less. Yet, as the funding for conventional psychotherapy went down, school admissions went up. Between 1975 and 1985, the number of clinicians holding M.D., M.S., and Ph.D. degrees doubled. By the end of this period, most of the new graduates were women.

The situation now, in the late 1990s, is that psychotherapy has become largely the province of females. The majority of psychiatrists is still male, but increasingly these doctors are leaving the practice of long-term psychotherapy for the more lucrative business of prescribing and monitoring medication. In other words, psychiatrists are doing less and less psychotherapy. This leaves the talking cure to psychologists, two thirds of whom are female, and to social workers and master's level counselors, whose membership is more than 70 percent female.* At the same time, the number of men applying to graduate school in these fields has been declining at the rate of 2 percent a year since the mid-1980s. Typically, a graduate class now has eight or more women and one or two men. For example, of the 101 master's-level mental health counselors who graduated from Boston College in 1995, 84 percent were women. Clearly, the field does not seem as attractive to men as it once did.

"There's just a certain attitude in the classroom that men are the enemy," said one male student who, like a member of any minority, feels invisible or as if his experience doesn't count. "Heterosexual men are accepted in the field only if they are, in a sense, demasculinized and impotent," said Ilene Philipson, who interviewed a large number of

---

* Until recently, the clergy has been overwhelmingly male. Nevertheless, by 1993 11 percent of pastors and priests were women. More and more women are seeking admission to seminaries, and with the exception of the Catholic Church, it looks as if women will soon equal or outnumber men.

students for her book *On the Shoulders of Women: The Feminization of Psychotherapy*. To the extent that either of these troubling statements is true, it suggests that as women gain control over psychotherapy, they will encourage the kind of men who seem least likely to exploit clients sexually. Will this exclude the Jungs, Ferenczis, and Perlses? Does it matter?

When men leave a profession it changes, and not for the better. As has happened in the past with bank tellers and book editors, for example, the pay goes down, the status drops, requirements for training relax, and the work itself becomes more routine. It is not pleasant to admit, but the most respected careers are associated with men. When they leave a profession, the money seems to go with them, and when this happens, the work tends to become deskilled, declassed, and degraded.* The men who remain in the field gravitate to managerial positions. In universities they are department heads. In clinics, they are directors. In psychology, in particular, the tension that has long existed between those who see themselves as scientists and those who see themselves as therapists has become increasingly associated with gender. In terms of common stereotypes, coldly objective males run programs staffed by touchy-feely females. This division leads some observers to say that the feminization of psychotherapy is a form of resegregation. Men handle business while women cope with feelings.

The present generation of therapists and counselors is well aware of these many changes. They no longer expect to start their careers earning an hourly rate of $100 while sitting in a gracious office treating attractive neurotics according to their own plans. Instead, they are far more likely to be working as fee-for-service clinicians; they will earn about $30 for each client they see while sitting in a concrete block

---

* This may sound harsh, but it's true. Deskilled refers to the lowering of admission requirements for graduate school. On average, students entering a field where $20,000 to $30,000 is a common starting salary will be less well educated — less skilled — than students applying for programs whose graduates can expect to earn $60,000 to $70,000 right away. Declassed refers to status. The title "psychologist" used to be considered important, but as numbers rise, salaries fall, and the title is increasingly associated with women, the status of the occupation drops. Degraded refers to the quality-of-life on the job itself. Most psychologists and psychiatrists are saying that "it's not as much fun anymore." I believe they are referring to the increasing restrictions and paperwork and the decreasing pay.

cubicle managing chronic patients on Medicaid according to someone else's plan for treatment.

That is the bad news. The good news is that women now form the majority of psychotherapists and are free to refashion the field to the extent that social and economic forces allow. Naturally, there are many agendas. One group calls for a spring cleaning. Locate and evict the bad apples, these women say, and make therapy a safe haven, free from all manner of abuse. Another group wants to rebuild the whole house rather than clean it. Their goal is social justice, and not only in psychotherapy. Still a third group is more interested in changing the therapeutic process itself. In some ways the three agendas pull together; in other ways they don't. When it comes to the question "Will the feminization of psychotherapy lead to a serious new investigation of the therapist-client bond?" there is considerable disagreement.

The spring cleaners are primarily concerned with controlling the lustful side of men. This is an old concern, and women have gone after this behavior in every arena, therapy included. In the professional literature, references to "tragic distortions," "the alarming topic," "the shocking practice," "the victimized patient," and of course to that "helpless figure . . . caught in the coils of a sexually abusing therapist" suggest that punishment and eviction are top priorities for certain authors. So does the acronym chosen by the Canadian Health Alliance to Stop Therapist Exploitation Now — CHASTEN — which literally means to correct by punishment or by suffering. Likewise, at a conference on countertransference given by Cambridge Hospital and the Harvard Medical School in 1994, a large portion of the time was spent listing possible diagnoses for therapists who act on attraction. When all their problems and perversions had been presented, a woman in the audience reflected the tone of the meeting by asking, "How can anyone rehabilitate abusive therapists? I mean, they're such slime. They've broken a sacred trust. I couldn't sit in the same room with them."

For the founders of BASTA as well, sexual desire is especially dangerous to the disenfranchised or powerless, and abusers need to be identified and forcefully swept out of the profession. Nancy Avery and her colleagues not only teach their clients to spot danger early — for example, by telling them that men in power first signal their sexual desire with a public gesture like a hug, which alerts every woman who witnesses it that this man is available for "something" — but they also explain that the public hug is one of the ways men "systematically program women for compliance." In other words, women are socialized to accept a great deal of seductive behavior, either without noticing it or without objecting to it by men who are the enemy. "We teach them about the snakes." Avery further believes that a woman is rarely wrong when she gets the feeling that "an authority" is staring at her or complimenting her in ways *he* finds personally satisfying. When a woman says abuse has occurred and a man says it hasn't, Avery sides with the woman. "We've seen it too often," she said. Until the imbalance of power between males and females is drastically reduced, women need to be given all the support they can get and the benefit of every doubt.

"And I am upset by that attitude," stated the psychiatrist from Georgia whose patient returned to her previous doctor and married him. From Dr. Johnson's point of view, good as well as bad male doctors are being singled out for punishment in a kind of backlash against men. The spring cleaning has gone too far. "We are putting each other on trial with the merest shreds of evidence. We are creating a climate where no one will take on the most difficult clients or make themselves vulnerable by going out on a limb. Now all the people I respect — or respected — either have lawsuits pending or have become Mr. Milquetoasts. What's the message to doctors? We'll punish you for taking risks on the patient's behalf."

For nearly forty years Dr. Johnson has taught clinical psychiatry in a large medical school. He also has a private practice — the old-fashioned kind, where patients work for years to learn where their problems come from and how to handle them differently. Using the experience gained in private practice to illustrate his lectures, Dr. Johnson used to tell his students that "I do things every day that could send me to court." Statements like this used to be common among clinical professors, and students soon realized their professors were trying to tell them something: a good doctor cannot rely entirely on accepted medical practices. Desperate people sometimes require desperate measures, and an experienced doctor will try a strange variety of techniques to reach a person in pain. "I don't say that anymore," Dr. Johnson said sharply. "I've become cynical about my profession."

Dr. Johnson's growing cynicism took a giant step forward three years ago, when he was accused of sexual misconduct. A woman who had been a patient of his for more than five years — "I'd kept her out of the hospital, and I was seeing her at a reduced rate" — threatened to complain to an ethics committee that Dr. Johnson wasn't paying *enough* attention to her. When she requested more frequent meetings, he disagreed. When she wanted longer meetings and tried to get them by refusing to leave his office, he called the police. When she began seeing a second therapist, he called it split care and insisted on gradually ending therapy with her. As Dr. Johnson sees it, termination was the last straw for the patient. She left in a rage, shouting from the waiting room that she would sue him. Months later, when he was in the hospital undergoing surgery, she made good on her threat. First she filed a complaint to the state psychiatric association and then to the state's Department of Registration, charging that Dr. Johnson had abused and deprived her — specifically, that he had fondled her when he had agreed to sit on a bench next to her for several minutes. Although admitting that those minutes sitting next to him were the "only time I felt soothed in my whole life," she also saw in them a promise of more attention, a promise the doctor did not fulfill.

Just out of the hospital, Dr. Johnson found himself in a four-round fight. In various ways he had to prove that he was blameless, first to his peers in the association, then to the state, next to his insurance company, and finally in a civil court of law. "I asked my friends who had gone through this what it was like. 'It's awful,' they told me. 'It will take up all your time and dominate your thinking. It becomes an obsession.'"

And so Dr. Johnson began three years of meetings and hearings. At times he was treated cordially. "Stop right there," the insurance inspector told him. "I know the rest of the story. Let me tell *you* what happened next." "And he did," said Dr. Johnson. "He knew the way these things play out. It was kinda reassuring." But at times he was treated like a low-life criminal by his peers.

"You have forty-five minutes," a psychiatrist said as she turned on a tape recorder. "Talk."

"I don't belong here," Johnson thought to himself over and over again as the machine hummed. "I am not being asked for information. I am being punished by people who actually do not want to know anything about me, my patient, or the case."

That was an eye-opener. Johnson felt he'd been slammed onto the wrong conveyor belt and was being ground up. He guessed that his patient was going through much the same ordeal. *"No one is listening,"* he said in horrified amazement.

Dr. Johnson eventually battled his way through all four rounds of the fight. He emerged with a reprimand (for not keeping conventional records), a whopping bill from two attorneys, a dropped suit, and a broken heart.

"This is *my* organization," he said of the Georgia Psychiatric Association. "These are *my* people — I trained half of them — and they put me on trial. They know me. They know my reputation, and yet no one trusts anyone anymore. I am so upset by this loss of trust. I would not go to medical school today — not the way things are now."

While there is another side to this story, as we have seen, patients as well as doctors complain that the process by which allegations of sexual misconduct are investigated is brutally punishing. In short, when punishment rather than mutual understanding is the goal, both doctors and patients feel deeply wronged. Dr. Betz, the psychologist from a Pacific Northwest board of examiners, feels that we will see more complaints in the near future and that many will feel like punishments to both doctor and patient. He is sad about the misunderstandings but glad that therapy is being cleaned up. Men like Dr. Johnson, on the other hand, suspect that the cost of a totally sanitized therapy is the exile of male therapists and the adoption of defensive, no-risk practices. The new problems that are bound to follow, he said, will not make many people happy, including women.

~~~

For other feminist psychotherapists, getting sex out of therapy is only a small part of a much larger program, just as punishment is a small part of social justice. Believing that all psychotherapy delivered to a woman by a man, even the most ethical, is sexist in that it represents an attempt by a powerful member of society to manipulate someone less powerful, some feminists are hoping to overturn the old social order, which protects men's interests above all else. But how are they to do this from their consulting rooms and university offices?

For them, the education of young women is a top priority. When they get together to discuss today's "climate of real intimidation" or to insist that "male domination is the severest illness in our country," one of the questions they examine most closely is, What forces people to behave decently? These women correctly understand that social justice cannot rest on rules and reprimands alone. When an imbalance or injustice is held in place by deep feelings such as greed, anger, and lust or, as some would say, by genetic programming, something stronger is needed — taboos. Taboos are more effective than regulations because the consequences are more serious. Disobey a law, and the result is a fine or imprisonment, but break a taboo, and the result is expulsion from the community. The current arrangement of taboos protects men first and women and children second, but feminists are trying to rearrange them. Understanding the taboos that keep our social order steady — always unfair to some, but steady — helps to explain further both the form and the fury of the debate surrounding doctor-patient sex.

Generally thought of as sacred prohibitions, taboos exist in every culture to protect both the strongest and the weakest members of society. For example, social stability was maintained for centuries in the Western world by making it a serious transgression to challenge the belief that the white patriarch should lead and direct the lives of everyone else. In some parts of the world it would have been shocking even to consider a different arrangement. That two women could raise a family, for example, or that a black man could hold political office seemed so threatening as to be unthinkable. These arrangements would have broken a taboo. At the same time, it was considered desirable to protect women, children, and minorities — the weakest members of society. "The rule of thumb," for example, stated that a husband was not to beat his wife with anything that exceeded the diameter of his thumb. Ludicrous as it sounds today, it was considered protection, and the rule put into words a taboo that existed against brutish violence. However, the first activity — bringing down or replacing a white male — was so much more threatening to the social order that men were protected far more vigorously than women, children, or minorities. So taboos protect the individuals that society deems are of greatest value first, and only then do complementary taboos extend protection to others.

In an astonishingly short time — as social changes go, in the blink of an eye — some taboos are being rearranged. In certain small groups they are even being reversed, so that *any* instance of abuse to a woman, child, or member of a minority is considered more serious than dismantling a white man's career. Just as the Victorian patriarch's word went unquestioned a hundred and fifty years ago, now some employers just as automatically believe the client, not the therapist or clergy. By and large, this is a great relief to women and their children, who for centuries had no voice with which to express their mistreatment. Although the majority still find it difficult to get what they feel is an unbiased hearing, a few women in a few situations find that the advantage has passed to them. The new protection has, however, a rather unexpected cost.

One of the consequences of regulating a society with taboos is that certain hypocrisies become prevalent because they function as pressure valves. When the white patriarch was protected by taboos that made it demonic or perverted to think of replacing him, he was forced to hide activities that tarnished his image as the good and essential citizen. If he could not live up to the ideal image of a provider and instead had a mistress or read pornography or was intractably lazy, he was obliged to pretend that he spent all his time being the good family man. He went to the club. He dozed behind a newspaper. He hid his mistress. At the very least, he dressed the part of the good man who deserved respect. He became a hypocrite.

Now, as a new arrangement of taboos evolves and women are given increased protection, they too must pay a price. They must try or at the very least pretend to fit the image of the woman-worthy-of-protection. We all know who she is: kind, nurturing, and somewhat childlike, she never maliciously invites sex or violence down upon her — ever. She is an innocent person rather than villainous or dangerous. If she becomes entangled in a steamy affair with her analyst, she must adopt the role of blameless victim if she wants the new protection. If she refuses this role and presents herself (or is presented) as a hungry, wild, and passionately self-centered Bacchante, for example, she will be denied the protection. Considered a pervert who threatens the good name of all women, she will be thrown out of the community. When Dr. Margaret Bean-Bayog wrote sadomasochistic sexual fantasies about Paul Lozano, she stepped outside the image of a woman-worthy-of-protection. Obscenities were painted on her car. Women insulted her in the supermarket. She received hate mail and obscene phone calls. As one of her biographers,

Gary Chafetz, remarked, "She pushed all the hot-button topics, not the least of which was female sexuality. It's not acceptable in our country for an older woman to fantasize about a younger man the way she did."

So the protection of taboos has a price. Just as the protection of regulations against specific social injustices both helps and hurts the same individuals — making it more likely that I will have a profession, for example, but limiting my freedom within that profession — so taboos constrict the behavior of the same women they protect. To complicate this picture still further, there is no simple revolution going on, with power being taken from males and given to females. Instead, there is a proliferation of social revolutions, and it becomes increasingly difficult to generalize about American values or to reach a consensus. There is no longer a single set of clearly recognized taboos for everyone — nor is there likely to be. For better or worse, a problem like doctor-patient sex must be dealt with by people who remain divided in their allegiances in complicated ways.

~~~

In addition to punishing the bad apples and, more broadly, changing conventions, the new female practitioners have also sought to change the therapeutic process itself by focusing on relationships. Making their presence felt first in marriage and family therapy, female theorists and practitioners have virtually taken over this field. In the 1980s the big names were men; today the leaders are women. Even as clinicians are urged by managed care companies to trim therapy to a kind of problem-solving technique, women have insisted that a client's ability to relate to others be studied. They maintain that being in an authentic relationship is the core of a person's life, and that women, especially, live within networks of these relationships. They are the natural teachers, therefore, of this essential skill.

As might be expected, the relational model of psychotherapy emphasizes being rather than doing, supporting rather than challenging, and mothering rather than fathering. "Above all," wrote Philipson in her overview, "psychotherapy is seen as a collaborative effort, not founded in objectivity and detachment, but empathy and engagement. The relational model's understanding of the clinical situation, therefore, corresponds much more readily to what is traditionally thought of as women's ways of being in the world." In other words, therapy is supposed to offer the client a real relationship with the therapist. They are "healing partners." Filling in for both a good mother and a comforting friend, the relational therapist helps her client form a collaborative relationship, which in turn becomes a foundation for further explorations for both of them. As Ferenczi said of mutual analysis, certain phases "represent the total giving up of all force and all authority on both sides. They give the impression of two children of the same age, who have been terrified, and who tell each other about their experiences. Because they have the same fate, they understand each other completely, and instinctively seek to comfort each other."

And they are open with each other. "I find you attractive" or "I feel tired when you arrive, as if I anticipate the burden you carry" are fine statements for the new relational therapist to make. Attempting to guide but never to gain power over her client, she tries to find and then walk the thin line that separates the kind professional from the therapist who is actually a friend and thus caught in a dual relationship. But can this actually be done? As Ferenczi knew and as the detailed study of any single case of relational therapy quickly reveals, guiding another person without exerting power over him or her represents a radical departure from conventional therapy. Although a few therapists deny that there is a conflict between being professional and being in a real relationship, my impression is that many relational therapists say they are collaborating as equals but are actually guiding and taking responsibility for what goes on in therapy, as if they were still the senior partners they have always been.

In spite of the difficulties involved in setting therapy up as a discussion between equals, some women devoted to relational therapy insist that the risk of slipping into a dual relationship — be it a friendship or even an erotic liaison — is no more dangerous than the risk of humiliation and manipulation that is part of conventional therapy.

"All life-giving relationships are infused with both erotic power and danger," maintained the Reverend Ms. Carter Heyward in a book about her own unsatisfactory therapy. *When Boundaries Betray Us* describes her attempt to establish an authentic relationship with a therapist who did not think it wise to risk the danger. Eventually Heyward came to the conclusion that for her, at least, the absence of a true relationship was more harmful than the unpredictable twists and turns that might occur as such a relationship evolved. This is the heart of relational philosophy.

Heyward brought to therapy a question that women often bring to a new lover — and to a therapist. "Is all the energy and intensity I feel," they ask, "proof that I am a passionate woman with armloads of gifts to give? Or am I actually a desperately hungry woman with a frightening number of needs?" It is a tricky question, so closely intertwined are love and foolishness, and so dependent is the answer on what has been created by two personalities, not just one. It is also an important question to answer — one that can haunt an entire life if not addressed.

Heyward had been wrestling with this question in all its various forms since her adolescence. Describing herself as "an overly enthusiastic teenage dyke, a young adoring woman who needed more than they [her teachers] could give," she had repeatedly thrown herself at "a big, strong woman," only to be rebuffed. "Again and again, I had been sent away, ashamed of being so needy and, evidently, too demanding." Was she "crazy," she began to ask herself, or simply a passionate woman in a culture that fears the force of love? When Heyward turned forty-two, she entered therapy to find out. She was tired and sad at this time in her life, anxious to guide her future onto a better track. She called a lesbian psychiatrist whose name had been given to her and explained her predicament.

Heyward's eighteen months of therapy got off to a wonderful start, but for reasons that many therapists would be uncomfortable just thinking about. "I'd found my helper," Heyward said to herself twenty minutes into the first meeting; later she realized that she had responded to three feelings. First, she felt relaxed around this doctor, whom she calls Elizabeth Farro. Second, she sensed Farro's "strong desire" to work with her — the doctor was intrigued. And third, Heyward had a clear sense that the relationship that would develop between them would be mutual. She would give to her doctor as well as get, teach as well as learn. They were embarking on this journey together.

For several months Heyward poured out her troubles and frustrations to Farro and left the office each week feeling lighter and stronger. She was growing to love this woman, she thought. Well, not exactly love, she corrected herself, but she was certainly transferring that mountain of passion and hope that had so bedeviled her in the past onto her doctor.

Because she herself was often the recipient of this kind of adoration from the young seminarians she taught in divinity school, she recognized a transference when she saw one. So did Dr. Farro. "It's important that I be clear with you and that you understand me," Farro told Heyward when she first mentioned that she hoped they would eventually grow beyond the transference and become friends. "Since we met here in this office, we will not be friends. Ours is a professional relationship. Is that clear?"

Heyward stared at her blankly as confusion and rejection hit her broadside. Had she merely imagined that the two were helping and healing each other? That they were *both* excited and pleased by these weekly visits? Was she *that* crazy? But perhaps the problem lay in a different direction. Was therapy a journey with so many restrictions that the therapist couldn't genuinely like or love the client regardless of how the client felt about her doctor? Heyward stopped her car on the way home from Farro's office and thought. Was this or was it not a *real relationship?* She didn't want a virtual relationship or an "as if" relationship or a you-can-like-me-and-I'll-pretend-to-like-you relationship. She wanted the real thing.

During the next several months Heyward became increasingly frustrated. At first she told herself that Farro would come around to her point of view and see that mutuality, the shared journey, was the basis of all authentic relationships both in and out of therapy. "Intuitively, I knew that any relationship that cannot, on principle, grow more fully mutual is not a right or trustworthy relationship," she wrote in her journal. Although she did not know it, she was raising for Farro exactly those issues that a patient had raised for Ferenczi more than fifty years earlier. This woman had challenged Ferenczi to tell her the truth — namely, that he didn't like her — and his eventual willingness to admit that she was right not only prevented her despair (she said) but also gave the therapy its first real chance to work. Ferenczi concluded that patients actually know how the doctor feels about them and that they want love and comfort from him. He agreed to his patient's request for mutual analysis — another name for a fully mutual relationship — and also managed to extract himself and his patient from this level of intimacy when it was time to turn his attention to others. But it was neither safe nor easy. Nevertheless, Ferenczi believed it essential to tolerate "the unbearable upheaval" of being honest. He must love his patients *and* do the hangman's work of disabusing them of the fantasy that his love was the ultimate answer to their problems. Anything less, he said, was a game.

Unfortunately for both Heyward and Farro, their therapy evolved into just such a game. The harder Heyward pushed for friendship, the more stubbornly formal Farro became, until the old scenario that had sent Heyward into therapy in the first place was repeating itself in every detail. The confusion between passion and neediness again rose up to torment her. Apparently she was too demanding for everyone, even a therapist.

Inadvertently, Heyward performed an interesting experiment on her own therapy. For a few months she gave up her own point of view and behaved as a client is supposed to behave. Gradually the focus of the treatment shifted from her concern for her therapist's friendship to an episode of child abuse that might have happened — probably happened. Almost certainly happened? It was a long and ultimately futile detour, but during this period Heyward felt a confusing blend of reassurance and humiliation — her reward for fitting into Farro's conventional framework. The two were in step now, a team. As Farro led and Heyward followed, both looked for abusive episodes in Heyward's past. Yet for the first time Heyward "began to believe I really was in some way crazy." When she abruptly returned to her demand for friendship, her doctor became furious and blew up.

The therapy ended on a sour note. As far as Farro was concerned, Heyward was a spoiled brat who insisted on getting her own way. Heyward felt that Farro was unbending *and* dishonest. Not only had her rigid control led to what Heyward calls abusive therapy, but Farro did not have the courage to say that she felt so powerfully drawn to Heyward that she was afraid of getting in over her head. Had she admitted this, Heyward wrote, "It would have been an altogether different kind of wound — inflicted by love and loss rather than by such an experience of emotional betrayal and relational contempt." (It is worth noting that this is the same distinction that was so important to Spielrein and many others. If the therapist admitted his affection, then the wound from impossible love was tolerable. If he refused to acknowledge his feelings, then he contemptuously betrayed the relationship.)

"It is important that . . . those of us who work as healers . . . understand how badly abusive we can be by withholding intimacy and authentic emotional connection from those who seek our help," Heyward concluded. "For 'abuse' is not simply a matter of touching people wrongly. It is [also] a refusal to touch people rightly. We . . . are as likely to destroy one another and ourselves by holding tightly to prescribed role definitions as we are by active intrusion and violation."

Heyward is by no means the only patient to assert that a therapist's refusal to acknowledge love is a form of abuse. When the British clinician Janice Russell gathered clients together for a research project on sexual abuse, one woman claimed that her therapist mishandled the erotic feelings in therapy so badly that "he really made me feel like an idiot." When this woman admitted to her therapist that she had a crush on him, he refused to make house calls, ripped up a love letter that she sent him, and told her that she was embarrassing him. Constance Dalenberg has observed this same disastrous humiliation when therapists flirt, then deny any feelings of affection. And in the next chapter we will see still another woman, the psychologist Annie Rogers, who felt so betrayed and abandoned when her therapist refused to discuss their mutual feelings of affection that she went back into therapy to sort out her feelings about love in the intimate hour so that she would neither hurt nor seduce the patients she loved.

The philosopher George Santayana wrote that "where one's gift is, there will one's faith be also." Women, with their age-old gift of forming and maintaining relationships, are putting their faith in the restorative power of true connection — be that friendship, collaboration, love, or the interlocking web of dual relationships we call community. In so doing, they are beginning to examine the role that love plays in therapy. This is an enormous step forward. As a number of top clinicians go about the work of refashioning psychotherapy, they are asking, How can love be included and acknowledged in the intimate hour without leading to abuse? Clearly these women are not out to deregulate desire, but their appreciation of affectionate bonds is leading them to reconsider the traditional boundaries between therapist and client. At the same time, some of their colleagues, especially those I refer to as spring cleaners, propose the opposite. Using professionalism as the latest bundling board or glass wand to separate all therapists from all clients at all times, they believe that boundaries formed by rules, ethics, and laws are needed to keep love out of the consulting room and to punish offenders. For them, a serious reexamination of why more than three quarters of all therapists say they are sexually attracted to clients at some point in their career is a sneaky way of opening a door they have worked very hard to shut.

What is likely to happen? My feeling is that, on balance, relational therapists will be far more open about love in therapy, especially in the increasingly common situation where both doctor and patient are women. They are likely to learn a lot, not about all kinds of love, but about the maternal and fraternal alliances that develop in treatment. Conceptualizing therapy as the ministrations of a compassionate parent and thus setting up the powerful taboo against incest as a barrier against acting on desire, many female clinicians will find it easier than men to address the varied attractions they feel in the intimate hour. However, I do not believe their new willingness to discuss love will be extended to male-female bonds, nor are male clinicians in a position to remedy this exclusion. They are already too vulnerable to accusations of abuse. Also working against the possibility of an open discussion are the socioeconomic changes in therapy itself — its takeover by women and the substantially shorter length of most treatment. Both are likely to reduce the incidence of sexual entanglement between therapist and client. As this happens, and the number of unethical therapists sinks toward the .4 or 0 percent level found when female clinicians are studied, doctors and patients will breath a sigh of relief, and any pressure to discover why entanglements occur will dwindle. Other problems, such as how fatherless adolescent boys and chronic male schizophrenics can be treated by women when male clinicians are in short supply, are already replacing sexual problems and coopting the interest of serious researchers. Nonetheless, the question of what role love plays in therapy will always remain even if it is not actively studied. After all, therapy is merely an extension of natural processes — our attempt to speed up or intensify Everyman's capacity to rebound from grief and misfortune. Thus therapists must always work the way people themselves work, with their heads and their hearts. The emphasis placed on love or logic — intimacy or business contracts — fluctuates with the times, and therapy will both influence and be influenced by our culture's choice of how to relate to each other in the next century.

9

The Active Ingredients
of the Intimate Hour

The quality of the therapeutic relationship has consistently been shown to be more important than the therapist's theoretical outlook.

— *Kalman Glantz and John Pearce*

You have to be nuts about your patient if it's going to work. . . . Hate isn't bad. That's another expression of intense interest, but neutrality or indifference won't accomplish a thing.

— *Max Day*

The idea that a therapist can cure his patient with love is alarmingly naive.

— *Glen Gabbard*

At the end of our tour through erotic entanglements, we are left with three questions: Is a close doctor-patient bond essential to effective therapy? Is love a part of that bond? And if so, why can't we say so? If the answers to the first two of these complex but not unanswerable questions are both no, the way is clear to try to get love and sex out of therapy; but if the answers are both yes, then we need to understand and manage the affection rather than throw it out or pretend it is something else. In other words, if we can even approximately define the role that love may play in therapy, we will know whether the primary question that now faces doctors and patients is: How can we keep love *in* therapy but manage its excesses? Or, how can we get love and attraction *out* and still be helpful?

Although many researchers have discussed the paternal and fraternal affections that develop between doctor and patient, few have dared to inquire what part personal magnetism, charisma, passion, and the like play in therapy. Throughout the history of the talking cure, it has been assumed that these strong and unreasonable emotions are too close to sexual desire to have any place in the treatment room. Not only the public but clinicians as well have been squeamish about the role of love. As Chertok asserted in a paper on Mesmer, "The appearance of sexuality continues to be an obstacle, a stumbling block, preventing researchers and practitioners from pursuing their investigations." In the few instances where clinicians have suggested that therapy rests on intense mutual affection, their ideas have been swept under the rug.

Although we have repeatedly backed away from doctor-patient attraction, there is nonetheless an enormous literature on what doctors supposedly do *to* their clients to fix them. These studies provide at least a partial picture of what makes therapy work and give us a sampling of the kinds of active ingredients that doctors have considered over the years. "Outcome studies" try to determine what therapy does to the people who seek it. The data gathered from interviews, questionnaires, symptom checklists, and observations are notoriously difficult to interpret, and it is not surprising that in the past forty or fifty years, several waves of research on what makes therapy work have come booming onto the beach. Depending on the focus of the investigations — the client, the illness, the technique, the social context, or even the therapist — and on the concepts of cure and improvement being used, these studies have come up with vastly different prescriptions for good therapy.

The apparent indecision about what fixes patients is in large part due to the elusive nature of the term "doing better." Often the client, the therapist, and the client's family have contradictory expectations of what ought to happen. For example, a seventeen-year-old may view successful treatment as convincing her parents to lift all curfews, her therapist may be aiming to keep the girl in school, and the parents want her to start obeying their rules. In addition to these different definitions of "fix," an accurate measurement of doing or feeling better is unbelievably tricky. Few studies follow patients and controls (people similar to the patients but receiving no therapy) for five or ten years after treatment to see if the help or the harm persists. Nor do many studies manage to circumvent "the demand effect," the powerful tendency for clients to tell investigators (or tests) what they think they want to hear. Even among the handful of sophisticated studies that have been undertaken, few manage to combine patients' subjective feelings, performance in the family and on the job, and clinicians' impressions into meaningful profiles of change. These are only a few of the difficulties that beset "outcome research." Nevertheless, some forty years of investigations have yielded several generalizations.

In 1952 the British researcher H. J. Eysenck rocked the clinical world by publishing a paper showing that therapy did not work. Reviewing nineteen studies of psychotherapy, he concluded that the passage of time was just as good as treatment. Stung, other therapists jumped into outcome research, and soon many were criticizing Eysenck's work. For example, many of his controls had actually been hospitalized and thus, it was argued, had received informal therapy from hospital staff. When larger, more sophisticated reviews were made of many hundreds of psychotherapy studies, it was found (to everyone's relief) that therapy was helpful after all. At least for most people with most kinds of problems, it was more helpful than no therapy at all. What clinicians were surprised to learn, however, was how little therapies differed in their ability to help. Whether a behaviorist set up a step-by-step plan to encourage an anorexic to eat or an analyst listened from behind a couch, the patient felt better and ate more. Nor did it matter much how long the doctor and patient took to discuss the problem. Even people seen once and put on a waiting list felt better just thinking about the help they were going to receive. Of course, there were individual exceptions, but when a thousand or more cases were combined and the average effects rather crudely considered, it seems that many kinds and amounts of therapy were helpful. (In 1995, a *Consumer Reports* survey of seven thousand people showed that long-term treatment was more effective than short-term treatment.)

But how helpful? Clinicians began to ask themselves if it was fair to say that therapy for an anxious, hysterical woman like Sabina Spielrein was successful if it enabled her to leave the asylum and enter medical school but left her overcome by leaden feelings of depression and occasional thoughts of suicide?

The argument over how much therapy helps the average patient is a long one, and it generally pits the practicing clinician against the academic researcher. Clinicians generally feel that therapy can take care of between 70 and 80 percent of a patient's presenting problems or symptoms, whereas researchers, with their more rigorous techniques but more limited contact with patients, feel on average that 30 percent improvement is a more realistic expectation. Both agree, however, that therapy is more helpful than no therapy at all.

That almost any kind and amount of therapy can produce modest improvement in a patient was not an easy pill for clinicians to swallow, but more difficult still was the finding that the therapist's formal training counted for little. Certain people were naturally good therapists, the studies suggested. Others were not. But formal training and degrees did not change the latter into the former. As had been shown as early as 1979, in a small but neatly designed experiment that compared the results of therapy provided by experienced doctors to that provided by college professors with no formal training, it didn't matter who did the listening as long as they listened well. Hundreds of studies have now been run on this aspect of outcome research, and, *on average,* the thousands of people involved did just as well with a college professor or concerned housewife as with a social worker, psychologist, or psychiatrist. This is not to say that there is no difference among clinicians, only that formal training in techniques — the ability to write behavioral contracts or to interpret the transference or to score a Rorschach inkblot test — does not seem to be what helps the patient. Exceptionally good clinicians are found among medically trained psychoanalysts, and exceptionally good ones are found among mental health aides with two years of college.

But if the mastery of specific skills and theories isn't essential to a therapist's success, what is? The active ingredients discovered thus far fall into two broad categories — the personal relationship that develops between doctor and patient, and the quicker, often nonverbal interventions such as laying on of hands, being put on a waiting list, receiving a prescription, and confession. Although a two- or three-year relationship with a therapist differs enormously from being put on a waiting list, both help. For example, when the search for the active ingredient of therapy got under way in the 1960s and '70s, one of the ideas examined was that psychotherapy helps because it is a secular form of confession.

Another idea was that the physical presence of the doctor — his magnetism or strength of character, not his ability to relate — had the power to cure. Although neither idea is particularly popular today, recent research has shown that, indeed, sitting alone in a room relating distressing events *to a tape recorder that is not turned on* or writing a letter that will never be sent but that nonetheless is full of emotional details, makes people feel better. Specifically, this kind of private confession, if made with feeling, reduces tension, enhances the functioning of the immune system, and reduces visits to the infirmary. Something similar takes place when the powerful doctor makes a physical appearance. A doctor is both an amulet and a placebo, and we know now that the hope that these symbols raise actually causes helpful chemical changes in the believer.*

The physical presence of the doctor — the handshake, the laying on of hands, the "gift" of a prescription, or the ritual massage — are still popular components of psychological healing in many countries, as is confession. Each seems to help by reducing tensions and raising hopes. Nonetheless, neither is usually enough by itself to change profoundly the way a patient sees himself or interacts with the world. For that, a personal relationship must be formed with someone (although not necessarily a therapist), and like the new language or dialect that a different kind of relationship actually is, it must be practiced, practiced, practiced.

Before outcome research tentatively explored the idea that the relationship is the active ingredient of therapy, simpler studies focused on the personalities of effective therapists. Dozens of investigations revealed that three general qualities are characteristic of effective therapists — accurate empathy, nonpossessive warmth, and genuineness. In other words, the ability to manage complex human relationships is the essential skill of a good therapist. No one claims that this ability is the only ingredient of successful therapy, but it is likely to be present when

* There is a disturbing story by Franz Kafka in which peasants roughly strip a doctor and force him to lie with a sick youth in a desperate attempt to cure a dying boy. Outside, children are playing in the heavy snow and singing: "Strip his clothes off, then he'll heal us, / If he doesn't, kill him dead! / O be joyful, all you patients, / The doctor's laid with you in bed!" One of Kafka's points was that the doctor has no control over what his patients believe about his powers. (Franz Kafka, "A Country Doctor," in Richard Reynolds and John Stone, eds., *On Doctoring: Stories, Poems, Essays* [New York: Simon & Schuster], pp. 96–100.)

good things happen. Ineffective therapists, on the other hand, are characterized as authoritarian. Seeming to know what is right for the patient beforehand, these therapists shame their clients into facing their failures and push them into uncomfortable changes. Studies have also been made of the personalities of successful and unsuccessful clients; to no one's surprise, it was found that, on average, the healthier a client is to begin with, the better he or she will feel after therapy. The clients most in demand came to be known as YAVIS — young, attractive, verbal, intelligent, and successful.

Most recently, attention has turned from the exclusive study of either therapist or client and has begun to focus on the relationship. Successful therapy is now seen as a three-way fit among doctor, patient, and the goal toward which they wish to work. Not only must the relationship between doctor and patient be understanding, warm, and genuine — and one that takes place where the patient is comfortable on the stairway — but the two must also agree on both the general and specific aims of their exploration. In terms of therapy's specific aims, is the clinician being called on to help a child deal with a sudden fear of going to school? Or to ameliorate the tension that pervades an entire family? Is a doctor being asked to comfort? Get a patient back to work? Prevent a divorce? Such goals are often spelled out early in therapy, increasingly so as managed care companies stress the economic aspects of improvement. Getting better often means staying out of the hospital and being back on the job. This may seem mercenary, but it is consistent with the philosophy of insurance companies in other fields. Medical doctors are far less likely to be reimbursed for training patients to adopt healthier ways of living than for helping them meet their responsibilities in spite of smoking, overeating, and not exercising.

When it comes to identifying the broader, underlying goal of therapy, there is no such precision. Partly it is the result of psychotherapy's curious pluralism. There are dozens upon dozens of recognized schools of thought, each with a different approach to therapy and a different long-term goal. Love, work, feel better, grow up — it is difficult to get clinicians to agree on a single, overarching goal. Some speak of enhancing a patient's "true self" so that individuals become clearer, truer versions of themselves. Some talk of autonomy and differentiation, some of remaining in a "right relationship." But the grand goal remains vague. There is no standard test to measure overall progress that is recognized by all psychotherapists. Symptom checklists, on which a client checks off such bothersome symptoms as insomnia, dry mouth, racing thoughts, and fatigue, are used to measure one kind of progress as are ratings of independent living, which equate well-being with the ability to care for oneself. Usually, however, the deep or underlying goals of therapy go unmeasured and unspecified except in the most general way. But they still have to fit. Doctor and patient have to agree on how therapy can lead toward a good enough life. Thus, in a productive three-way fit, the doctor's and the patient's general and specific expectations of what therapy is supposed to do fit together, their personalities work together, and their philosophies of life are compatible.

"But how can I tell if the patient and I make a good match?" asked a young therapist at a seminar given by the Boston psychoanalyst Max Day. "What's the signal I'm looking for?"

"I'm crazy about the patient and the patient is crazy about me," replied Dr. Day promptly. "That's the signal. It takes about ten seconds to say to yourself, 'I want to be with this person.' If this attraction doesn't take place, don't see them."

"Attraction?" replied the intern in a horrified voice.

"Human interest. Enthusiasm," Dr. Day said with a smile. "The therapist's enthusiasm is essential. Her communication that *you* are important, *this therapy* is important, *I* am important — it's this conviction that is one of the most potent ingredients in the cure. Some therapists concentrate on the damnedest things, but if they have enthusiasm and conviction — it works."

So therapy, with its accurate empathy and nonpossessive warmth, is not just any old relationship between two people who fit together but a high-energy, enthusiastic relationship between doctor and patient — a mutual investment made by two people who want to spend time together. This is "the undeniable bond" that Mesmerists spoke of and "the somnambulist passion" that hypnotists observed. Dr. Day suggests that it doesn't much matter what the therapist calls this investment — behavior modification, suggestion, analysis — or even what the therapist thinks he or she is investing — encouragement, instruction, affection — as long as the doctor brings to the task a certain heartfelt fervor.

Thinking back to clinicians like Jung, Ferenczi, Rank, and even

Douglas and Dr. Norman, we have seen that a mutual investment of personal energy and concern has characterized private practice in many periods of psychotherapy. It has been far less common in public psychiatric hospitals, where until recently the only relationships with patients were assumed to be distant and formally structured. However, a few clinicians have now begun focusing on respectful personal relationships even on the back wards. In one article, "Client as Colleague," it was suggested that among the chronically and profoundly ill, doctor and patient do best when they decide together who the patient wishes to become, what changes need to be made if this is to happen, and how to proceed.

Still another acknowledgment of the importance of the relationship is found in a recent study of what patients remember of therapy. Several years after their treatment, it was discovered that clients remembered being particularly helped by — of all things — calling their therapist by his or her first name and hearing stories from the therapist's life. These clients had forgotten the relief they may have felt from confessing or the reassurance they gained from learning, but they remembered the relationship — the part that felt mutual.

The emphasis placed on the doctor-patient relationship is not merely a Western phenomenon. In comparing witch doctors to psychiatrists, E. Fuller Torrey pointed out that the details and duration of the relationship may vary enormously, from patients in Africa who move into the homes of their doctors for several years to patients who see the doctor only briefly — but it is always a relationship. Torrey maintained that "although some therapists strive to keep their own personality out of the therapy, they are never entirely successful. In all cultures of the world, therapy remains a relationship between two people."

One more aspect of this relationship needs to be discussed before we compare therapy to love. This is mutuality. It is easy to slide over the term "doctor-patient relationship" without stopping to think what therapy means for the doctor. Everyone knows that the patient will be affected by the therapist; in fact, many patients talk as if they have made room inside themselves to carry the therapist around with them. And clinicians can be heard talking unself-consciously among themselves about "the honeymoon period" with a new client or an abrupt "divorce" that occurred when a client walked out of the office. This sounds as if they too are solidly part of the relationship. But are doctors really affected by patients? Do they let them inside?

Two well-known healers, Bruno Bettelheim and Henri Nouwen, used a great variety of metaphors for healing, but the one each returned to again and again was hospitality — the hosts or hostesses and their guests. "You ought to prepare for a new patient the way you prepare for an honored guest in your home," Bettelheim used to tell his students. Or from Nouwen: "This hospitality . . . requires that he allow others to enter his life, come close to him and ask him how their lives connect with his. Nobody can predict where this will lead us, because every time a host allows himself to be influenced by his guests he takes a risk not knowing how they will affect his life. But it is exactly in common searches and shared risks that new ideas are born, that new visions reveal themselves, and that new roads become visible."

Therapists can be dramatically changed by their clients. Two stories have stuck in my mind. One comes from the past. Long ago, just as therapy started mixing science into its art, one Johann Christoph Blumhardt was called on to exorcise a girl who people believed was possessed and whom we would call psychotic. Blumhardt confronted the girl, who flew at him in a rage and tried to destroy him. Using only the power of his mind, Blumhardt cured her. Then, he said, the real story began, for while she went on to learn about the workings of the mind — in fact, she became his assistant — he was transformed still more completely. He reported that he became an utterly changed man with a great faith in Jesus, who, he said, had helped him cure the patient.

The second story is modern and involves a psychoanalyst who had a profitable practice and a fine reputation. He was known to be bright, conscientious, and caring, and people would wait for months to become his patient. Gradually, however, he began making strange accusations, to the point that patients complained and his wife became alarmed. She urged him to seek treatment himself, but he refused. Soon he believed that everyone was out to get him. In desperation, his wife begged one of his colleagues to help. This man entered treatment with the troubled analyst, and for an hour every day he pretended to struggle with an insidious paranoia that was gradually taking over his mind. The analyst became fascinated by his colleague's terrible problem. Yes, he said, he thought he could help him. In the process, he cured himself.

Every clinician I have told this story to responds with a similar, although less dramatic, version. All of us have found ourselves giving patients earnest explanations of feelings or behavior that we notice with a shiver are equally apt for ourselves. And we have all given advice or interpretations that, unbeknownst to the client, are being urged on both doctor and patient simultaneously. "The psychotherapy relationship is two-sided, whether we acknowledge it or not," wrote Annie Rogers in *A Shining Affliction.* "[It] is an interchange of love, longing, frustration, and anger in the vicissitudes of a real relationship."

Stories like these emphasize both the *reciprocal nature* of the therapeutic relationship — an aspect rarely considered until recently — and the *unpredictability* of the process. This combination is unsettling. If therapy is combustible, first lighting a fire under the patient, then altering the doctor profoundly, and if these potentially dramatic changes can take place unexpectedly, as in the case of Blumhardt's conversion, then no wonder the report on Mesmerism concluded that "the danger is reciprocal." As we address the place love may play in psychotherapy, it is wise to remember that we are not just talking about what is best for the patient. We are really discussing what kind of relationship *both* doctor and patient find useful, sustaining — and manageable.

Having ascertained that effective therapy usually involves a genuine, well-matched, unusually attentive, mutual relationship, we may suspect that some form of love or at least affection is operating in the intimate hour. But what is it? Clinicians have tied themselves in knots trying to state what they feel for patients in discreetly obscure ways, and they have largely succeeded — succeeded, that is, in remaining obscure. Some give their feelings professional names like accurate empathy and nonpossessive warmth; others use metaphors from the physical world like magnetism; others rely on ordinary terms like parental concern or hospitality; and the more articulate select poetic names like attentive wonderment. Almost none goes on to state *in personal terms* what it is about their own response to patients that leads them to describe therapy as "this kind of loving [which is] not reducible to other more familiar forms" or as anything else. Although clinicians routinely complain about how vague our descriptions of the doctor-patient bond are, if they are prompted to review their own cases for signs of personal involvement, there seems to be a powerful urge either not to look closely or not to speak. When it comes to *impersonal* discussions of the relationship, however — what ought to happen in the consulting room or what other clinicians feel and do — then practitioners acknowledge that the average therapist enters into a variety of relationships. Some feel parental, some fraternal (or collegial), and some seem to be romantic. They admit that there may also be a bond that is a mixture of these or different from all of them — a "rare and inexplicable feeling" that for Hillman is most like "the love of an old man, the usual personal content of love voided by coming death, yet still intense, playful, and tenderly, carefully close."

Let us then examine the roles that paternal and fraternal relationships play in therapy and the one that sexual attraction either plays or points to. Are there ways in which feeling like a parent, a friend, a teacher, and even a could-have-been or a might-have-been lover advance the work of therapy?

~~~

The Old Testament tells the story of the Lord's instructing Solomon to build a temple that would house the ark of the covenant and thus be the most holy of holy places. The covenant itself was to be encased in a vault topped by a fabulous sculpture representing Jehovah's complicated relationship with Israel. Two winged cherubim, each fifteen feet high and made "from the wood of the oily tree" covered with gold, stood upon the vault looking intently at each other — sometimes. But how could this be? How could a sculpture simultaneously represent God and Israel in an intensely intimate interaction — being "woven one inside the other," as the Talmud puts it — and also being at odds with each other, separate. The apparently contradictory descriptions of the sculpture found in the Bible sparked a rabbinical discussion in the third century A.D. that came up with two answers. Either the cherubim were placed on the vault at an angle to each other so that the viewer had to use his own imagination or intuition to know whether they were weaving their thoughts together or looking past each other, *or* the angels were mounted on magical hinges. Without warning the hinges might move, and the two would no longer be engaged with each other for real.

In all of our lives, intimacy proceeds like the weaving of angels on hinges. At any given moment two people may speak to each other openly, from the heart, and weave their thoughts together into a fabric of unpredictable pattern, which is often called a friendship or relationship. But they are doing more than producing a joint creation or adding color to each other's cloth. In being "woven one inside the other," they are also creating each other in much the same way that the birth of a child creates a mother and a father or the death of a wife creates a widower. As a skillful therapist and a responsive client do, they call each other into existence — until the hinges move. By acts as grand as death and greed and as trivial as missed phone calls and moments of annoyance, a hinge moves and the intimate connection is broken. Together and apart, together and apart, the angels move, and our lives unroll in small acts of mutual creation and dissolution. Such is intimacy.

The idea that we weave each other into existence or, more broadly, that we and our personal worlds constantly create and destroy each other is a radical one. Psychologists call it counterintuitive, meaning that common sense suggests the opposite. Common sense, or more accurately convention, sees an individual as separate from everything else — a stable, predictable entity. He or she has unfolded according to the physical and temperamental specifications laid down at conception and has then been pushed ahead or held back by circumstance. The result seems to be an individual who both changes slowly but who also stays the same in important ways. We rely on this stability. We don't want to wonder if our friends and relatives have changed overnight. But the useful concept of stability may be overrated.

At least since Freud's time, there has been an increasing appreciation of the complex interactions that create and then maintain individuals. Freud realized that an individual cannot be understood in isolation — indeed, cannot come into existence in isolation. Physically, mentally, and emotionally, he or she is composed of a million proposals and responses to the surrounding world. Like a wave in the ocean, whose size and shape are determined at every instant by the wind and the configuration of the sea floor, the individual is not an object but a dynamic interaction of forces. Each of us is a little cyclone that depends for our very existence on the surrounding heat. Of course, we are not passive like waves and cyclones. Unlike these inanimate expressions of weather, we actively modify the very forces that shape us. We "train" our parents. We "educate" our partners. We "mold" our therapists. But no matter who is shaping whom at any particular instant, only these responsive interactions bring forth what we call personality.

The idea that a human being can develop something called individuality and thereby stand apart from the crowd — lonely but also victorious — is a peculiarly Western phenomenon. The martyrs of Western civilization from Socrates through Christ and since have given their lives for the right to leave the path of least resistance and separate themselves from what they often saw as the unreflective masses. Socrates would have insisted that something beyond physical care of the body must take place if a person's character is to develop fully. Although it is no accomplishment to have a separate body — it happens automatically and miraculously at birth — it is both a psychological and a social achievement to become an individual: psychological, because it requires a difficult and continual rearrangement of natural urges and desires; social, because as Freud discovered, this rearrangement only takes place in relationships. (Social also because only a flexible society can tolerate the strain of being made up of individuals.) But how is the development of character or individuality actually supposed to happen?

Current thinking on development suggests that there are no true individuals in the womb. A fetus is merged with his or her mother and even for a time after birth seems to expect that food and warmth will automatically be provided, just as they were before birth. If this expectation could be met and, as in the womb, every single one of the baby's needs could be provided so promptly and so perfectly that the baby was not even aware of wanting anything, many child psychologists believe that a separate person would never develop. Instead, there would be a very large baby securely attached to a preoccupied mother. (If you've ever tried to marry such a unit, you already understand that becoming an individual is not automatic.) In other words, the world must be responsive and give much more than food and shelter, but it cannot provide everything to perfection if the baby is going to learn to become a self. The hinges draw the angels together, but they also must carry them apart.

In an unusual interpretation of Freudian psychoanalysis, Jonathan Lear maintained, in his book *Love and Its Place in Nature,* that Freud's genius was in understanding how the frustrated desire to be perfectly loved drove the undifferentiated infant into the arms of the world and, if all went moderately well, into a lifetime of being an individual. Parental love rather than fraternal or romantic is the guiding metaphor in this explanation.

In simplest terms, parents express their love for their baby by caring for it as best they can, which is always imperfectly. As they feed and change it, they validate the baby's experiences by reflecting its moods back to it like a mirror.

"Waaa," says Baby.

"Oh, you are wet and miserable," says Mother. "Come, let me change you."

"Waa," Baby says again.

"Poor thing," says Mother. "You must be hungry."

But the mother is being more than a mirror. More organized and competent than her infant, she is caring for it emotionally and physically far better than the baby can care for itself. Freud believed that the child knows this and tries hard to get the mother to do everything just as she did before birth. But because the baby cannot get everything it wants, he or she gradually comes up with a disappointing but useful compromise that Freud called "identification." *As will later occur with lovers and therapists,* the baby seems to say "I love the way you respond to me and care for me. You do a much better job of it than I do. I feel so good when you give me a hundred percent of your loving attention, so . . . stay focused on me forever! If I can't get you to agree, then I'll be sad and disappointed — but I will also try to copy your way of loving me."

Freud maintained that each time the self doesn't get the magically perfect love it dreams of, it identifies with the less-than-perfect parent, lover, or therapist and draws its pattern of caring inside. Such a self feels sorely disappointed. The dream of being perfectly loved and cared for by someone who finds him or her utterly captivating dies a slow and lingering death. So the self keeps trying and failing. Each time the cycle turns, he or she believes a little less in magic and, alas, a little less in his or her own irresistible fascination and importance. The self also learns how to survive these losses, namely by identification. The individual actively pulls inside an ever more productive way of caring for itself. We commonly call this combination of disappointment and learning "growing up." The process goes on continually as the emerging individual reorganizes his or her relationship both with the world outside and the desires inside — always trying to dance a little more smoothly with the beast, always trying to devise a more comprehensive peace treaty with the outside world. In a good-enough world, where parents, teachers, friends, counselors, employers, lovers, and others pay attention and respond caringly, the individual will continually identify with loving people and constantly rearrange his or her own frontiers. Through these loving relationships, he or she will continue becoming an individual. If, on the other hand, this same self is treated for years like an "it" — never looked at in the eye, never called by name, never touched by someone who deeply cares — then the wind dies and the wave sinks into the sea. Without loving relationships, individuals become robots or die.

Serious, long-term therapy continues and sometimes improves on the process that began with the loving acknowledgment of the infant by its mother and continued through friendships and love affairs. It recapitulates the basic cycle whereby a person is pushed to grow up by the partially frustrated desire to find the perfect loving caretaker. In therapy, the yearning for the magical doctor, the subsequent disappointment, and the process of identification can be seen as a controlled recapitulation of what is usually an uncontrolled and haphazard process. In those cases where doctors yield to romantic attraction or adopt patients and bring them into their homes, as occasionally happens, the controlled process gives way to yet another uncontrolled experiment. "Psychoanalysis is at its core committed to the process of individuation," maintained Lear, "and it will flourish or wither depending on the value we place on the individual and the development of individuals in society."

Even more generally, it seems that insofar as we achieve maturity and autonomy by being in relationships with caring and attentive persons — by being woven one inside the other — then anything that threatens relationships threatens individuals and vice versa. The two exist together in a society or they disappear together. Thus one could say that the health of the family in the United States is directly related to the health of the country's individuals — and again vice versa. For many of the same reasons, the health of long-term therapy, where long-lasting relationships between doctor and patient are formed, is tied to the health of individuals. If, as a society, we want a country full of people who think for themselves in diverse, creative, and even peculiar ways, then we need to encourage families and long-term therapy — two of the great workshops where individuals are formed.

Friendship or fraternal love plays a somewhat different role in therapy as in life. Although relational therapists are actively experimenting with the idea that a real relationship between equals is the goal of therapy, the true experiments on fraternal love in therapy have been performed in peer counseling and in the leaderless groups common in the recovery movement. Although no money changes hands and no leader with formal credentials is in charge — two factors that set these forms of counseling outside the mainstream — some research has been done on the effectiveness of leaderless therapy. Studies have found that less formal counseling methods are particularly good at providing support and at teaching what could be called "communal skills." The men and women who enter Alcoholics Anonymous or Overeaters Anonymous, for example, realize immediately that they are not alone. They are among a group of people who often become their friends and supporters. As this occurs, members develop greater interpersonal sensitivity. That is, they learn to listen more carefully to and communicate more clearly with one another. The weak point of peer counseling is the lack of opportunity to work out issues related to authority and conflict.

Although fraternal love is currently considered less essential and less valuable than parental or romantic love, the ancients considered true friendship to be "the crown of life: the school of virtues." By this they meant that it was a great achievement and pleasure not only to individuals but to the community as a whole. Friends, they understood, formed a network of like-minded individuals who cared about the same truth and worked together for its promotion. Friends formed communities and bridged the exclusiveness natural to families and individuals. They collaborated. They traveled together. They taught one another how to be good citizens. Of course, fraternal love does some of the same work that parental affection does, and friendship may pass easily into romantic love, but its special contribution both in and out of therapy is to help individuals form sustaining communities. It is not surprising that in a time of growing concern for the loss of traditional communities, relational therapy, with its emphasis on friends and networks of friends, should seem so appealing.

Now we turn to romantic love. If it is true that "a real man trembles like a frog about to leap whenever he sees a beautiful woman" or feels "a kind of choking longing, a yearning that goes nowhere" and of which he is ashamed to speak, then it is probable that the 95 percent of male clinicians and 76 percent of women who reported on a survey that they felt erotically attracted to certain clients were not exaggerating. Lust, romance, erotic attraction — they all come sidling into the consulting room — but what do they do there besides make trouble? A small handful of contemporary clinicians have been brave enough to describe in detail the love and longing they feel in the consulting room — providing they call it a not-quite-real experience and providing they have it under control at all times. An example is Michael Tansey's compassionate paper, "Sexual Attraction and Phobic Dread in the Countertransference."

Pointing out that "our profession remains paralyzed by phobic dread of countertransference that is sexual or desirous in nature" and arguing that an inability to examine these feelings sets the stage for either destructive acting out or harmful pulling back, Tansey advanced the idea that sexual feelings in therapy are common and that "we are all vulnerable to committing some form of transgression." He himself "became increasingly aware of sexual and romantic feelings [for a deeply depressed patient], accompanied by apprehension and guilt that interfered with my ability to become curious about my growing response."

If Tansey had said nothing more, he would have made a contribution to our attempted discussion of love in therapy nonetheless and his point is worth restating. As he became romantically interested in a woman who sat across from him in his office three days a week — perhaps noticing her tone of voice, almost surely noticing the shape of her body, her gestures — waves of anxiety made him so nervous that he couldn't stand to see what was going on. Something in his head kept shouting "No!" every time he noticed how lovely his patient was. What are we likely to learn about love in therapy if our most common reaction is to shut down in its presence? Happily, Tansey caught himself backing up and took another look.

He had been treating this particular patient for several years when he became aware of how attractive she was. He did not discuss his feelings with her, and he could not be sure whether his interest was the cause or effect of his patient's changing concerns. One day, however, his patient began sobbing and apologizing uncharacteristically. As Tansey leaned forward and made eye contact in hopes of comforting her, she screamed as if she were being raped. Her cries of fear and pleas for mercy continued throughout the session. Tansey was beside himself. After several more sessions, however, he came to believe that he had seen the breakthrough of previously repressed memories of childhood sexual abuse. Possibly the first signs of these returning memories had prompted Tansey's sexual interest in her or perhaps it was the other way around. In either case, his solicitous and unconsciously provocative leaning forward had triggered the eruption of these feelings.

Tansey's erotic feelings subsided quickly, and looking back he felt that the attraction he experienced was sending him a signal about his patient's repressed sexual conflicts that he initially missed. He concluded that the therapist-patient bond is sometimes a frighteningly sensitive conductor of intense and hidden feelings, and he said that he now has a new appreciation of how this bond can both help and hurt. How, for example, can he foster a strong enough bond to hold and help a deeply regressed patient without also creating a barrier rather than a bridge between her and more complete relationships outside the consulting room? In other words, when does a bond that looks and feels a lot like love hold and comfort a patient? And when does it bind the patient to the therapist and hinder further progress? Tansey argued for disentangling but not throwing out the bonds of love in therapy and for learning more about them.

Tansey's report is similar to a handful of others in that it allows love into the consulting room but only as a signal that something entirely different is going on in either the patient or the doctor. Thus, romantic or sexually exciting feelings are not a part of therapy in and of themselves.

More provocative accounts of erotic attraction in therapy come from men who are not themselves clinicians. For example, when the author D. M. Thomas reviewed an early book on the Jung-Spielrein affair, he speculated that eroticism is an essential component in psychoanalysis. Calling analysis a "metaphorical seduction," he pointed out that a needy, vulnerable young woman meets daily in private chambers with an older man. There she lies on a couch and is supposed to offer him her most intimate secrets. But she won't. She resists. The analyst probes deeper and deeper, getting closer all the time to the central secret. She resists with greater energy until at last he breaks through her defenses. In a flood of emotion, she loses her innocence. She knows and is known. At this point, the analyst is supposed to end the affair.

But *why* does a current of eroticism run through analysis, albeit in a subtle and nonphysical form? The British analyst Christopher Bollas tried to answer the question that Thomas didn't ask. In *Cracking Up: The Work of Unconscious Experience,* Bollas argued that between people who know each other well, a surprising amount of information goes back and forth in a form that never reaches consciousness, that is, that neither person is aware of. A useful metaphor is that the unconscious exchanges that accompany a twosome's conversation are something like the "temperament" of a language that coexists with its vocabulary. As people who speak several languages realize, they are not exactly the same person when they languidly slur their way through Portuguese, for example, as when they stride through German even if they are saying the same thing in both languages. Without being aware of it, they pass the ordinary events of daily living through different filters and produce accounts with distinct flavors and personalities to match. This subtle form of reinvention is immensely pleasurable, and people who speak multiple languages well sometimes describe it as the rather seductive capacity to jump in and out of various plays. Bollas called this pleasure the love of representation — of presenting oneself and of being received.

Psychotherapy is one of these plays. According to Bollas, every doctor and patient pair speaks a different language. Over the course of time, they learn each other's rhythm or unconscious signals (as well as each other's words). They learn each other's unspoken idioms until, paradoxically, they feel better understood during their silences than during their conversations. And they love using these private exchanges that call into being for this hour alone a slightly different patient and a slightly different doctor than exist anywhere else. Similar to the way a parent first prompts a baby to develop an identity of its own, the unconscious communication that fascinated Bollas is another way of encouraging a person to create him- or herself. Like so many other pleasures of giving and receiving, Bollas felt that this one was basically erotic. But would an ordinary person call unconscious exchanges sexy? What was he talking about? Although Bollas did not flesh out his idea with many particulars, he nevertheless maintained that "the aim of sexual urges is not simply bodily gratification, important as that is; in my view, the desire to populate the inner world with excitements and objects of desire is as significant." He seemed to say that doctor and patient constantly express their sexual natures by gently flirting. In each other's presence, their imaginations pass exciting ideas back and forth — not specific plans for seduction, but the kinds of pleasurable ideas that bubble up naturally in the minds of males and females.

From my own experience, I have found this to be true. I am aware of patients as males or females, and I often sense the undercurrent of exchanges that signal their gender. It is difficult to assign these signals specific meanings because they are not verbal and they don't translate easily, but they constitute a running acknowledgment that this patient seated across from me is a full-fledged man or woman. In addition to whatever else he or she is (or so often is not), remembering that each is an adult male or female is a respectful and profitable stance. It tells the patient that I know we are far more alike than different and goes a long way toward leveling the playing field. Human beings have a natural fear of strangers, and nowhere is this more evident than among the mentally ill and emotionally distraught. Yet our sexual nature counteracts this pervasive apprehension and allows connection and communication where apprehension would ordinarily reside. Consciously and unconsciously, the recognition that we are male or female operates in the intimate hour and is expressed in a variety of ways. Bollas insisted, and I agree, that close communication between sexual beings is one of the great pleasures we enjoy and that it can, without exaggeration, be called a mild form of sexual gratification.

Yet "analysts of most schools . . . shy away from describing its deep pleasure," said Bollas. "After all, how can this pleasure be justified? Better to emphasize the abstinence, the frustration, the pain, the travails, the pathologies, the resistances, the negative transferences, than to reveal the pleasure that is the source, the aim, and the gratified object of psychoanalysis. And as to cure? That pleasure should be a means of cure? That the free-associative process which gratifies the analysand's urges to express the self should be the essential means of transformation from pathology to well-being, that the analyst's technique should be his pleasure in the handling of the patient, that two people in such a place should acknowledge such a pleasure: this seems as yet an impossibility."

Why impossible? Because, said Bollas, Freud exiled the idea that analysis could be sexually gratifying in any way, and no one has dared say that although the concept got exiled, the pleasure did not. Predicting that most people in modern societies will repress and displace their sexuality rather than acknowledge it, Freud did the same thing to the sexually pleasurable aspects of the technique he invented.

"That psychoanalysis should be so gratifying is not a surprise," concluded Bollas. "That its theoreticians should shudder from this fact is a curious oblation of the pleasures of unconscious communication." Thus the mildly erotic pleasures of the doctor-patient relationship are offered up as a ritualistic sacrifice, in part perhaps to keep therapists safe from feeling too much pleasure, which could lead to action and the end of therapy, and in part because the Freudian tradition is not easy to contradict.

Although Bollas made a brave start at bringing attraction back into the conversation, he confined his discussion to unconscious exchanges, which by definition cannot ordinarily be noticed or described. Can we expand the conversation by looking at more accessible attributes of the doctor-patient relationship? For example, by comparing the Western concept of romance to what therapy is supposed to accomplish? If we can identify areas of concern that are common to both lovers and doctor-patient pairs, we may then be able to add some less esoteric reasons for saying that therapy involves or runs parallel to love.

Although it is easy to show that love has meant many different things over the ages, it is also true that certain central themes or ingredients have remained remarkably constant throughout the past eight centuries. It was during the twelfth century that courtly love crossed the Pyrenees and took root in southern France. Although in earlier times romantic love was understood to range from a painful delirium at its most violent to a longing for one's spiritual "other half" at its most moderate, the tradition of courtly love introduced an entirely new element. Instead of a temporary loss of reason or the soulful reaction to a psychic amputation, love became a way of life — and a superior way of life. With a new appreciation of women, who in ancient times were not considered even capable of friendship and in early Christian times were supposed to express little more than maternal love, courtly or romantic love was elevated to a particularly admirable way of dealing with another person.

Courtly love was not confined to sexual partners. Although erotic attraction was a basic ingredient, so were the constraining forces of loyalty and control. In fact, this new form of love was less a prelude to sex than it was a sustainable form of passionate attentiveness. Thus the new way of paying attention was enjoyed by many kinds of couples. Perhaps the most typical involved a married woman who was courted according to strict rules of conduct by an unmarried man of lower social standing. In this languorous context of frustrated or perhaps sublimated desire, knights and ladies studied in minute detail the intricacies of love's bittersweet contradictions. If they had both the passion and self-control to enjoy what was called "pure intimacy," then no sex entered the relationship at all. As they inched their way along this tightrope, they discovered many things about male and female patterns of thinking and feeling — discoveries that, like their music and poetry, still color our image of love.

In *The Double Flame: Love and Eroticism,* the poet-philosopher Octavio Paz points out five ways in which the twelfth-century "invention" of love has remained constant to the present time. First, there is the question of exclusivity. Love, in contrast to lust, desires only one person, one particular individual, and that has not changed. Second, Paz said, love has remained revolutionary. It involves an overturning of habitual patterns on both a personal and community level. A couple in love is outside the law, sometimes literally, as when Hitler passed a law forbidding Germans to have sex with non-Aryans, but more often figuratively, as when social, racial, ethical, or even geographical constraints must be overcome. In love, what has been separate is joined, and what has been united now comes apart and is rearranged.

Love has also overturned the usual understanding of domination and submission. The powerful willingly become weak. The weak find themselves with power they have not asked for. High-ranking ladies wrote perfumed notes to knights whose social station was so far below their own that they could not have communicated with each other in any way except through love. On the other hand, when a knight underwent the final test of pure intimacy and gazed unmoving upon his lady as she disrobed, he never used his superior physical strength to overpower her.

A fourth aspect of love that has persisted from the twelfth century is the tension between the fatefulness of love, its preordained quality, and its freedom. Lovers cannot explain their feelings with one *or* the other of these concepts, and again they find themselves forced to embrace a contradiction. Finally, lovers are still concerned with body and soul — with the changing, material part of the person that is subject to the accidents of time and with the immortal essence. As with domination and submission or destiny and freedom, lovers cannot adequately explain what they feel if they restrict themselves either to the timebound body or the timeless essence of their beloved.

As sketched above, the Western conception of romantic love both sounds like and does not sound like the relationship commonly established between doctor and patient. In romantic love, two people are attracted to each other exclusively, and within this intense and attentive union they actively confront the great existential themes of life — the ambiguities that surround tradition and innovation, power and submission, fate and freedom, body and soul. These are the topics that lie beneath their long and eager discussions. In therapy, on the other hand, the relationship is not exclusive, at least not from the doctor's point of view. Yet the concerns are similar. Doctor and patient are also revolutionaries, actively seeking to join what has not been joined and loosen or even break ties that still impede the client. Although therapy serves the interests of the dominant culture and tends to rein in rather than encourage true revolutionaries, yet within the range of behavior our culture allows, clinicians urge their patients to leave the beaten track and experiment with new ways of thinking, feeling, and behaving.

Similarly, therapy is focused on the other concerns of love. Questions of domination and submission are often played out *in* therapy in order to illustrate what the client is feeling and doing *outside* therapy. Fate and freedom walk into every session when a patient asks how much of her situation has been handed to her by fate and how much is of her own making or maintaining. Lastly, when it comes to a serious accounting of body versus soul — the flesh-and-blood person seated in the office chair versus the immutable essence that will last forever — therapy is divided in complicated ways between materialism and spirituality. Clinicians who seek to understand a person's problems as chemical misfortunes of the body do not consider the spirit, but others do, although often in secular terms. Thus it seems that doctor and patient join forces to take a new look at the world and to confront its eternal ambiguities together. They talk about the same things that lovers talk about, and like the knight and his lady, they use a curiously inhibited form of attraction both to overcome their differences and to personalize or energize the discussion.

The Arab women of Mecca and Medina, from whose songs of yearning courtly love arose, realized that if sexual tension didn't exist between a man and a woman, the man wasn't likely to pay attention to what the woman said; centuries later, Freud maintained that unless transference love developed, patients wouldn't pay attention to what their therapists said. Thus we return to the idea that courtliness, with its undercurrent of erotic attraction and its strict rules of conduct, is a way of being attentive that has been used in many social situations. The parallels that I suggest exist between courtly love and therapy — in both terms of topics discussed and process — make sense, not only of Thomas's metaphorical description of the erotic analysis, but also of Tansey's belief that romantic feelings can direct the clinician's attention and Bollas's belief that the gratifications of self-invention and representation are central to therapy. All these lines of thinking support the idea that feelings (not actions) of paternal love, fraternal love, and even of erotic pleasure are essential to the work that therapy tries to do.

In spite of assertions that love and pleasure advance psychotherapy, romantic love especially is not welcome in the consulting room. Among its disadvantages is that it draws too much attention to the disagreeable possibility that our veneer of rational control is not very thick, and that we are more suggestible and more creaturely than we wish to acknowledge. At least in the West, we want our treatments rational and scientific, not nonrational — which is to say emotional. We are suspicious of passion, altered states of consciousness, confession, and other states of mind that let go of logic and allow our less civilized natures to emerge.

Romantic love also draws too much attention to the therapist's personal life to be comfortably acknowledged. As Dr. Norman maintained, falling in love with a patient was like trying to do therapy in a hall of mirrors. Everything the patient said triggered so many emotional reactions that at the end of the hour the doctor found herself with as many questions about her own life as about the patient's. Why was she initially feeling such relief? Had she been tense and lonely without knowing it? Why such joy? Why such guilt?

"Love is the most dangerous thing to feel," said Max Day. "And if we talk about it, we really feel it. Hate is more manageable. We can focus primarily on what it is about *the patient* that enrages us."

As if making us uncomfortably aware of our primitive nature and our private lives were not enough, romantic love also undermines the clinician's special privilege. All love overcomes our natural fear of the foreign, and as a clinician acknowledges his affection for a patient, he is likely to see how little difference there is between doctors and patients — in fact, he may begin to regard them as natural pairs, like teachers and students, saints and sinners, cops and robbers. One cannot think of pairs of anything without noting their similarities, and psychologists love to point out that on personality tests policemen and criminals have remarkably similar profiles. And us? Are we linked in some deep and natural way to the emotionally and mentally disturbed? I suspect so, but without acknowledging the bond of affection between doctor and patient, we can skip over this rather obvious connection. "In love there is no condescension," Irving Singer stated in *The Pursuit of Love*. "To the extent that we are able to love, we act as if we are all alike — each of us, as in the words of the Negro spiritual, 'standing in the need of prayer.'"

Love also undermines the business decisions that clinicians make every day. Can you terminate with patients who have run out of money if you openly acknowledge that you share a special kind of love with them? As an employee of a managed care company, can you deny weekly therapy to a chronic schizophrenic patient who lives in a rented room and whose therapist says very clearly, "I am the only person in the world who loves this person"? Regardless of the good works that love may do in creating individuals and inspiring hope, affection clearly gums up the works on the business end of psychotherapy. Love may be the pathway to personal agency, but it is not the cornerstone of capitalism.

"Most mental health treatments of love are stale, antiseptic, and preachy," wrote Ethel Person, the author of *Dreams of Love and Fateful Encounters*. "They generally denigrate the experience of falling in love. In essence they downgrade romantic love and endorse some version of nonpassionate 'love' which is based on a rational decision to commit oneself to a person or situation."

In addition, practitioners call love "unrealistic," "a maladaptive effort to solve a dependency problem," "narcissistic," "childish and intrinsically humiliating," "self-destructive," and "embarrassing." The feelings

Romeo and Juliet had for each other have been cited as a good example of a "dyadic illness." For Freud, romantic love was "lust plus the ordeal of civility." These comments, reminiscent of those made centuries ago by struggling monks, suggest that clinicians are downright afraid of love.

"Of course we're afraid of love," said Dr. Norman. "I feel ashamed to call my feelings for a patient love. Caring, fondness — those are acceptable feelings, but not love. It was drilled into us in training that we're not supposed to need our patients at all. Love was a sign of sickness." Or from Henri Nouwen, "After so much stress on the necessity of a leader to prevent his own personal feelings and attitudes from interfering in a helping relationship, it seems necessary to reestablish the basic principle that no one can help anyone without becoming involved, without entering with his whole person into the painful situation, without taking the risk of becoming hurt, wounded, or even destroyed in the process. . . . Who can take away suffering without entering it?" And who can deny that the sadness of parting from patients can be painful enough without admitting that you have loved them and now, predictably, you are watching them leave your office and your life. Perhaps this is one more reason for not acknowledging love in the doctor-patient relationship. Perhaps we do not want to share Father Walsh's characteristic ache of the heart.

Of course, there are clinicians who do — do acknowledge love and do ache when their work with a patient is over. One of the more articulate and circumspect is Annie Rogers. As a clinician in training, she had been working with a five-year-old child for just a few months when he told her to make him a paper airplane and write on it "Happy Christmas, Ben, I Love You." "I write exactly what he wishes. Ben stands and looks at me, his dark eyes so clear I feel my heart bound. How quickly I have come to love him." In a daring description of two interlocking cases, the treatment of uncontrollable Ben and the treatment of her own breakdown and hospitalization, Rogers meticulously documented the diverse roles that love plays in psychotherapy in *A Shining Affliction.* As both clinician and patient she has experienced the near-miraculous help love offers and the stunning hurt it can deliver.

Rogers's story began as she started treating young Ben at a special school for disturbed children. Drawn to the child's wary hunger for affection, Rogers entered into his suffering only to discover gradually that it was her own. Within several months, she learned that Ben had not only been neglected as an infant, but that when placed in a foster home at eighteen months of age he was forgotten in his crib when the house caught fire. As he saw it, the Mama Bear who was essential for life was also radically unreliable. It was hard for him to know whether he should hate her, and probably perish, or try to make himself believe in her protective love by telling himself that her neglect was actually a punishment he deserved. In either case — endangered or bad — he was miserable. As Ben acted out his dilemma over and over again by playing make-believe games that passionately expressed his fears and hopes — his wish to kill the mothers that abandoned him and his wish to be rescued by them — Rogers was drawn down into terrors of her own. For one thing, she began to suffer a recurrence of the fracturing anxiety she felt at irregular intervals throughout her life. She saw an angel in the library. She heard music, close and in stereo, only to notice that she wasn't wearing earphones. For another, she realized that her beloved therapist was backing away from her. Not only did she announce that hugs were off limits now, but she increasingly acted on the belief that therapy revolves totally around the patient's problems rather than the relationship that doctor and patient are living out together. When Rogers complained that the sessions didn't feel right anymore, her therapist was ready with explanations that pointed to Rogers's deficiencies. Rogers tried everything to redirect her therapist's attention away from interpretations and back onto the awkward dance that therapy had become. Finally she threatened to kill her therapist with a toy gun and a knife. The therapist shut the relationship off like a tap. As Rogers grew more despondent, both from her inability to rekindle her therapist's affection and from watching Ben's heart-wrenching attempts to negotiate an untrustworthy world, she slipped into a profound state of confusion. Earlier bouts of this psychic shattering had earned her such labels as psychotic and schizophrenic.

Not long after Christmas vacation, Rogers was hospitalized. She was hallucinating in spite of medication and had apparently lost the power of speech. When a doctor in the hospital told her that he was going to try electroshock therapy, it was all she could do to summon the word "no." Luckily, her health insurance ran out before more experiments could be proposed, and she went to live with friends. As she left the hospital, her doctor told her to leave psychotherapy behind her — forever. Don't get any, he told her, and don't give any. Just take the pills.

Less than a week later, Rogers started seeing an analyst who became for her the model of what a good therapist can be. A quiet and unprepossessing man of great dedication, Dr. Blumenfeld waded deep into the water to take Rogers by the hand. He met her as often as she needed him. He encouraged her to call him in the middle of the night if she became anxious. He didn't stock his office with Kleenex because he was not afraid of tears. Nor was he afraid of love. He spoke freely of doctors loving their patients and patients loving and healing their doctors. They worked together for their mutual benefit, he told Rogers, or they didn't work at all. Over time, he lent Rogers the strength to see — as she was again helping Ben to see — that all her life she had received love that was mixed with fear and rejection. Although her parents abused her and her therapist abandoned her, all three of these people also loved her. This was as hard for Rogers to hear as it was for Ben — hard for anyone to hear — and for many months she alternated between insisting that her caregivers were good to her and complaining that they never loved her at all. Naturally she wanted to believe that she was worthy of love and that her parents and therapist loved her as best they could, but she was so confused that she could no longer believe in her own ability to recognize love when she saw it.

"Can I believe you?" she asked Blumenfeld when he told her that they loved her as well as hurt her. "Can I believe in [the original therapist's] first response, when she . . . held me?" "Yes," Blumenfeld answered. "That was her bravest moment with you, and even if she retreated from it later, you can believe in it." Nonetheless, he told Rogers, the unpredictable commingling of affection and rejection that she had received since birth was the most confusing and hurtful message of all.

A year after Rogers began seeing Ben and some six months after her own hospitalization, her internship at the school came to an end, and she was faced with leaving the patient she had grown to love. Because Ben's past paralleled her own and because he was the occasion for the acknowledgment of her own "forgotten" abuse, he had become a special partner on her life's journey. How could she say good-bye to him without reinforcing the idea that all loving people — all Mama Bears — disappear?

Leaving is never easy, and there is probably no such thing as a perfect end to a loving relationship in or out of therapy. Nevertheless, with great patience, Rogers showed Ben on the playroom calendar when their "good-bye day" would be, and she put into words with him the sadness they would feel at losing each other. They had snapshots taken of the two of them sitting together, and each took one as a keepsake.

"You look at me every day and don't you forget," he told her.

"I won't," she replied. "How could I ever forget?"

For a long time Rogers thought about what had happened to her and the people around her during that painful year; six years later she concluded, as Dr. Blumenfeld had before her, that healing is always two-sided and is always based on a loving relationship. Two stories and two ways of seeing the world come into therapy, she believed, and doctor and patient together "create a world and a new story. When this happens [each] participates in a new story and is healed within it." Rogers also learned that a clinician can hurt her clients either by being unmoved or by promising too much. The very worst hurt seems to come from a combination of the two — genuinely courageous affection followed by or combined with fear and rejection.

In short, Rogers concluded that it is necessary but not sufficient to love your patients. There is a need for care, humility, and control when handling an emotion as powerful as love, and for a clinician this means many kinds of support and guidance must be in place. Not only is guidance from theory and experience necessary as a clinician establishes loving relationships with clients, she now believes, but support from a supervisor and from personal, nonprofessional relationships as well. She echoes the understanding of celibate priests.

~~~

Having looked at how parental, fraternal, and romantic love advance the work of therapy — encouraging the formation of individuals and communities and stirring up an attentive dialogue on life's contradictions — can we finally grant these forms of love a legitimate place in therapy? Can we say that therapy is — or rather that it should be — an intense, intimate, and affectionate relationship intended, as are all such relationships, to call two people into existence and revitalize them? And can we further say that in some cases, if not all, therapy, like courtly love before it, uses a curiously inhibited form of sexual attraction to unite dissimilar people and heighten the relevance of the existential dilemmas they address? If we say yes to these proposals, we approach a dangerous conclusion: that love and possibly sexual attraction are *supposed* to be part of serious therapy and are *supposed* to remain unfulfilled. That certainly places psychotherapy in dangerous waters. As long as love and pleasure attend therapy in any guise, there will be misunderstandings between doctor and patient, as Dr. Betz has pointed out so clearly. In addition, talk will occasionally slip into action, and therapy will be lost to an erotic relationship that will probably hurt the patient. Finally, doctor and patient will *hurt each other* if they abandon their unspoken agreement to care about each other. Instances of all these liabilities fill earlier chapters.

We have come a long way from the first crude investigations of the active ingredient of the intimate hour and a longer way still from the one-sided discussions of exploitive erotic attraction that dominate the news today. Like the church built in Bari in honor of Saint Nicholas, we seem to have discovered that part of psychotherapy's beauty and power comes from a language that traditionally is not supposed to be spoken in a professional relationship any more than Muslim devotions are supposed to decorate a Christian church. There are currents of love between doctor and patient that run both beneath and parallel to parental, romantic, and fraternal love. We have heard this stated by many clinicians — "You cannot heal disturbed people without love." "No analysis can succeed in which we do not succeed in really loving the patient" — and we have heard it from patients, from Sabina Spielrein in the first years of this century to Annie Rogers in the last.

Many forms of intimacy weave their way through the intimate hour, and not everyone will have the same feelings or use the same words when it comes to describing them. The most problematic are feelings akin to romantic love. At their worst they presage the end of therapy and a precipitous flight into a complicated relationship that for many reasons is not likely to bring either party contentment. At their best, however, feelings of love between doctor and patient represent a special kind of impossible love — a pure intimacy — with multiple attractions and prohibitions and with passionate attentiveness on both sides. The doctor-patient relationship is not supposed to be an ongoing adventure the way a marriage or a love affair can be. It is not supposed to be the relationship within which doctor and patient work out the most intimate knowledge of themselves and of another person in the course of a lifetime, although certainly therapy has occupied this most central and important place even when neither person has so much as touched the other's hand. But in the normal course of events, the affectionate bond that develops between doctor and patient represents an initiation, a turning point on the path to a more satisfying life that, once negotiated, is left behind. Each patient comes in needing a different initiation, and each has a different way of leaving old fears and habitual constrictions. As this happens, a therapist is asked to love and support these people in many ways before finally doing "the hangman's work." For most therapists, one uncharted journey or another proves to be dangerous. I have discovered that almost every therapist has a love story. The vast majority of these attractions are not played out, but that doesn't mean that the relationships don't bring great joy and great heartbreak.

When the British analyst Harry Guntrip had finished his own analysis with the famous W. R. D. Fairbairn, a model of reticence, he wrote, "After I was finally leaving Fairbairn after the last session, I suddenly realized that in all that long period we had never once shaken hands, and he was letting me leave without that friendly gesture. I put out my hand and at once he took it, and I suddenly saw a few tears trickle down his face. *I saw the warm heart of this man.*"

And that, after all, is the essence of therapy — and love.

Conclusion

Hell is the only place outside heaven where we can be
safe from the dangers of love.
— *C. S. Lewis*

For more than a hundred years psy-
chotherapists have treated people suffering from mental illness, emotional distress, and the common vicissitudes of living. Except for brief
periods in restricted regions, it has been understood that sex and romance were not supposed to be part of such treatment, and that when
they were, the doctor had taken advantage of the patient. And yet in
every decade, in every country, and among practitioners of every school
of thought there have been doctors and patients who exchanged therapy
for a more physical relationship. Currently, it is fashionable to say that
all these erotic entanglements are sadistic acts — instances of a powerful person preying on a weaker one for personal gain. I have tried to
show that the reality is more complex. Among the many thousands of
such erotic liaisons that statistics suggest have occurred in the past
twenty-five or thirty years, there has been enormous variety. It does no
one any good — neither patients nor doctors — and advances no area of
understanding to insist that all these relationships are terrible and all are
the same.

Although we know the details of relatively few cases, it is clear that
the strength of the patient, the power differential between patient and
doctor, and the nature of the doctor's desire — lust versus love — are
each critical in determining the kind and the course of the entanglement. Not surprisingly, the so-called high-functioning clients are the

least likely to get hurt. When such women encounter a lecherous old goat in the consulting room, they have been known to slap him or spit on his Oriental carpet and leave. When the same kind of fairly confident woman meets a therapist who falls in love with her, she has been known to marry him. Both surveys and anecdotal evidence suggest that happy endings occur in some small percentage of cases.

On the other hand, when a patient is fairly vulnerable, she is more likely to be drawn into a harmful liaison. A typical example is Katherine, who was used by her married minister to add some excitement to his life. If the counselor has more honorable intentions, however, as did Douglas, then even a fairly vulnerable woman like Jeannette may remain in control of the situation enough to be unharmed or even to profit. The most severe harm inevitably occurs near the bottom of the therapy staircase, where patients, many previously abused, regard their doctors as having the power and authority of parents. In this situation, there is no way to avoid a bad result. If the doctor who crosses the ethical line is out for easy sex, his patient feels raped and reabused. If he is out for love, the result, ironically, is worse. Then the thoroughly confused patient is likely to feel all the ambivalence and powerlessness of an incest victim. In all cases of doctor-patient entanglement — every one of them — the therapy the two have been conducting together comes to an end. In most cases it is replaced by an unstable, unfair, and ultimately unpleasant liaison.

In spite of the consistency with which doctors have desired their patients, the history of the talking cure contains no sustained investigation of why this might be so. The idea that love or something like it might be an essential part of the therapeutic process is entertained only when doctors find themselves unable to help large numbers of suffering patients with traditional treatment. Mesmer with his animal magnetism, Breuer and Freud with their explosions of countertransference, and encounter groups with their prescriptions of free love all appeared on the scene when conventional treatment did not work for increasingly frustrated and discouraged people. When these radical treatments began to enter the mainstream, however, each was forced to pull back from the direct use of passion or sexual acts. All three methods of treatment still exist. All three continue to help people. But all three now deny they have any direct dealings with love.

There are many reasons that any form of cure-by-passion will be rejected by our culture. One is that it is too disturbing to believe that psychotherapy uses anything as unreasonable and unscientific as love to do its eminently reasonable work of restoring logic to its proper and dominant place in our minds and lives. Therapy is supposed to tame the passions with reason, not temper reason with passion. In a secular, democratic, and technologically advanced country, mainstream treatment must at least appear to be just that — secular, democratic, and technologically advanced. If it is not, we do not want to know about it. A second reason for not investigating love in therapy is that it would be bad for the business portion of psychotherapy. Love has always and everywhere broken down the barriers between "us" and "them," and an open acknowledgment of its necessity in therapy would force us to rethink and reorganize our mental health system. Psychotherapy is a big, multi-billion-dollar business in this country, and it is run like one.

So we have stumbled through a century of psychotherapy wondering why doctors keep falling for their patients but resolutely refuse to examine love's place in therapy. This may be changing. Although some feminists have worked so hard to protect their sisters from unscrupulous therapists that they have turned love into a dirty word, and although managed care companies have worked so hard to protect themselves from lawsuits that no one dares speak the word out loud, some clinicians have begun working for the right to reexamine the doctor-patient relationship and to say what they find. Especially in the new school of relational therapy, where the doctor-patient relationship is openly acknowledged as the active ingredient of the therapeutic process, women are asking what it is about this relationship that heals people. Freer to speak of love in therapy than men, female therapists and clergy like Annie Rogers and Carter Heyward are examining the love they feel for their clients and parishioners, and they are talking as well about the love they want from their own therapists. Therapy is a risky business, they conclude. It must have love — this is essential — and it must also have controls.

Other lines of thinking also argue for the presence of some form of love in psychotherapy. Outcome studies suggest that effective therapy involves an intense, intimate, and affectionate relationship between a doctor and patient who are well matched; developmental studies suggest that only in the loving presence of another person do we develop as individuals. Love seems to have other jobs in the world as well. Overcoming our natural fear of strangers, love lets us relate as fellow beings, and overcoming our resistance to change, it infuses whatever is discussed with energy and importance. Like the pure intimacy of courtly love, love in therapy unites dissimilar people and heightens the relevance of their dealings. Moreover, in group therapies, fraternal love supports the members as they learn to relate to one another as good citizens.

Therapy seems to depend on all kinds of love as it prompts people to expand their sense of themselves and to take their place in the world. Although in therapy affection is rarely expressed physically or called by name, that doesn't mean it isn't a common part of treatment. Analysts like Bollas argue that doctors and patients unconsciously enjoy a pleasure that is "the essential means" of transforming pathology into well-being. Consistent pleasures rarely dissociate themselves from love: where you find one, you are likely to find the other.

If it appears that I am working awfully hard to make the point that love and pleasure are the very stuff of therapy, it is because so many years of naysaying have been piled in the way of this rather obvious conclusion and because the consequences of such an assertion are so distasteful to so many. For if we conclude that love is essential to therapy, we must be prepared to manage rather than eliminate all the problems that surround the doctor-patient interaction. We will need to handle the inevitable misunderstandings that arise, and we must deal with the results when doctors cross the ethical line. Rather than turn our back on the complexity of intimacy in therapy, we will have to study this strange partnership of friends who are not exactly friends, of parents who aren't related to their "children," and of admirers who are never supposed to act. And that is not all.

Once we begin investigating the doctor-patient relationship, we will need to pass on what we learn to young therapists, who may not understand or want to understand that with love comes many kinds of frustration and sadness. Those too are parts of the job. In short, acknowledging love means rethinking a lot of things — training, educating the public, correcting and rehabilitating therapists, and helping patients recover from bad experiences. I am not hopeful that much of this will happen, at least not quickly, for I think it more likely that the problem of doctor-patient erotic entanglements will be replaced rather than examined. As therapy itself changes so substantially and becomes for most people a brief encounter, and as women increasingly find themselves treated by female clinicians, I think sex in therapy will decline and be replaced by a larger but not unrelated problem: How do all of us, in and out of therapy, wish to do business with each other in the twenty-first century? As intimates? Surrounded by the problems of love? Or as business partners? Surrounded by the complexities of economics and legalities? If psychotherapists and even the clergy desert the path of love, who is left in the public realm to champion intimacy?

"Does that discourage you?" asked Father Walsh as he shifted his large body and inadvertently flipped the cat onto the floor.

"Yes," I admitted. "I don't like to see intimacy on the run — leaving the classroom, the consulting room, the doctor's office."

"And you're afraid that people won't see the danger in time?"

"Exactly."

Father Walsh twisted around in his wicker chair until he could look down the street in front of the rectory where nothing seemed to move in the summer heat. "Our job," he began slowly, still looking down the empty street, "our job is not to lead people back to the old days when they trusted priests and doctors and all the other authorities. Nor is our job to push them toward a premature solution in hopes of simplifying their lives. And ours."

"But instead?" I prompted.

"We are companions on the journey," he said, turning to face me squarely. "Our job is to suffer these confusing times along with our people. We will wait *with* them until a new way emerges. Sometimes we will urge patience — 'Don't oversimplify,' I tell them. 'Don't jump to conclusions.' And sometimes we will urge daring action. But year after year, we will stay with them as they change, and all the while we will keep saying, 'I am a witness that love works.'"

We are indeed companions on a journey, one that often seems to progress too quickly along a road that winds too sharply. As we move ahead through problems as potentially divisive as sex between doctor and patient or former patient, let us take the time to listen to *all* the stories that we hear along the way.

Notes

Introduction

page

2 "Some day I'll have": "Psychiatrists and Sex Abuse," *Boston Globe* (Oct. 4, 1994), p. 14.

"Both students and experienced therapists": Nancy Bridges, "On Loving and Being Loved: Psychodynamic Meanings and Management of Attraction in Psychotherapy," Cambridge Hospital Seminar, April 1994.

4 "I saw almost too well": Aldo Carotenuto, *A Secret Symmetry: Sabina Spielrein Between Jung and Freud* (New York: Pantheon, 1982), p. 20.

"I do believe I am capable": Ibid., p. 21.

"Sometimes when he just strokes": J. G. Gaarlandt, *An Interrupted Life: The Diaries of Etty Hillesum* (New York: Pantheon, 1984), p. 16.

Whereas all of them: J. Marmor, "Sexual Acting Out in Psychotherapy," *American Journal of Psychoanalysis*, 22 (1972): 7.

In these early years: T. J. Akamatsu, "Intimate Relationships with Former Clients: National Survey of Attitudes and Behavior Among Practitioners," *Professional Psychology: Research and Practice*, 19 (1988): 454–58.

5 "a psychopathic male therapist": Thomas Gutheil and Glen Gabbard, "Obstacles to the Dynamic Understanding of Therapist-Patient Sexual Relations," *American Journal of Psychotherapy*, 46 (1992): 516.

"the woman patient": Sydney Smith, "The Seduction of the Female Patient," in Glen Gabbard, ed., *Sexual Exploitation in Professional Relationships* (Washington, D.C.: American Psychiatric Press, 1989), p. 58.

"caught in the coils": Ibid., p. 63.

Two women tried to bring charges: Gutheil and Gabbard, "Obstacles to the Dynamic Understanding," p. 519.

10 "The [current] standard of care": Miriam Greenspan, in Carter Heyward, *When Boundaries Betray Us: Beyond Illusions of What Is Ethical in Therapy and Life* (New York: HarperCollins, 1993), pp. 199, 200.

12 "If a patient approaches": Thomas Gutheil and Glen Gabbard, "The Concept of Boundaries in Clinical Practice: Theoretical and Risk-Management Dimensions," *American Journal of Psychiatry*, 150 (1993): 195.

"Professional organizations invariably": Jane Ussher, *Women's Madness: Mysogyny or Mental Illness?* (Amherst: University of Massachusetts Press, 1991), pp. 180, 182.

I. A HISTORY OF SEXUAL ENCOUNTERS IN PSYCHOTHERAPY

19 "that it was impossible": John Kerr, *A Most Dangerous Method: The Story of Jung, Freud and Sabina Spielrein* (New York: Knopf, 1993), p. 193.

20 In his opinion: Ibid., p. 128.

"slandered and scorched by the love": Ibid., p. 209.

"very close to [an indiscretion]": Ibid., p. 219.

Critics condemned the new treatment: Ibid., pp. 379, 189.

21 "Americans in general were uncomfortable": Ibid., pp. 233, 241.

Melanie Klein, who believed: M. Goodman and A. Teicher, "To Touch or Not to Touch," *Psychotherapy*, 25 (1988): 494.

22 And female analysts reported: Ethel S. Person, *Dreams of Love and Fateful Encounters: The Power of Romantic Passion* (New York: Penguin, 1988), p. 257.

The most notorious of these: J. Marmor, "Sexual Acting Out in Psychotherapy," *American Journal of Psychoanalysis*, 22 (1972): 5.

23 The examples that abound: Popular books written from the victim's point of view include L. Freeman and J. Roy, *Betrayal* (New York: Stein and Day, 1976); E. Walker and T. Young, *A Killing Cure* (New York: Holt, 1986); B. Noel and K. Watterson, *You Must Be Dreaming* (New York: Poseidon Press, 1992); and C. Bates and A. Brodsky, *Sex in the Therapy Hour: A Case of Professional Incest* (New York: Guilford Press, 1989).

1. Early Romantic Explosions

25 "That couldn't be me": Aldo Carotenuto, *A Secret Symmetry: Sabina Spielrein Between Jung and Freud* (New York, Pantheon Books, 1982), p. 19.

27 She noticed that with neither: John Kerr, *A Most Dangerous Method: The Story of Jung, Freud and Sabina Spielrein* (New York: Knopf, 1993), pp. 69, 70.

If on a Monday she felt: Carotenuto, *Secret Symmetry*, p. 16.

28 Gross had gotten into: Kerr, *Most Dangerous Method*, pp. 186–88.

"My dear," he wrote: Ibid., p. 197.

"it is only with great difficulty": Carotenuto, *Secret Symmetry*, p. 168.

She seemed to read his thoughts: Kerr, *Most Dangerous Method*, p. 171.

29 Jung became Spielrein's "poet": p. 223.
    she thought of the project: Ibid., p. 226.
    "life means nothing to me": Ibid., p. 205.
    "I am looking for a person": Ibid.
30 "The doctor knows his limits": Ibid., p. 206.
    "Spielrein flew into one of her": Carotenuto, *Secret Symmetry*, p. 97.
    "Dear Professor Freud": Ibid., p. 92.
31 "Just think, Professor": Ibid., p. 99.
    Jung told Freud: Kerr, *Most Dangerous Method*, 218.
    Freud responded: Ibid., p. 219.
    In exchange for her silence: Ibid., p. 221.
32 "Despair gave me courage": Ibid., pp. 294–95.
    Again Spielrein burned for Jung: The account of Spielrein's torturous nights is
    from Carotenuto, *Secret Symmetry*, pp. 12, 13.
33 then send a letter to Freud: Ibid., p. 183.
    Equally duplicitous, Freud: Kerr, *Most Dangerous Method*, p. 470.
    Jung meanwhile complained: Carotenuto, *Secret Symmetry*, p. 184.
34 Freud and Jung broke: Kerr, *Most Dangerous Method*, p. 437.
35 "I sincerely want to learn": Letter of Sabina Spielrein to Carl Jung, 1919. Aldo
    Carotenuto, *Tagebuch einer Heimlichen Symmetrie*. Freiburg: Kore, 1986.
    "I have lit in you a new light": Jung to Spielrein, 3 April 1919, Ibid.
    "The love of S. for J.": Carotenuto, *Secret Symmetry*, p. 190.
36 "Whatever the specific contributions": Bruno Bettelheim, in Ethel S. Person,
    Dreams of Love and Fateful Encounters: The Power of Romantic Passion (New
    York: Penguin, 1988), p. 252.
    He called this feminine force: Kerr, *Most Dangerous Method*, p. 504.
    These remain as expressions: Ibid., p. 507. The plaques and their inscrip-
    tions contain ambiguities that allow them to be read as referring to either
    Spielrein or Jung. For example, the bear is the national animal of Switzerland,
    Jung's country, as well as being designated in Jung's journal as Russian. In the
    second inscription, the word "body" may be translated "womb," and the light
    may be understood as belonging to either Jung or Spielrein or both. In
    addition, Jung certainly knew that the North Star, or polestar — "the star of
    every wandering bark" — is in the constellation Ursa Minor, the Little Bear.
    This too may have expressed his tie to Spielrein. Such complex interweaving
    of symbols was characteristic of Jung. E.C., personal communication.
38 "Profound changes took place": Person, *Dreams of Love*, p. 253.
    Or, in the same vein: Ibid., pp. 252–53.
    Subsequent critics: Jeffrey Moussaieff Masson, *Against Therapy: Emotional
    Tyranny and the Myth of Psychological Healing* (New York: Atheneum, 1988),
    p. 176.
39 "My personal well-being": Eva Brabant, Ernst Falzeder, and Patrizia Giam-
    pieri-Deutsch, eds., *The Correspondence of Sigmund Freud and Sandor Ferenczi*,

Vol. I, 1908–1914 (Cambridge, Mass.: Belknap Press/Harvard University Press, 1994), p. 87.

39 "Evidently I have [found] *too much*": Ibid., p. 88.

40 "When . . . I first learned": Ibid., p. 319.
He even tried to have a fling: Ibid., p. 263.
And later, "she has proved": Ibid., p. 297.
Freud could see that Ferenczi: Ibid., p. 319.
Finally, on December 30, 1911: Ibid., p. 323.
"At that," wrote Ferenczi: Ibid., p. 324.

42 "Patients at some level": In Masson, *Against Therapy*, p. 77.
"I tried to pursue the Freudian technique": Judith Dupont, ed., *The Clinical Diary of Sandor Ferenczi* (Cambridge, Mass.: Harvard University Press, 1988), p. 186.
"Mrs. Ferenczi felt": Ibid.

43 "You have not made a secret": Freud, in J. Marmor, "Sexual Acting Out in Psychotherapy," *American Journal of Psychoanalysis*, 22 (1972), 4.
"And then you are to hear": Freud, in Dupont, *Clinical Diary*, p. 3.

44 "Your fear that I might develop": Ibid., p. 4.
"I tend to think": Ibid., pp. 92–93.
It seemed to him that: Ibid., p. 93.

45 "the hangman's work": Ibid., p. 53.
The technique had some daunting problems: Ibid., p. 94.

46 Not only did patients tattle: Paul Roazen, *Freud and His Followers* (New York: Allen Lane, 1976), p. 110.

47 The first to admit that she tinkered: Noël Fitch, *Anaïs: The Erotic Life of Anaïs Nin* (Boston: Little, Brown, 1993), p. 6.
When her father: Anaïs Nin, *Incest: From a Journal of Love. The Unexpurgated Diary of Anaïs Nin, 1932–1934* (New York: Harcourt Brace Jovanovich, 1992), p. 100.
"I rush to my passion": Ibid.

48 In her diary, she recalled: Fitch, *Anaïs*, p. 125.

49 "Today we kissed madly": Nin, *Incest*, p. 59.
"He reproaches me": Ibid., p. 134.

50 Although Rank was short: Ibid., p. 291.

51 Nin began analysis with Rank: Ibid., pp. 293, 292.
Nin realized that it was: Ibid., p. 302.

52 Two days after that she announced: Ibid., p. 334.
"On Tuesday I decided": The seduction scene comes from her diaries, Ibid.

53 When Nin returned to Rank's office: Ibid., p. 336.
"June 6, 1934." Ibid., pp. 338–39.
When Nin caught herself: Ibid., p. 358.
"not love, but revenge": Ibid., p. 341.

54 "Will Rank be another victim": Ibid.

"I have found love": Ibid., p. 366.

55 "the doctor came": Ibid., p. 385.

"*I* am dying now": Fitch, *Anaïs*, p. 177.

57 "It's a case of nontherapeutic touch": Laurie Abraham, "Dr. Smith Goes to Sexual-Rehab School," *New York Times Magazine* (Nov. 5, 1995), p. 48.

2. Variety and Surprise

58 The story of Etty Hillesum and Julius Spier is based on Hillesum's diary, which was published by J. G. Gaarlandt as *An Interrupted Life: The Diaries of Etty Hillesum* (New York: Pantheon, 1984).

60 These alternated with: Ibid., p. 16.

"When we wrestled": Ibid.

62 "A quick wrestle": Ibid., p. 55.

63 "Does he kneel": Ibid., p. 64.

64 "Something has happened to me": Ibid., p. 52.

"There are no wasted": Ibid., p. 83.

"Last night, when I bicycled": Ibid., p. 75.

66 "I feel so sure": Ibid., p. 108.

67 "A few months ago": Ibid., p. 107.

69 She became the equal: Ibid., p. 75.

73 The story of Esalen and the therapies developed there is taken in large part from Walter Truett Anderson, *The Upstart Spring: Esalen and the American Awakening* (Reading, Mass.: Addison-Wesley, 1983).

75 Schutz, with an unbounded belief: Ibid., p. 294.

76 The story of Fritz Perls's relationship is taken from the interviews of Perls and Marty Fromm published by Martin Shepard as *Fritz* (New York: Bantam, 1976).

78 "I was frigid and vicious": Ibid., p. 81.

79 Later Fromm realized: Ibid., p. 84.

80 "Well, Marty": Ibid., p. 89.

81 "We ended up": Ibid., p. 93.

"In this life you don't": Ibid., p. 78.

3. Recent Intimacies

84 "We wish to stress": Thomas Gutheil and Glen Gabbard, "The Concept of Boundaries in Clinical Practice: Theoretical and Risk-Management Dimensions," *American Journal of Psychiatry*, 150 (1993): 189.

85 "It is a rape": in "Psychiatrists and Sex Abuse," *Boston Globe* (Oct. 4, 1994), p. 14.

"depending on how": Margaret Burroughs, *The Road to Recovery: A Healing Journey for Survivors of Clergy Sexual Abuse* (Chatham, Mass.: Island Scribe, 1992), p. 4.

86 She said she was trying: J. L. Herman, N. Gartrell, S. Olarte, M. Feldstein, and R. Localio, "Psychiatrist-Patient Sexual Contact: Results of a National Survey, II: Psychiatrists' Attitudes," *American Journal of Psychiatry,* 144 (1987): 167.

89 threatened with expulsion: Kenneth S. Pope, Janet L. Sonne, and Jean Holroyd, *Sexual Feelings in Psychotherapy: Explorations for Therapists-in-Training* (Washington, D.C.: American Psychological Association, 1993), p. 25.

Stating that "if only": William Masters and Virginia Johnson, *Human Sexual Inadequacy* (Boston: Little, Brown, 1970). Also Pope, Sonne, and Holroyd, *Sexual Feelings in Psychotherapy,* p. 270.

90 An early one, launched: J. C. Holroyd and A. M. Brodsky, "Psychologists' Attitudes and Practices Regarding Erotic and Nonerotic Physical Contact with Patients," *American Psychologist,* 32 (1977): 843–49.

A far larger study: Gartrell et al., "Psychiatrist-Patient Sexual Contact, I, Prevalence."

relationships with *former* clients: T. J. Akamatsu, "Intimate Relationships with Former Clients: A National Survey of Attitudes and Behavior Among Practitioners," *Professional Psychology: Research and Practice,* 19 (1988): 454–58.

Four percent of clergymen: Attorney Linda Jorgenson, videotape of her presentation, "Sexual Misconduct," for the Episcopal Diocese of Massachusetts.

And among social workers: Lucille Gechtman, "Sexual Contact Between Social Workers and Their Clients," in Glen Gabbard, ed., *Sexual Exploitation in Professional Relationships* (Washington, D.C.: American Psychiatric Press, 1989), pp. 27–38.

In one of the rare: K. M. Mogul, "Ethics Complaints Against Female Psychiatrists," *American Journal of Psychiatry,* 149 (1992): 651–53.

91 Two thirds of the respondents: Gartrell et al., "Psychiatrist-Patient Sexual Contact."

But four fifths of the respondents: Holroyd and Brodsky, "Psychologists' Attitudes."

"The profession itself": Jeffrey Moussaieff Masson, *Against Therapy: Emotional Tyranny and the Myth of Psychological Healing* (New York: Atheneum, 1988), p. 181.

"When the subject of a survey": "Sex Surveys: Does Anyone Tell the Truth?" *American Demographics,* 15 (1993): 9–10.

92 our country's roughly 1.2 million: This figure is based on the Department of Labor's 1993 *Employment and Earnings Statistics* for psychologists, social workers, and clergy, as well as on U.S. Census figures for psychiatrists.

At one extreme, social scientists: Martin Williams, "Exploitation and Inference: Mapping the Damage from Therapist-Patient Sexual Involvement," *American Psychologist,* 47 (1992): 418.

At the other extreme: "Psychiatrists and Sex Abuse," *Boston Globe* (Oct. 4, 1994), p. 14.

The Episcopal bishop Barbara Harris: Burroughs, *Road to Recovery* p. 3.

93 What did social workers: Gechtman, op. cit., p. 29.

a full 98 percent: Herman et al. "Psychiatrist-Patient Sexual Contact."

105 "It is alarming that the topic": Thomas Gutheil and Glen Gabbard, "Obstacles to the Dynamic Understanding of Therapist-Patient Sexual Relations," *American Journal of Psychotherapy*, 46 (1992): 515, 516.

II. THE CURRENT SITUATION

110 "every available case of sex": Barbie Taylor and Nathaniel Wagner, "Sex Between Therapists and Clients: A Review and Analysis, *Professional Psychology*, 7 (1976): 593–601.

111 Chesler's stories illustrated: Phyllis Chesler, *Women and Madness* (New York: Avon, 1972), p. 157.

112 "those women were in denial": This kind of statement is typical of books that try to dramatize doctor-patient entanglements. An example is Peter Rutter, *Sex in the Forbidden Zone* (London: Unwin Hyman, 1990), or Sydney Smith, "The Seduction of the Female Patient," in Glen Gabbard, ed., *Sexual Exploitation in Professional Relationships* (Washington, D.C.: American Psychiatric Press, 1989).

115 This would represent a very large: Personal communication from Constance Dalenberg, Ph.D., at the Trauma Research Institute in San Diego, and Lynn Shepler, M.D., J.D., at the Thorne Clinic in Pocasset, Mass.

4. As Wolves Love Lambs

117 An exquisite example: This account of lost innocence is taken from Aldous Huxley, *The Devils of Loudun.*

119 Although emotional thugs: Not only did the large survey run by Gartrell et al. find that most doctors had become entangled with a client only once, but Andrea Celenza, who speaks on the rehabilitation of therapists, asserted that most therapist-clients were one-time offenders (Seminar on Countertransference, Cambridge Hospital, Cambridge, Mass., April 1994). See also Gary Schoener and John Gousiorek, "Assessment and Development of Rehabilitation Plans for Counselors Who Sexually Exploited Their Clients," *Journal of Counseling and Development*, 67 (1988): 227–32.

120 Lovestruck or lovesick therapists: Stuart Twemlow and Glen Gabbard, "The Lovesick Therapist," in Glen Gabbard, ed., *Sexual Exploitation in Professional Relationships* (Washington, D.C.: American Psychiatric Press, 1989), p. 74.

"the sadistic wish to destroy": Ibid., p. 84.

129 When sexual abuse at the hands of a lunatic: Ibid., p. 73.

Suzanne King, a Boston psychiatrist: "Sex Scandal Costs License of Brookline Psychiatrist," *Boston Globe* (Aug. 12, 1994), p. 29.

Even when a big national survey: Gartrell et al., "Psychiatrist-Patient Sexual Abuse, I, Prevalence," pp. 1126–31.

"It is, of course, possible": J. Marmor, "Sexual Acting Out in Psychotherapy," *American Journal of Psychoanalysis*, 22 (1972): 7.

131 One way that such creativity: Frank Barron, in Marvin Goldwert, *The Wounded Healers: Creative Illness in the Pioneers of Depth Psychology* (New York: University Press of America, 1992), p. 7.

And why, asked Laura Brown: Laura Brown, "Harmful Effects of Posttermination Sexual and Romantic Relationships with Former Clients," *Psychotherapy*, 25 (1988): 252.

As Kalman Glantz and John Pearce pointed out: Kalman Glantz and John Pearce, *Exiles from Eden* (New York: W. W. Norton, 1989), p. 28.

132 "the genes that hold culture": E. O. Wilson, *On Human Nature* (Cambridge, Mass.: Harvard University Press, 1978), p. 167.

They are primed: When Chairman Mao asked Henry Kissinger for his secret, namely how such a fat man got so many women, Kissinger is supposed to have replied, "Power is the greatest aphrodisiac."

133 As E. O. Wilson maintained: Wilson, *On Human Nature*, p. 82.

According to a British clinician: Janice Russell, *Out of Bounds: Sexual Exploitation in Counselling and Therapy* (London: Sage, 1993), p. 50.

Perhaps therapists who have been: Goldwert, *Wounded Healers*, p. 58.

134 When a group of psychiatrists: Gartrell et al., "Psychiatrist-Patient Sexual Abuse, I, Prevalence," pp. 1126–31.

fairy godmother complex: Natalie Eldridge, "Power in Therapy," presented at Learning from Women, Boston, April 29–30, 1994.

The few studies available: Ibid.

Becoming a fully functioning: Personal communication, Alan Flashman, a child psychiatrist who teaches at the Hebrew University in Jerusalem.

136 "Many people enter therapeutic": E. Mark Stern, "Humanists Confront Template," *Division 32 Newsletter of the American Psychological Association* (spring 1995): 7.

138 "Well, I am dying now": Noël Fitch, *Anaïs: The Erotic Life of Anaïs Nin* (Boston: Little, Brown, 1993), p. 177.

"Return to me in this moment": John Kerr, *A Most Dangerous Method: The Story of Jung, Freud and Sabina Spielrein* (New York: Knopf, 1993), p. 205.

139 "the typical patients are those": S. A. Avrill, D. A. Beale, B. Benfer, et al., "Preventing Staff-Patient Sexual Relationships," *Bulletin of the Menninger Clinic*, 53 (1989): 387.

Other hallmarks: The characteristics of Borderline Personality Disorder are listed in the *Diagnostic and Statistical Manual IV* (Washington, D.C.: American Psychiatric Association, 1994).

Although the disorder: Janice Cauwels, *Imbroglio: Rising to the Challenges of Borderline Personality Disorder* (New York: W. W. Norton, 1992), p. 27.

140 What little research there is: Although Pope, Sonne, and Holroyd (*Sexual Feelings in Psychotherapy* [Washington, D.C.: American Psychological Press, 1993]) argue that there is not enough information to be certain that women who have been abused are more likely to be become entangled with therapists, the *Harvard Mental Health Letter* (Jan. 1993, p. 7) reports otherwise. Also, people who work with abused women believe that they are particularly vulnerable. Constance Dalenberg of the Trauma Research Institute in San Diego is one.

Regardless of the historical period: Kenneth Pope, Patricia Keith-Spiegel, and Barbara Tabachnik, "Sexual Attraction to Clients: The Human Therapist and the (Sometimes) Inhuman Training System," in Kenneth S. Pope, Janet L. Sonne, and Jean Holroyd, *Sexual Feelings in Psychotherapy: Explorations for Therapists-in-Training* (Washington, D.C.: American Psychological Association, 1993), p. 224.

5. Transference and the Power Imbalance

142 "If the patient's advances": Sigmund Freud, "Observations on Transference-Love," *Complete Psychological Works,* Standard Edition, Vol. 12, translated and edited by J. Strachey (London: Hogarth Press, 1958), p. 166.

"Frau C. has told me": Freud, in John Kerr, *A Most Dangerous Method: The Story of Jung, Freud and Sabina Spielrein* (New York: Knopf, 1993), p. 391.

143 "a large share of what is": Judith Dupont, ed., *The Clinical Diary of Sandor Ferenczi* (Cambridge, Mass.: Harvard University Press, 1988), p. 93.

"The Psychology of Transference": Jung, in Aldo Carotenuto, *A Secret Symmetry: Sabina Spielrein Between Jung and Freud* (New York, Pantheon, 1982), p. 208.

"The patient's destiny": Ibid., p. 210.

144 "Long ago I settled": Personal communication from Robert Blanchard, former director, Thorne Clinic, Pocasset, Mass.

145 Both in religion and therapy: Ethel S. Person, *Dreams of Love and Fateful Encounters: The Power of Romantic Passion* (New York: Penguin, 1988), p. 243.

145 In other words, patients' ongoing attempts: Irving Singer, *The Pursuit of Love* (Baltimore: Johns Hopkins University Press, 1994), p. 10.

146 "the history of madness": Roy Porter, *A Social History of Madness: The World Through the Eyes of the Insane* (New York: Dutton, 1989), p. 39.

Franz Anton Mesmer: Marvin Goldwert, *The Wounded Healers: Creative Illness in the Pioneers of Depth Psychology* (New York: University Press of America, 1992), p. 33.

147 Apparently Oesterline writhed: Léon Chertok, "Psychotherapy, Suggestion

and Sexuality: Historical and Epistemological Considerations," *British Journal of Psychotherapy*, 5 (1988): 95.

148 Mesmer mesmerized Mesmer: M. A. Gravitz, "The First Use of Self-hypnosis: Mesmer Mesmerizes Mesmer," *American Journal of Clinical Hypnosis*, 37 (1994): 49–52.

149 "The danger is reciprocal": Chertok, "Psychotherapy," p. 97.
In England, magnetism: Porter, *Social History of Madness*, p. 56.

151 When power is misused: Report of the Ethics Committee, 1994, *American Psychologist*, 50 (1995): 708.
Although an Exploitation Index: Richard Epstein, Robert Simon, and Gary Kay, "Assessing Boundary Violations in Psychotherapy: Survey Results with the Exploitation Index," *Bulletin of the Menninger Clinic*, 56 (1992): 150–66.
the Therapist-Patient Sex Syndrome: Kenneth Pope, "How Clients Are Harmed by Sexual Contact with Mental Health Professionals: The Syndrome and Its Prevalence," *Journal of Counseling and Development*, 67 (1988): 222–26.

152 One small survey: J. Bouhoutsos, J. Holroyd, H. Lerman, B. Forer, and M. Greenberg, "Sexual Intimacy Between Psychotherapists and Patients," *Professional Psychology*, 14 (1983): 185–96.
No questions were asked: Kenneth Pope and Valerie Vetter, "Prior Therapist-Patient Sexual Involvement Among Patients Seen by Psychologists," *Psychotherapy*, 28 (1991): 429–38.

153 "patients vary in the degree": Thomas Gutheil and Glen Gabbard, "Obstacles to the Dynamic Understanding of Therapist-Patient Sexual Relations," *American Journal of Psychotherapy*, 46 (1992): 521, 523.
a whopping 95 percent: Shirley Feldman-Summers and Gwendolyn Jones, "Psychological Impacts of Sexual Contact Between Therapists of Other Health Care Practitioners and Their Clients," *Journal of Consulting and Clinical Psychology*, 52 (1984): 1059–61.
Ten were heterosexual: Ibid., p. 1056.

154 The author of a self-help book: Peter Rutter, *Sex in the Forbidden Zone* (London: Unwin Hyman, 1990), pp. 73, 81.
At the other extreme: Because this position is so unpopular and is so regularly equated with the proponent's insensitivity rather than his or her observations, the two doctors who advocated the idea were not willing to do so publicly — another indicator that the doctor-patient sex furor is about redressing social injustice, not studying human behaviors.
(It is estimated that: *Harvard Mental Health Letter* (January 1993), p. 7.

6. There Oughta Be a Law

160 In 1990, for example: Robyn Dawes, *House of Cards: Psychology and Psychotherapy Built on Myth* (New York: Free Press, 1994), p. 11.

Fewer therapists say they believe: Stanton Jones, "A Constructive Relationship for Religion with the Science and Profession of Psychology," *American Psychologist,* 49 (1994): 184.

161 For example, when New Jersey: Katie Roiphe, *The Morning After: Sex, Fear, and Feminism on Campus* (Boston: Little, Brown, 1993), p. 61.

162 "a sex-abuse industry": M. S. Wylie, "The Shadow of a Doubt," *Networker* (September–October 1993): 22.

"salute to the flag": R. T. Hare-Mustin, J. Maracek, A. Kaplan, and N. Liss-Levinson, "Rights of Clients, Responsibilities of Therapists," *American Psychologist,* 34 (1979): 3.

163 Thus an ethics committee sat down: The story of how this code of ethics evolved is drawn from Dawes, *House of Cards,* pp. 255–58.

Although . . . only a single article: S. Shopland and L. VandeCreek, "Sex with Ex-Clients: Theoretical Rationales for Prohibition," *Ethics & Behavior,* 1 (1991): 37–38.

164 As one of the members: Dawes, *House of Cards,* p. 257.

165 "act as if posttermination sex": Shopland and VandeCreek, "Sex with Ex-Clients," p. 37.

166 Yet the APA feels people: Dawes, *House of Cards,* p. 258.

By contrast, in the United Kingdom: Janice Russell, *Out of Bounds: Sexual Exploitation in Counselling and Therapy* (London: Sage Publications, 1993), pp. 7, 111.

167 Summing up the pros and cons: L. H. Strasburger, L. Jorgenson, and R. Randles, "Criminalization of Psychotherapist-Patient Sex," *American Journal of Psychiatry,* 148 (1991): 859.

Wisconsin was the first state: Melba Vasquez, "Sexual Intimacies with Clients After Termination: Should a Prohibition Be Explicit?" *Ethics & Behavior,* 1 (1991): 56. For legislative trends among therapists and clergy, see Sally Johnson, "Legal Issues in Clergy Sexual Boundary Violation Matters," in Katherine Ragsdale, ed., *Boundary Wars* (Cleveland: Pilgrim Press, 1996).

168 "Sexual intercourse under pretext": Irwin Perr, "Medico-legal Aspects of Professional Sexual Exploitation," in Glen Gabbard, ed., *Sexual Exploitation in Professional Relationships* (Washington, D.C.: American Psychiatric Press, 1989), p. 221.

169 What the client must prove: J. Edelwich and A. M. Brodsky, *Sexual Dilemmas for the Helping Professional* (New York: Brunner/Mazel, 1989), p. 220.

When the *Boston Globe:* "Psychiatrists and Sex Abuse," *Boston Globe* (Oct. 4, 1994), p. 14.

170 "damages vary tremendously": Perr, "Medico-legal Aspects of . . . Exploitation," p. 223.

179 "We feel that the Church": Although this is taken from an open letter that was made public in 1995, I have been asked not to give the reference for fear of compromising the confidentiality of Attorney Blake's clients.

185 "This case had a terrorizing effect": Gary Chafetz and Morris Chafetz, *Obsession: The Bizarre Relationship Between a Prominent Harvard Psychiatrist and Her Suicidal Patient* (New York: Crown, 1994), p. 252.
"because the seriously ill": Ibid., pp. 172, 253.
"I think the reason managed care": Alexander Vuckovic, in Neil Miller, "Managing McLean," *Boston Globe* (Sept. 10, 1995), p. 70.

186 In Massachusetts, for example: Ibid., pp. 25, 28.
It is not surprising: Ibid., p. 70.

187 A peculiar form of sadism: Personal communication from Constance Dalenberg, Trauma Research Institute, San Diego.

189 Among clinicians, it is the males: H. M. Schulte and J. Kay, "Medical Students' Perceptions of Patient-Initiated Sexual Behavior," *Academic Medicine*, 69 (1994): 842.

7. Repairing the Damage

199 As Katie Roiphe noted: Katie Roiphe, *The Morning After: Sex, Fear, and Feminism on Campus* (Boston: Little, Brown, 1993), p. 37.

200 Research on hundreds: See for example, George Goethals and Richard Reckman, "The Perception of Consistency in Attitudes," *Journal of Experimental Social Psychology*, 9 (1973): 491–501.

201 "These kinds of explanations": Martin Seligman, "Seligman Recommends a Depression 'Vaccine,'" *APA Monitor* (October 1994): 4.
Because "most [psychotherapeutic] technologies": David Kipnis, "Accounting for the Use of Behavior Technologies in Social Psychology," *American Psychologist*, 49 (1994): 168. See also E. Herman and N. Chomsky, *Manufacturing Consent* (New York: Pantheon, 1988).
"There is no place": Judith Herman, "Women's Pathways to Healing," presented at Learning from Women, Boston, April 29–30, 1994.

202 "means really to be out of harm's way": James Hillman, *A Blue Fire* (New York: Harper & Row, 1989), p. 278.

203 Among sterile ways of dealing with betrayal: Ibid., pp. 279–80.
"The paranoid demand": Ibid., p. 280.
"It may well be that betrayal": Ibid., p. 281.
"a kind of loving": Ibid.
"There is no cure": Jan Bauer, *Impossible Love or Why the Heart Must Go Wrong: The Hidden Meaning of Love's Disasters* (Dallas: Spring Publications, 1993), p. 195.

204 Based on Arabic folk legends: My retelling is based on Nizami, *The Story of Layla and Majnun* (Boulder, Colo.: Shambhala, 1978), and Diane Wolkstein, *The First Love Stories from Isis and Osiris to Tristan and Iseult* (New York: HarperCollins, 1991).

208 It also appears from the majority: Janet Sonne and Kenneth Pope, "Treating

Victims of Therapist-Patient Sexual Abuse," in Kenneth Pope, Janet Sonne, and Jean Holroyd, *Sexual Feelings in Psychotherapy: Explorations for Therapists-in-Training* (Washington, D.C.: American Psychological Association, 1993), p. 255.

Gary Schoener and: Gary Schoener and John Gonsiorek, "Assessment and Development of Rehabilitation Plans for Counselors Who Have Sexually Exploited Their Clients," *Journal of Counseling and Development,* 67 (1988): 227–32.

210 Dr. Constance Dalenberg: Personal communication.

216 "honest, loving service": David Rice, *Shattered Vows: Priests Who Leave* (New York: William Morrow, 1990), p. 111.

III. WHY CAN'T WE TALK
ABOUT LOVE?

8. Women Refashion Psychotherapy

227 In a poem about Orpheus: Edward Hirsch, "Orpheus: The Descent," *Earthly Measures,* in *New York Times Book Review* (May 15, 1994), p. 27.

229 Although there were only thirty-five: Ilene Philipson, *On the Shoulders of Women: The Feminization of Psychotherapy* (New York: Guilford Press, 1993), pp. 25ff.

230 Under President Ronald Reagan: Ibid., p. 39.

the number of . . . degrees doubled: Ibid., p. 58.

This leaves the talking cure: These figures are based on the Department of Labor's 1993 *Employment and Earnings Statistics.* Until recently, the clergy has been overwhelmingly male. By 1993, however, 11 percent of pastors and priests were women. More and more women are seeking admission to seminaries, and with the exception of the Catholic Church, it looks as if the number of women will soon equal or outnumber men.

At the same time, the number of men: Philipson, *On the Shoulders of Women,* p. 1.

"There's just a certain attitude": A student quoted in Ibid., p. 61.

"Heterosexual men": Ibid., p. 62.

232 "helpless figure": Sydney Smith, "The Seduction of the Female Patient," in Glen Gabbard, ed., *Sexual Exploitation in Professional Relationships* (Washington, D.C.: American Psychiatric Press, 1989), p. 63.

236 "climate of real intimidation": Judith Herman, "Women's Pathways to Healing," presented at Learning from Women, Boston, April 29–30, 1994.

238 "She pushed all the hot-button topics": Gary Chafetz, personal communication.

"Above all . . . psychotherapy": Philipson, *On the Shoulders of Women,* p. 126.

239 "represent the total giving up": Ferenczi, in Jeffrey Moussaieff Masson,

Against Therapy: Emotional Tyranny and the Myth of Psychological Healing (New York: Atheneum, 1988), p. 88.

"All life-giving relationships": Carter Heyward, *When Boundaries Betray Us: Beyond Illusions of What Is Ethical in Therapy and Life* (New York: HarperCollins, 1993), p. 171.

240   "an overly enthusiastic teenage dyke": Ibid., p. 30.

241   "It's important that I be clear": Ibid., p. 34.

"Intuitively, I knew": Ibid., p. 64.

Nevertheless, Ferenczi believed: Judith Dupont, ed., *The Clinical Diary of Sandor Ferenczi* (Cambridge, Mass.: Harvard University Press, 1988), p. xix.

242   Yet for the first time: Heyward, *When Boundaries Betray Us*, p. 87.

"It would have been an altogether different": Ibid., p. 180.

"It is important that": Ibid., p. 194.

243   When the British clinician: Janice Russell, *Out of Bounds: Sexual Exploitation in Counselling and Therapy* (London: Sage, 1993), p. 39.

9. The Active Ingredients of the Intimate Hour

246   "The appearance of sexuality": Léon Chertok, "Psychotherapy, Suggestion and Sexuality: Historical and Epistemological Considerations," *British Journal of Psychotherapy*, 5 (1988): 97.

247   In 1952 the British: E. Fuller Torrey, *Witchdoctors and Psychiatrists: The Common Roots of Psychotherapy and Its Future* (New York: Harper & Row, 1986), p. 197.

247   At least for most people: Ibid., p. 201.

What clinicians were surprised to learn: A discussion of the myth of expertise is found in Robyn Dawes, *House of Cards: Psychology and Psychotherapy Built on Myth* (New York: Free Press, 1994), pp. 54–63.

(In 1995, a *Consumer Reports* survey: Martin Seligman, "The Effectiveness of Psychotherapy: The Consumer Reports Study," *American Psychologist*, 50 (1995): 965–74.

The argument over how much therapy: Scott Sleek, "What Treatments Have Proven Effective?" *APA Monitor* (October 1995): 40–42.

248   That almost any kind: Dawes, *House of Cards*, p. 56.

As . . . early as 1979: Ibid. and Torrey, *Witchdoctors and Psychiatrists*, p. 44.

249   Specifically, this kind of private: J. Pennebaker, J. Kiecott-Glaser, and R. Glaser, "Disclosure of Trauma and Immune Function: Health Implications for Psychotherapy," *Journal of Consulting and Clinical Psychology*, 56 (1988): 239–45.

Dozens of investigations: Torrey, *Witchdoctors and Psychiatrists*, pp. 41–43.

the ability to manage: Hans Strupp, "The Psychotherapist's Skill Revisited," *Clinical Psychology: Science and Practice*, 2 (1995): 70.

251   "the undeniable bond": Chertok, "Psychotherapy, Suggestions," p. 100.

252 "Client as Colleague": Robert Heinssen, Philip Levendusky, and Richard Hunter, "Client as Colleague," *American Psychologist,* 50 (1995): 522–31.

Several years after their treatment: Penny Ramsdell and Earle Ramsdell, "Dual Relationships: Client Perceptions of the Effect of Client-Counselor Relationship on the Therapeutic Process," *Clinical Social Work Journal,* 21 (1993): 195–212.

"although some therapists": Torrey, *Witchdoctors and Psychiatrists,* p. 38.

253 "You ought to prepare": Bruno Bettelheim and Alvin Rosenfeld, *The Art of the Obvious: Developing Insight for Psychotherapy and Everyday Life* (New York: Knopf, 1993), p. 65.

"This hospitality . . . requires": Henri Nouwen, *The Wounded Healer* (New York: Doubleday, 1972), p. 104.

Johann Christoph Blumhardt: This story is recounted by Aldo Carotenuto in *A Secret Symmetry: Sabina Spielrein Between Jung and Freud* (New York, Pantheon, 1982).

254 "The psychotherapy relationship is two-sided": Annie Rogers, *A Shining Affliction: A Story of Harm and Healing in Psychotherapy* (New York: Viking, 1995), p. 319.

"this kind of loving": James Hillman, *A Blue Fire* (New York: Harper & Row, 1989), p. 281.

255 "the love of an old man": Ibid., p. 282.

259 "Psychoanalysis is at its core": Jonathan Lear, *Love and Its Place in Nature* (New York: Noonday Press, 1991), p. 22.

260 Although no money changes hands: Irving Yalom, *The Theory and Practice of Group Therapy,* 3d ed. (New York: Basic, 1985), pp. 427–28.

"the crown of life": C. S. Lewis, *The Four Loves* (New York: A Harvest/HBJ Book, 1960), p. 87.

"a real man trembles": Bohumil Hrabal, *Dancing Lessons for the Advanced in Age* (New York: Harcourt Brace, 1995), in the *New York Times Book Review* (Nov. 26, 1995), p. 19.

"a kind of choking longing": Kalman Glantz and John Pearce, *Exiles from Eden* (New York: W. W. Norton, 1989), p. 169.

95 percent of male clinicians: Kenneth S. Pope, Janet L. Sonne, and Jean Holroyd, *Sexual Feelings in Psychotherapy: Explorations for Therapists-in-Training* (Washington, D.C.: American Psychological Association, 1993), p. 205.

261 "our profession remains paralyzed": Michael Tansey, "Sexual Attraction and Phobic Dread in the Countertransference," p. 1. Paper presented on April 18, 1993, at an American Psychological Association panel discussion, "Love, Passion, Desire, and Dread in the Countertransference."

"we are all vulnerable": Ibid., p. 2.

262 Calling analysis a "metaphorical seduction": D. M. Thomas, review of Aldo Carotenuto, *A Secret Symmetry,* in *New York Review of Books* (May 13, 1982), p. 3.

263 "the aim of sexual urges": Christopher Bollas, *Cracking Up: The Work of Unconscious Experience* (New York: Hill and Wang, 1995), p. 43.

264 "analysts of most schools": Ibid., p. 46.

265 "That psychoanalysis should be so gratifying": Ibid., p. 47.
   Courtly love: For a discussion of the development of courtly love, see Theodore Zeldin, *An Intimate History of Humanity* (New York: HarperCollins, 1995), pp. 72–85, and Octavio Paz, *The Double Flame: Love and Eroticism* (New York: Harcourt Brace, 1995).

266 In *The Double Flame:* Paz, *The Double Flame,* pp. 123–61.

268 We are suspicious of passion: Torrey, *Witchdoctors and Psychiatrists,* pp. 92ff.

269 "In love there is no condescension": Irving Singer, *The Pursuit of Love* (Baltimore: Johns Hopkins University Press, 1994), p. 94.
   "Most mental health treatments": Ethel S. Person, *Dreams of Love and Fateful Encounters: The Power of Romantic Passion* (New York: Penguin, 1988), p. 17.
   The feelings Romeo and Juliet had: Stuart Twemlow and Glen Gabbard, "The Lovesick Therapist," in Glen Gabbard, ed., *Sexual Exploitation in Professional Relationships* (Washington, D.C.: American Psychiatric Press, 1989), p. 73.

270 "lust plus the ordeal of civility": Freud, in Singer, *Pursuit of Love,* p. 130.
   "After so much stress": Henri Nouwen, *The Wounded Healer* (New York: Doubleday, 1972), pp. 72–73.
   "I write exactly what he wishes": This account is from Rogers, *A Shining Affliction,* pp. 72ff.

272 "Can I believe you?": Ibid., p. 157.

273 "create a world and a new story": Ibid., p. 256.

275 "After I was finally leaving Fairbairn": Harry Guntrip, in Janet Malcolm, *Psychoanalysis: The Impossible Profession* (New York: Vintage, 1982), p. 156.

Bibliography

Anderson, Walter Truett. *The Upstart Spring: Esalen and the American Awakening.* Reading, Mass.: Addison-Wesley, 1983.

Bates, C., and A. Brodsky. *Sex in the Therapy Hour: A Case of Professional Incest.* New York: Guilford Press, 1989.

Bauer, Jan. *Impossible Love or Why the Heart Must Go Wrong: The Hidden Meaning of Love's Disasters.* Dallas: Spring Publications, 1993.

Bettelheim, Bruno. Review of *A Secret Symmetry: Sabina Spielrein Between Jung and Freud.* In *New York Review of Books* 30 (June 30, 1983): 39.

———— and Alvin Rosenfeld. *The Art of the Obvious: Developing Insight for Psychotherapy and Everyday Life.* New York: Knopf, 1993.

Bollas, Christopher. *Cracking Up: The Work of Unconscious Experience.* New York: Hill and Wang, 1995.

Brabant, Eva, Ernst Falzeder, and Patrizia Giampieri-Deutsch, eds. *The Correspondence of Sigmund Freud and Sandor Ferenczi,* Vol. 1, 1908–1914. Cambridge, Mass.: Belknap Press/Harvard University Press, 1994.

Brown, Laura. "Harmful Effects of Posttermination Sexual and Romantic Relationships with Former Clients." *Psychotherapy,* 25 (1988): 249–55.

Carotenuto, Aldo. *A Secret Symmetry: Sabina Spielrein Between Jung and Freud.* New York: Pantheon, 1982.

Chafetz, Gary, and Morris Chafetz. *Obsession: The Bizarre Relationship Between a Prominent Harvard Psychiatrist and Her Suicidal Patient.* New York: Crown, 1994.

Chertok, Léon. "Psychotherapy, Suggestion and Sexuality: Historical and Epistemological Considerations," *British Journal of Psychotherapy,* 5 (1988): 94–104.

Dawes, Robyn. *House of Cards: Psychology and Psychotherapy Built on Myth.* New York: Free Press, 1994.

Dupont, Judith, ed. *The Clinical Diary of Sandor Ferenczi.* Cambridge, Mass.: Harvard University Press, 1988.

Feldman-Summers, Shirley, and Gwendolyn Jones. "Psychological Impacts of Sexual Contact Between Therapists of Other Health Care Practitioners and Their Clients," *Journal of Consulting and Clinical Psychology,* 52 (1984): 1059–61.

Fitch, Noël. *Anaïs: The Erotic Life of Anaïs Nin.* Boston: Little, Brown, 1993.

Freud, Sigmund. "Observations on Transference-Love," *Complete Psychological Works,* Standard Edition, Vol. 12, translated and edited by J. Strachey. London: Hogarth Press, 1958, pp. 157–73.

Gaarlandt, J. G. *An Interrupted Life: The Diaries of Etty Hillesum.* New York: Pantheon, 1984.

Gabbard, Glen, ed. *Sexual Exploitation in Professional Relationships.* Washington, D.C.: American Psychiatric Press, 1989.

Glantz, Kalman, and John Pearce. *Exiles from Eden.* New York: W. W. Norton, 1989.

Goldwert, Marvin. *The Wounded Healers: Creative Illness in the Pioneers of Depth Psychology.* New York: University Press of America, 1992.

Goodman, M., and A. Teicher. "To Touch or Not to Touch," *Psychotherapy,* 25 (1988): 492–500.

Gutheil, Thomas, and Glen Gabbard. "Obstacles to the Dynamic Understanding of Therapist-Patient Sexual Relations," *American Journal of Psychotherapy,* 46 (1992): 515–25.

Herman, J. L., N. Gartrell, S. Olarte, M. Feldstein, and R. Localio. "Psychiatrist-Patient Sexual Contact: Results of a National Survey, II: Psychiatrists' Attitudes," *American Journal of Psychiatry* 144 (1987): 164–69.

Heyward, Carter. *When Boundaries Betray Us: Beyond Illusions of What Is Ethical in Therapy and Life.* New York: HarperCollins, 1993.

Hillman, James. *A Blue Fire.* New York: Harper & Row, 1989.

Holroyd, J. C., and A. M. Brodsky. "Psychologists' Attitudes and Practices Regarding Erotic and Nonerotic Physical Contact with Patients." *American Psychologist* 32 (1977): 843–49.

Kerr, John. *A Most Dangerous Method: The Story of Jung, Freud and Sabina Spielrein.* New York: Knopf, 1993.

Lear, Jonathan. *Love and Its Place in Nature.* New York: Noonday Press, 1991.

Marmor, J. "Sexual Acting Out in Psychotherapy." *American Journal of Psychoanalysis* 22 (1972): 3–8.

Masson, Jeffrey Moussaieff. *Against Therapy: Emotional Tyranny and the Myth of Psychological Healing.* New York: Atheneum, 1988.

Masters, William, and Virginia Johnson. *Human Sexual Inadequacy.* Boston: Little, Brown, 1970.

Middlebrook, Diane. "The Analyst and Her Appetites," a review of *Karen Horney: A Psychiatrist's Search for Self-Understanding,* edited by Bernard J. Paris. New Haven: Yale University Press. In *Washington Post,* Jan. 29, 1995.

Nin, Anaïs. *Incest: From a Journal of Love. The Unexpurgated Diary of Anaïs Nin, 1932–1934.* New York: Harcourt Brace Jovanovich, 1992.

Nouwen, Henri. *The Wounded Healer.* New York: Doubleday, 1972.

Paz, Octavio. *The Double Flame: Love and Eroticism.* New York: Harcourt Brace Jovanovich, 1995.

Person, Ethel S. *Dreams of Love and Fateful Encounters: The Power of Romantic Passion,* New York: Penguin, 1988.

Philipson, Ilene. *On the Shoulders of Women: The Feminization of Psychotherapy.* New York: Guilford Press, 1993.

Pope, Kenneth S., Janet L. Sonne, and Jean Holroyd. *Sexual Feelings in Psychotherapy: Explorations for Therapists-in-Training.* Washington, D.C.: American Psychological Association, 1993.

"Psychiatrists and Sex Abuse," *Boston Globe.* Oct. 4, 1994, pp. 1ff.

Ragsdale, Katherine, ed. *Boundary Wars.* Cleveland: Pilgrim Press, 1996.

Rogers, Annie. *A Shining Affliction: A Story of Harm and Healing in Psychotherapy.* New York: Viking, 1995.

Roiphe, Katie. *The Morning After: Sex, Fear, and Feminism on Campus.* Boston: Little, Brown, 1993.

Russell, Janice. *Out of Bounds: Sexual Exploitation in Counselling and Therapy.* London: Sage Publications, 1993.

Schoener, Gary, and John Gonsiorek. "Assessment and Development of Rehabilitation Plans for Counselors Who Have Sexually Exploited Their Clients," *Journal of Counseling and Development,* 67 (1988): 227–32.

Shepard, Martin. *Fritz.* New York, Bantam, 1976.

———. *The Love Treatment: Sexual Intimacy Between Patients and Psychotherapists.* New York: Peter Wyden, 1971.

Torrey, E. Fuller. *Witchdoctors and Psychiatrists: The Common Roots of Psychotherapy and Its Future.* New York: Harper & Row, 1986.

Williams, Martin. "Exploitation and Inference: Mapping the Damage from Therapist-Patient Sexual Involvement," *American Psychologist,* 47 (1992): 412–21.

Wilson, E. O. *On Human Nature.* Cambridge, Mass.: Harvard University Press, 1978.

Zeldin, Theodore. *An Intimate History of Humanity.* New York: HarperCollins, 1995.

Acknowledgments

The most and the most surprising help came from E.C., whose story appears in this book. Throwing herself with great energy into the search for a fair and satisfying understanding of what happens when doctor and patient are dangerously attracted to each other, she amassed an astonishing collection of insights, clippings, references, clever ideas, new leads, and additional stories. For plain goodwill, this woman is unmatched. And for passionate devotion, "Father Walsh" has no peer. The hours spent with him were a delight. Thanks also to the other men and women, doctors and patients, attorneys and clients, counselors and residents, clergy and parishioners, who have talked with me. Each added the private details of experience that I believe turn caricatures of good and evil into living, breathing people.

This book was unexpectedly difficult to write. Much of the time I felt caught between the stupefying banality of political correctness on the one side and the insensitive arrogance of people in power on the other. There were times when I wanted to put my entire cast of characters on an island, where they would be forced to cooperate in order to survive. In my imagination I would yell, "Just work it out, and get back to me with the answer!" But understanding an issue as complex and as idiosyncratic as doctor-patient attraction — both lust and love — proceeds slowly and circuitously. It takes time and relentless attention. In the end, I am amazed all over again at the ingenuity and perseverance of human beings. And, dear Miriam Altshuler, at their patience.

Index